Volunteering and Society in the 21st Century

Colin Rochester
Roehampton University, UK

Angela Ellis Paine
Institute for Volunteering Research, UK

Steven Howlett
Roehampton University, UK

with

Meta Zimmeck

First published in hardback 2010
First published in paperback in 2012 by
PALGRAVE MACMILLAN

Palgrave Macmillan in the UK is an imprint of Macmillan Publishers Limited,
registered in England, company number 785998, of Houndmills, Basingstoke,
Hampshire RG21 6XS.

Palgrave Macmillan in the US is a division of St Martin's Press LLC,
175 Fifth Avenue, New York, NY 10010.

Palgrave Macmillan is the global academic imprint of the above companies
and has companies and representatives throughout the world.

Palgrave® and Macmillan® are registered trademarks in the United States,
the United Kingdom, Europe and other countries.

ISBN: 978–0–230–21058–5 hardback
ISBN: 978–0–230–36772–2 paperback

This book is printed on paper suitable for recycling and made from fully
managed and sustained forest sources. Logging, pulping and manufacturing
processes are expected to conform to the environmental regulations of the
country of origin.

A catalogue record for this book is available from the British Library.

A catalog record for this book is available from the Library of Congress.

10 9 8 7 6 5 4 3 2 1
21 20 19 18 17 16 15 14 13 12

Printed and bound in Great Britain by
CPI Antony Rowe, Chippenham and Eastbourne

Volunteering and Society in the 21st Century

Dedicated to the memory of Irene Rochester (1941–2007)

Contents

Tables

Figures

Abbreviations

AVM	Association of Volunteer Managers
BME	Black and Minority Ethnic
CLG	Communities and Local Government
CSV	Community Service Volunteers
HOOVI	Home Office Older Volunteers Initiative
ICT	Information and Communications Technology
IiV	Investing in Volunteers
ILO	International Labour Organization
IVR	Institute for Volunteering Research
IYV	International Year of Volunteers
LEAP	Learning, Evaluation and Planning
LETS	Local Exchange Trading Schemes
LLI	Long-Term Limiting Illness
LSE	London School of Economics and Political Science
MS	Muscular Dystrophy
NGO	Non-Governmental Organisation
PQASSO	Practical Quality Assurance System for Small Organisations
PSA	Public Service Agreement
U3A	University of the Third Age
UN	United Nations
VE	Volunteering England
VFI	Volunteer Functions Index
VDS	Volunteer Development Scotland
VIAT	Volunteering Impact Assessment Toolkit
VIVA	Volunteer Investment and Value Audit
VSO	Voluntary Service Overseas
WVS	World Value Survey

Acknowledgements

This publication brings together the findings from our own research, but also that of many other researchers, to whom we are grateful. In particular, we have drawn heavily on the work of the Institute for Volunteering Research and our thanks go to all our colleagues that have contributed to the work of the team there over the years. We are equally grateful to all those respondents who have participated in our research. We hope we have done justice to all your ideas, experiences and reflections. We are grateful to our publishers, for their patience, support and guidance. Thanks must also go to our families who have supported us throughout.

The authors and publishers would also like to thank the following for permission to reproduce copyright material: the Office of the Third Sector for Table 4.1 on page 43, Table 14.1 on page 194 and Figure 14.1 on page 198; The Indiana University Press for Table 5.2 on page 61; the International Society for Third Sector Research (ISTR) and Johns Hopkins University for Figure 5.1 on page 64; and John Wiley and Sons Ltd for Figure 13.1 on page 185.

Foreword

When we wrote the original hardback edition of *Volunteering and Society in the 21st Century* we were very much aware that a general election would take place a few months after its publication. And, like just about everyone else in Britain, we expected that this would result in a change of governing party. In the event, the outcome of the election was a new government formed by a coalition of the Conservatives and the Liberal Democrats which took office in May 2010. While it is not unusual for incoming administrations to emphasise the extent to which they embody a new approach to governing, the Coalition has made a break with the past a central feature of its rhetoric. It has explicitly rejected the 'mistakes' of earlier governments and set in train a major reshaping of the state and a transformation of the relationship between government and society. Little more than a year after the election it may be too early to judge how far the Coalition has succeeded in implementing its programme of radical change and to assess the impact and the implications of its attempts to remould the state. We can, however, begin to chart the ways in which the Coalition's policies may be changing the environment in which voluntary action takes place and, more specifically, to examine the nature and likely impact of its approach to promoting and supporting volunteering.

We can identify four aspects of the Coalition's overall policy programme which are likely to impact on volunteering. The first of these is David Cameron's 'big idea' or vision of the Big Society. While much, but not all, of the detailed implementation of this policy stream remains obscure the broad thrust of the idea is clear; much of what we have looked to the state to organise and provide is intended to become the responsibility of concerned citizens acting in a voluntary capacity. The second key policy strand – the localism agenda – can be seen as complementary to the 'Big Society' project. It involves the introduction of a 'right to challenge' through which voluntary and community sector groups will be able to 'express interest in taking over the running of a local service' and local authorities, when selling assets, will have to allow community groups sufficient time to present a bid and raise funding. The third important component of the Coalition's policies is the drive to reduce public expenditure; the funding of voluntary and community sector organisations, many of which involve volunteers in their work, has been reduced by an amount estimated to fall between £3.2 billions and £5.1 billions. And, finally, the government's commitment to privatisation and to embedding the values and mechanisms of the market into public services will increasingly define the space occupied by volunteers and volunteering.

While the Coalition's approach to promoting and supporting volunteering more explicitly differs from that of its predecessor in a number of ways, it does not represent a complete break with the past. The ways in which it is seeking to promote and support voluntary action are very similar although the focus of the activities, the philosophy underlying the approach and the methods used to operationalise it may be different. Like New Labour did before it, the Coalition is attempting to promote volunteering from the top downwards and outwards. It has introduced a number of funding programmes aimed at stimulating volunteering within various sections of society; it is endeavouring to create pro-volunteering social norms; it is trying to make it easier for people to volunteer; and it is attempting to provide better support for providers of opportunities for volunteering.

While its programme targets some of the groups which New Labour selected as priorities (young people and the over sixties) it has a broader focus which encompasses informal as well as formal kinds of volunteering and emphasises community action as well as the delivery of services. Furthermore, the philosophy underpinning the Coalition's approach is very different to that of New Labour. Although some of the rhetoric on the need for social action has appeared radical enough for bidders for the contract to train 'community organisers' to boast of their understanding of the work of Saul Alinsky and Paolo Freire, the driving force behind it is the need to fill the gaps left by a shrinking state. Further evidence of this approach is provided by the *Giving* White Paper which defines volunteering as the 'giving of time' and thus analogous to philanthropy – the 'giving of money'. Volunteering is seen not as a complement to state action but as part of the mix of resources needed to replace it.

The other key difference between the Coalition's approach to promoting voluntary action and that of its predecessor lies in the ways in which policy is implemented and how progress is evaluated. It has rejected both New Labour's 'culture of control' and its bespoke organisational solutions. In the first place it has abandoned – for the moment at least – the attempts made by its predecessor to prescribe outputs, set targets and measure outcomes in detail in favour of allowing the organisations it funds greater flexibility to implement programmes as they judge fit while accountability has been scaled back to the provision of management information and self-assessment. In the process, however, it has thrown the baby out with the bathwater and cancelled the Citizenship Survey which had provided high quality longitudinal data on volunteering since 2001. In the second place it has taken an axe to a number of quangos and other specialised vehicles set up by New Labour to implement its initiatives and dismantled the network of 'strategic partners' through which the previous government spread its influence across the voluntary and community sector.

Overall, the impact of the policies and the programmes of the Coalition on volunteering have been mixed. On the one hand, the vision of the Big Society and the localism agenda hold out the prospect of an enhanced and broader role for voluntary action which is reinforced by the government's interest in informal as well as formal kinds of volunteering, while the bonfire of detailed targets and the scaling down of volunteering's infrastructure (perhaps better described as superstructure) provides the conditions under which a diverse range of activities may flourish. On the other, the expectations that volunteers and volunteer-involving organisations will be ready and able to replace the shrinking state in many areas of activity are challenging at best and unrealistic at worst. And the ability of many organisations to rise to the occasion has been undermined by deep cuts to the financial support they have received from local authorities. And, in any case, the adoption of the commissioning model of outsourcing public services clearly favours the corporate sector and the largest voluntary sector organisations in which volunteers play a very subordinate part – if they are involved at all.

To what extent have this latest turn of the policy wheel and the reshaping of the environment in which volunteering takes place challenged the key arguments of our book? How different might it have been if we were writing it today? The key thread running through *Volunteering and Society in the 21st Century* was the argument that we needed to replace the narrow view of volunteering embodied in what we called the 'dominant paradigm' with a broader, more inclusive 'round-earth' account of voluntary action. Arguably, the Coalition has taken some steps in that direction by its focus on informal as well as formal volunteering and its drive for volunteers to take on the management of services and assume responsibility for community assets in the place of paid local government officers. On the other hand, much of the philosophy underlying the emphasis on informal volunteering and the rationale behind the coupling of giving time with giving money is still based on a narrow and traditional view of why people volunteer. Informal volunteering is seen as a series of acts of kindness to those less fortunate than ourselves and, more generally, people who give their time as an expression of their philanthropic impulses. While the Coalition may have changed the terms on which we discuss and challenge the dominant view of what volunteering is and why people engage in it, it has not removed the need for a continued search for a more rounded map of voluntary action.

Volunteering and Society in the 21st Century also identified some key challenges or threats to volunteering. In the first place, we were concerned about the ways in which volunteering needed to maintain its independence from the state. We argued that governments could encroach on the autonomy of voluntary action in a variety of ways. These include direct means such as making some forms of volunteering compulsory or the recruitment of volunteers by government agencies for their own purposes and indirect impacts from attempts to set the agenda for volunteering (for example, by prioritising certain social groupings or activities) and create an environment in which volunteering can flourish. Like its predecessors, the Coalition government has been reluctant to introduce compulsory volunteering (although there are elements of this in its requirement for unemployed people to undertake 'mandatory work activity') and engage in the direct recruitment of volunteers (although, in the wake of the riots and looting in many English cities in August, 2011, there have been suggestions that its National Citizen Service programme should be enlarged and extended).

The Government's indirect impact on volunteering, however, could involve more significant changes in the priorities for voluntary action and to the environment in which it takes place. While the Coalition shares New Labour's emphasis on volunteering by young people – the agency created to address this – v – was spared in the cull of pet programmes and non-departmental public bodies (although it has had its funding scaled down) and National Citizen Service has been introduced – it has extended its areas of interest to informal volunteering and disadvantaged communities. And this rebalancing of the priorities has been matched by radical changes in the volunteering environment. These can be seen from two very different perspectives. On the one hand, the shrinking of the state is seen as having made space for a flowering of voluntary action hitherto 'crowded out' by the activity of statutory agencies. On the other hand, the Big Society can be viewed as placing unwelcome burdens on ordinary citizens who may be ill equipped to shoulder them while increasing the gulf in the level and quality of civic participation between the most 'comfortable' areas and their more disadvantaged counterparts.

The advent of the Coalition has therefore had some impact on the way in which the actions of government influence voluntary action. It has, however, made less impression on the other challenges we identify in the book – changing the image of volunteering; making it more inclusive; and defending its spirit from formalisation. It is, of course, quite possible that the new emphasis on informal volunteering, the deployment of community organisers in disadvantaged areas and the challenge to all citizens, wherever they live, to rise to the challenge of the 'Big Society' will help to change the image of volunteering and make it more socially inclusive. It is also possible that these changes will have the effect of reinforcing the differences between those who participate and those who do not. It is, of course, too early to assess their impact. The influence of the change of government and the change of policies this has brought about on the pressure of formalisation on volunteering is also difficult to evaluate. On the one hand, informal volunteering has been recognised but other pressures for more formal approaches have continued and, perhaps, been intensified. If volunteers are to take responsibility for providing services and managing community resources we would expect the demands for accountability and the pressures of regulation to drive them along the path to more formal methods of organisation. And, more generally, the marketisation of public services comes with a plethora of bureaucratic provisions.

The world in which volunteering takes place in Britain has changed since we wrote and published the original hardback edition of this book. Some of the impacts of these changes are clearer than others and the long-term outcome of the new government's flagship 'Big Society' project remains a matter of speculation; we cannot yet see where this leap in the dark will take us. While some of the landscape for volunteering in the 21st century remains obscure and some of its has visibly changed in the last fifteen months we believe that the account we have given of the nature and condition of voluntary action; the theoretical and practical challenges it faces; and the ways in which our understanding of volunteering might develop are still very much as we argued in the original edition of our book.

Colin Rochester
Angela Ellis Paine
Steven Howlett

Contributors

Colin Rochester has taught and conducted research on voluntary action at the London School of Economics and Political Science (LSE) and Roehampton University. His publications include *Juggling on a Unicycle: A handbook for small voluntary agencies* (LSE, 1999) and *Voluntary Organisations and Social Policy: Perspectives on change and choice* (with Margaret Harris; Palgrave, 2001).

Angela Ellis Paine is director of the Institute for Volunteering Research, where she has spent the past nine years researching volunteering. She has authored numerous reports, including co-authoring *Helping Out: A national survey of volunteering and charitable giving* (Cabinet Office, 2008).

Steven Howlett is a senior lecturer at Roehampton University leading the non-profit management master's degree. He has previously worked at the Institute for Volunteering Research.

Meta Zimmeck is a visiting fellow of the Centre for the Study of Voluntary and Community Activity at Roehampton University, specialising in voluntary and community sector research. She was head of the Voluntary and Community Research Section in the Home Office for six years and was responsible for a complex portfolio of research and evaluation.

1
Introduction

Great expectations

In the words of the Independent Commission on the Future of Volunteering (2008: p. 3) in England, 'volunteering has never had it so good'. While voluntary action has been a consistent feature of most societies (Hodgkinson, 2003) the current weight of expectation about the contribution it can make to individual development, social cohesion and addressing social need has never been greater, and it has a more prominent place on the agenda of public policy than ever before.

This is a global as well as a national phenomenon. The potential for voluntary action to contribute to the fight against key global issues was recognised by the United Nations' (UN) General Assembly in 1997 by the designation of 2001 as the International Year of Volunteers (IYV) (UN General Assembly, 2005). Volunteering was seen (by the UN Commission for Social Development, quoted in Hodgkinson) to offer skills, energy, expertise and local knowledge. All of this was seen to have the potential to assist governments in delivering better public programmes and policies. According to the Secretary-General's report on the follow-up to IYV, it was a powerful force for the achievement of the Millennium Development Goals (UN General Assembly, 2005).

At the European level, we have seen the launch of a *Manifesto for Volunteering in Europe* devised and promoted by a network of 38 volunteer development agencies and volunteer centres (European Volunteer Centre, 2006). This makes the claim that 'voluntary action is...an important component of the strategic objective of the European Union of becoming the most competitive and dynamic, knowledge-based economy in the world' (p. 5).

Nationally, the promotion of volunteering is more firmly established than ever as a priority for government action. As a policy stream, it stretches back beyond the 'Make a Difference' initiative launched by John Major in 1992 (Davis Smith, 2001) to the establishment of the Volunteer Centre UK (now Volunteering England [VE]) in 1973 (Brenton, 1985). In May 2006, a more recent Prime Minister, Tony Blair, included in his list of key challenges for the government and for his new Minister for the Cabinet Office and Social Exclusion the need to 'increase overall levels of volunteering across all age ranges and backgrounds' (Blair, 2006). This followed the setting of targets in the Public Spending Rounds of 2002 and 2004. The first of these aimed at a 5 per cent increase in voluntary and community sector activity by 2006 while the second added a specific reference to greater involvement 'amongst those at risk of social exclusion including people with no qualifications, people from Black and Minority Ethnic (BME) communities and people with disabilities or limiting long-term illnesses' (Harries, 2005). Volunteering is also seen as a means of delivering a whole range of government policies over and above social inclusion which include sustainable communities, health and social welfare, rural communities, education, criminal justice and anti-social behaviour.

The commitment of successive governments to the promotion of volunteering has led to significant funding for a series of initiatives aimed at specific groups and for measures aimed at strengthening the infrastructure of volunteering. The former have included projects and programmes aimed at the unemployed, older people, and the younger age group while the latter have included major investment aimed at rationalising the network of national and local bodies which promote and support volunteering and developing and disseminating expertise through the ChangeUp programme which represents a major investment in the effectiveness of the voluntary and community sector.

The unprecedented level of interest in volunteering has been reflected by the appointment in 2006 – by the England Volunteering Development Council (a body established in 2004 to provide a high-level representative and advocacy mechanism for volunteering) – of the Commission on the Future of Volunteering whose remit was to develop a long-term vision for volunteering in England. Chaired by the Liberal Democrat peer, Julia Neuberger, the Commission collected 'a huge amount of written evidence' and 'travelled the country to hear hundreds of oral testimonies from those within the volunteering world' (Commission on the Future of Volunteering, 2008: p. 7). It published its Manifesto in January 2008 (ibid.) and a report on the response to its public consultation a little later in the same year (Gaskin et al., 2008). Many of the recommendations made by the Commission have been accepted and acted upon by the current government – including the agreed investment of £4 million in new training programmes for volunteers and volunteer managers and a further £2 million to create a new access to volunteering fund for disabled people. Gordon Brown's administration has also demonstrated their interest in volunteering by the appointment, in June 2007, of Baroness Neuberger as the Government's volunteering champion with a specific brief to look at 'how the public services can make better use of volunteers' (http://www.cabinetoffice.gov.uk/third_sector/volunteering/volunteering_champion.aspx).

The growing expectations of policy-makers has been matched by increasing aspirations on the part of practitioners working in agencies which promote and support volunteering and organisations which involve volunteers in their work. VE and its counterparts in other countries of the United Kingdom have provided volunteering with a national infrastructure which has both raised its profile and helped to develop a more 'professional' approach to recruiting and managing volunteers. The development of what is increasingly referred to as a 'volunteering industry' and the growing perception that volunteer management is a specialist profession has been underlined by the development of quality standards, training for those who manage the work of volunteers, and the establishment of a professional body for volunteer managers.

This growing interest has been accompanied by the development of a body of research both in the United Kingdom and across the world. Important data about participation in volunteering have been provided by the series of Citizenship Surveys conducted by the Home Office and the Department of Communities and Local Government (CLG) since 2001 (Attwood et al., 2003; CLG, 2008; Home Office, 2004), and a major new survey of volunteering and charitable giving was published in 2007 (Low et al., 2007). A key role has also been played by the Institute for Volunteering Research (IVR), a partnership between VE and the University of East London which was established in 1997. As well as undertaking a large body of its own research during more than ten years of its existence, IVR has also disseminated the work of other scholars through its journal, *Voluntary Action*, which was published between 1998 and 2008.

This book

This book attempts to meet this unprecedented level of interest in volunteering by gathering together in a single volume what is known about the phenomenon of volunteering, the principles and practice of involving volunteers in a variety of organisational settings and the emerging and enduring challenges for voluntary action in the 21st century. The focus of the book is the United Kingdom but it is informed by and, in turn, is intended to inform international perspectives on voluntary action. As well as findings from the research undertaken by IVR and the wider British literature on volunteering, we will draw on wide range of literature from outside Britain to help us understand the nature of volunteering in the United Kingdom, patterns of participation in voluntary action, the kinds of challenges faced by volunteer-involving organisations and the dynamics of the interaction between volunteering and government. As well as a wealth of research-based and theoretical literature from the United States and Canada, our sources include evidence from Australia and the work of European scholars. We have tried to place the key features of UK volunteering in an international context to highlight what it has in common with voluntary action elsewhere in the world and identify the ways in which it is different and distinctive.

The book is aimed at three kinds of reader. In the first place, it is intended to provide a comprehensive and authoritative text for a number of academic audiences – not only the small but growing number of undergraduate and postgraduate students (and their teachers) who have a specific interest in voluntary action but also across the much broader spectrum of the curricula of public and social policy, government and community studies. Second, we have aimed it at the growing body of practitioners including those who manage volunteers, those who lead volunteer-involving organisations and the managers and staff of national and local volunteering infrastructure bodies. To this end, we have striven to make the contents accessible as well as authoritative. This aspiration is also important in terms of our third target audience, policy analysts and policy-makers across a wide range of areas of public policy and provision, not only the more obvious areas such as health and social welfare, community cohesion, social inclusion and public participation but also the environment, the arts, and sports and recreation.

The book consists of four main sections. In the first of these – which consists of Chapters 2 to 5 – we attempt to provide an overview of volunteering and delineate its salient features. Chapters 2 and 3 aim to create what we have called, following David Horton Smith (2000), a 'round-earth' map which captures the full extent of the phenomenon and the rich variety of the forms it can take. In Chapter 2, we explore the scope and range of the subject and attempt to clarify discussion of the concept of volunteering by developing a conceptual map based on three different perspectives, examining the value base of volunteerism and identifying its core characteristics. Chapter 3 follows this analysis by looking at ways of categorising and classifying volunteering opportunities and volunteers to ensure that we capture the full range and variety of voluntary action and the different ways in which people engage in it. It will also enable us to identify the distinctive characteristics of specific kinds of volunteering activities and the ways in which people engage with them.

Chapter 4 focuses on levels of volunteering and patterns of participation in the United Kingdom. We discuss the number of people engaged in volunteering and who these volunteers tend to be – their demographic and socio-economic characteristics. We also discuss the areas of social life to which volunteers contribute and the roles and functions they perform. The chapter draws on the Citizenship Survey, which is a household survey of approximately 10,000 adults in England and Wales (plus BME boost sample of approximately 5,000). Initially conducted by the Home Office and subsequently by CLG, the Citizenship Survey has been run every other year since 2001. We supplement these data by drawing on several other smaller studies from each of the four home countries.

Chapter 5 attempts to set this information in an international context. Do other countries have a similar profile, or does the United Kingdom have a lot more, or a lot fewer, volunteers? What are the different ways in which volunteering is viewed by people and supported by policy? The chapter looks at some of the data available from a selection of surveys before examining theories scholars have used to attempt to explain differences. It is through the application of these theories that we begin to understand that participation is the result of complex historical contexts and that similar rates are not necessarily the result of comparable driving forces.

The second section of the book – Chapters 6 to 8 – focuses on the changing world in which volunteering takes place. Chapter 6 summarises the key societal changes which are likely to make an impact on voluntary action. We look in turn at demographic trends, the changing relationship between the individual and society, and contemporary values and mores. In the final part of the chapter, we draw out some of the key implications of these changes for the future of volunteering and the practices of volunteer-involving organisations. Chapter 7 has been contributed by Meta Zimmeck. She concentrates on the ways in which successive governments have attempted to promote and encourage volunteering and reviews the impact of these actions and policies on volunteering and volunteer-involving organisations. The section is brought to a conclusion by Chapter 8 which discusses the ways in which volunteering itself is changing. It begins by looking at the phenomenon of short-term or episodic volunteering and the growing diversity of the activities undertaken by volunteers. It then reviews two areas in which the numbers of volunteers have been growing rapidly – employer supported and transnational volunteering. The chapter then looks at the challenges posed by the growth of virtual volunteering and trends in volunteering as activism before concluding by reviewing the rediscovery and repackaging of mutual aid under the banner of Timebanking.

The third section – Chapters 9 to 12 – is devoted to issues of organisation and management. Chapter 9 discusses motivation – why people choose to give freely of their time for voluntary action. It begins by outlining some of the methodological problems with researching motivations and looks at a selection of theories relating to volunteer motivation. Next, it looks at survey data, primarily from the United Kingdom, disaggregating motives across different demographic groups. After reviewing a selection of studies in an attempt to see how thinking about theoretical perspectives can add meaning to research, the chapter concludes by looking at how volunteer-involving organisations make use of these ideas.

This is followed by a look at retention – what makes people stay (or not) in organisations once they have taken the decision to become involved. Chapter 10 reviews the findings of studies into retention and ultimately finds that, while each of these attempts has some explanatory power, the research evidence is often contradictory when considered as a whole. However, it argues that, by engaging with different models and perspectives and recognising that while we will not find 'the answer', we may be in a better position to interpret what factors are more likely to be successful in helping retention.

Chapter 11 looks at how the work of volunteers can be organised and coordinated. It begins by tracing the development of volunteer management and highlighting the ways in which policy and practice have led to the increasing adoption of a formal approach based on the ways in which paid staff are managed. This model of management, it argues, is dominating the idea of best practice to the exclusion of less formal methods which are likely be more useful and appropriate for some volunteer-involving organisations. The chapter then looks at the ways in which values and organisational contexts influence the practice of management before looking at the strengths and weaknesses of the two approaches.

The section is completed by Chapter 12 which addresses the growing need for volunteer-involving organisations to be able to demonstrate the impact of the work of their volunteers. It discusses the ways in which the assessment of the impacts of volunteering have been conceptualised and undertaken. It considers who is impacted upon by volunteering and what those impacts are. It explores methodological issues faced in assessing these impacts; alongside, some of the tools created help meet the challenge. In particular, it draws on the work by the IVR in the development of its *Volunteering Impact Assessment Toolkit* (VIAT) (involving two of the authors of this book), which aims to assist organisations in a 'D-I-Y' assessment of the impact of volunteering across a range of stakeholders.

The final section of the book – Chapters 13 to 16 – draws on the earlier material to discuss four enduring challenges for volunteering. The first of these – Chapter 13 – explores volunteering's continuing problem with narrow and stereotypical public perceptions and the enduring challenge of trying to overcome a negative and unhelpful image. It reviews the nature of those perceptions and looks at the implications of them for volunteer-involving organisations, distinguishes between the different perspectives represented by image, brand, culture and vision and reviews a number of different ways in which they might be deployed to change the perception of volunteering.

The challenge discussed in Chapter 14 is the problem of ensuring that those who volunteer reflect the diversity of the population at large. There are some key demographic groups whose involvement is comparatively rare. This chapter explores the reasons behind these uneven patterns of volunteering and identifies the steps that are needed to make volunteering more inclusive. It reviews what we know about the different kinds of barriers which prevent more people from volunteering and discusses what is being done and can be done to overcome them and meet the challenge of making volunteering truly inclusive.

Chapter 15 focuses on the concern that the autonomy of volunteering may be under threat from the encroachment of the state and its agencies. It reviews some general ideas about the relationship between the state, civil society and democracy before concentrating on four ways in which governments can undermine the independence of voluntary action – by introducing compulsion, by developing government-sponsored volunteering, by seeking to set the agenda for voluntary action and by creating the environment within which it takes place.

The chapter then discusses what governments should and should not do and the need for volunteering to develop institutions through which government can be challenged.

The section is completed by a discussion of the fourth of our challenges to the future health and vitality of volunteering – the challenge of formalisation. One of the key features of the growth of public and community interest in volunteering has been the development of what has been called a 'volunteering industry' with its national and local infrastructure organisations; an emerging body of professionally trained volunteer managers, quality standards and performance measures, all adopted to improve the quality of the volunteering experience. Chapter 16 discusses the impact of these changes and critically assesses the extent to which the advantages of this formalisation of volunteering should be balanced against the loss of flexibility, informality and spontaneity which accompanies them.

The book ends with Chapter 17 in which we attempt to draw together the key themes of the book and set an agenda for future action and the research which should underpin and inform it. The chapter highlights the impact of the 'dominant paradigm' on the ways in which volunteering is commonly understood and discussed, and it assesses the extent to which we have been able to sustain our 'round-earth' view of voluntary action in the face of a research literature which is largely bounded by the narrow perspective of 'volunteering as service'. It discusses the extent to which we have been able to extend our analysis beyond this 'flat-earth' view of volunteering and bring a more nuanced approach to the discussion of key issues and topics. The chapter concludes by outlining an alternative vision of volunteering as a broad, heterogeneous and untidy field of human activity rather than simply the activities undertaken by the contemporary 'volunteering industry' and argues that securing a healthy future for voluntary action depends on understanding and promoting that complexity.

2
Making Sense of Volunteering: Perspectives, principles and definitions

Introduction: a 'round-earth map' of volunteering

This chapter and the one that immediately follows it represent an attempt to make sense of volunteering by capturing the full extent of the phenomenon and the rich variety of the forms it can take. We start from the premise that the general perception of volunteering is based on what David Horton Smith (2000) has called, in a different context, a 'flat-earth map'. In other words, the picture most people have of voluntary action is incomplete; while some of its features are clearly defined, many more of them are 'dark matter' (ibid.) which remains relatively unknown and largely unexplored.

The need to 're-conceptualise what we mean by volunteering without undermining its intrinsic value' was one of the key issues identified by Justin Davis Smith (now chief executive of VE) in the keynote speech he made at the launch of the Independent Commission on the Future of Volunteering (Davis Smith, 2006). The importance of devising an inclusive but robust concept of volunteering has been underlined by a number of studies which have found that one important barrier to participation in voluntary action is a general lack of knowledge or understanding of the diversity of the possible activities, organisational settings and the people involved (see, for example, Hankinson and Rochester, 2005; IVR, 2004a; Rochester and Hutchison, 2002).

Chapters 2 and 3 are therefore designed to provide a comprehensive and accurate 'round-earth map' of volunteering. In this chapter, we will explore the scope and range of the subject and attempt to clarify discussion of the concept of volunteering by

- presenting three perspectives on voluntary action and bringing them together into a conceptual map of the territory;
- exploring the values base of voluntarism and drawing out some key principles and
- identifying its core characteristics and using them to explore the boundaries of volunteering.

In Chapter 3, we look at ways of categorising and classifying volunteering opportunities and volunteers. This is to ensure that we capture the full range and variety of voluntary action and the different ways in which people engage in it. It will also enable us to identify the distinctive characteristics of specific kinds of volunteering activities and ways of engaging with them in order to avoid treating volunteers and volunteering as if they were homogeneous.

Three perspectives

The dominant paradigm

In the United Kingdom, the United States and a number of other similar societies, a very high proportion of the discussion about volunteering – by practitioners, policy-makers and researchers alike – is concentrated on one very specific view of the phenomenon which we can describe as the 'dominant paradigm'. There is evidence that this view of volunteering is no longer accepted as a comprehensive account of the field; the latest major text (Musick and Wilson, 2008) not only emphasises the activist strand in voluntary action (see below) but also notes that it had been largely neglected within the dominant paradigm. But the paradigm remains powerful; the report and recommendations of the Neuberger Commission (Commission on the Future of Volunteering, 2007, 2008) were framed by it. This approach involves a series of narrow definitions of volunteer motivation, the areas of social life in which volunteers are active, the organisational context within which volunteering takes place and the ways in which volunteering roles are defined.

Motivation.   While it is increasingly acknowledged that there is a rich cocktail of explanations of why people become volunteers (these are discussed in Chapter 9), the dominant view of volunteering is that it is essentially an altruistic act often seen as the 'gift' of one's time and thus analogous to the gift of money which defines philanthropy. In this view, people become volunteers in order to help others who are less fortunate than themselves.

Areas of activity. Volunteering is seen as taking place in the broad field of social welfare where it helps to provide care, support, advice and other activities for the benefit of people in need such as children, older people, people with disabilities or mental and physical health issues and people living in poverty or social exclusion.

Organisational context. From this perspective, opportunities for volunteering are provided by large, professionally staffed and formally structured organisations. While these are most likely to be charities or third sector organisations, they also include statutory agencies like hospitals and schools. Volunteers provide them with a significant additional resource in the form of unpaid labour and are increasingly treated as 'human resources' which need formal and skilled management of a similar kind to that provided for paid staff.

Volunteer roles. The work undertaken by volunteers is generally thought of as defined in advance by the volunteer-involving organisations. People are recruited for specific roles, and this may involve a process of selection, induction and, in some cases, training.

This view of volunteering has been described by Lyons and his colleagues (1998) as the 'non-profit paradigm'. It has been shaped in part by research carried out by academics in the fields of economics, law and management studies, largely in the United States, where the emphasis is on the comparatively large, well-staffed and bureaucratic non-profit organisations. In the United Kingdom, it has gained ground as a result of the drive by successive governments to give voluntary agencies a greater role in the delivery of public and social services and to invest in third sector infrastructure organisations. This has given greatest prominence to larger organisations in general and, in the specific case of volunteering, to those who deploy the largest numbers of volunteers.

In turn it has helped to shape what is now sometimes called the 'volunteering industry' and the emergence of a discrete new profession of volunteer management. This has involved the development by the Volunteering Hub (part of the government's strategy for building voluntary sector capacity) of a National Training Strategy for Volunteer Management and the drafting of National Occupational Standards for

Volunteer Managers (Commission on the Future of Volunteering, 2007) followed by the formation, in April 2007, of the Association of Volunteer Managers (AVM) (see also Chapter 16).

A different perspective – the civil society paradigm

Lyons et al. (1998) contrast this 'non-profit paradigm' with the approach to voluntary action which is predominant in other parts of the world including much of Europe and the developing countries of the South. This 'civil society paradigm' has its academic roots in political science and sociology and involves very different definitions of the volunteers' motivations, the areas of activity in which they are involved, the organisational context for their activities and the kinds of roles they play.

Motivation.   Rather than an altruistic or philanthropic desire to help other, less fortunate people, the motivation for those engaged with this kind of voluntary action is seen to be rooted in self-help and mutual aid. Their activities are based on the ability of people 'to work together to meet shared needs and address common problems' (Lyons et al., 1998: p. 52).

Areas of activity.   There are two broad differences between the kinds of activity undertaken by 'civil society' volunteers and those who are thought of as working within the 'non-profit paradigm'. In the first place, their involvement in social welfare is less likely to be focused on delivering care and other services than in offering mutual support in self-help groups or campaigning for improvements in provision. Second, their activities extend beyond social welfare to other areas of public policy such as transport, town planning and the environment.

Organisational context.   The key organisational forms through which this kind of voluntary action is seen to be pursued are associations based entirely on the work of volunteers and self-help groups rather than non-profit agencies with paid managers and staff. Recently, there has been a growing interest in these organisations in both the United States where they are called 'grass-roots associations' and in Britain where they are seen as part of a 'community sector' (Rochester, 1997, 1998).

Volunteer roles.   Within this paradigm, volunteers are not seen as helpers who are recruited to play specific roles within the organisation but members of the association who provide it with leadership and, between them, undertake all of its operational activities. The role to be played by the member activist in this kind of organisation 'cannot be defined in advance' but 'will be developed over time in the light of experience, personal growth and reflection' (Rochester, 1999/2007: p. 9).

This kind of voluntary action is sometimes called 'horizontal' volunteering to distinguish it from the 'vertical' kind found in the 'non-profit paradigm' and can be characterised as activism rather than unpaid help. Its scale and importance are often underestimated, but the number of grass-roots associations, community groups and self-help groups and the contribution they make to the quality of life and living conditions (Rochester, 1997) are very large indeed. Their low profile may be due in part to the size of the individual organisations and the perception that, unlike staffed non-profit or voluntary agencies, they are seen as run for the benefit of their members rather than the public as a whole.

A third view – volunteering as serious leisure

We are indebted to Lyons et al. (1998) for rescuing 'volunteering as activism' from the shadow of the dominant paradigm of 'volunteering as unpaid work or service' but now need to add a third view of volunteering which is 'volunteering as serious leisure'. In a sense, it is simple common sense to view volunteering as a leisure time activity, and it has been identified as such by scholars for more than thirty years (Stebbins, 2004, for example, quotes studies by Bosserman and Gagan from 1972 and David Horton Smith from 1975). Until recently, however, this perspective has been largely neglected by scholarly writers on volunteering. This lack of interest may be explained by the association of leisure with ideas of fun and frivolity which are at odds with the serious business of much voluntary action and with terms like 'amateur' and 'hobbyist' which are often used pejoratively. Now, however, the idea of volunteering as leisure – and, most importantly, as 'serious leisure' – has been explored in a series of publications by Stebbins (see, for example, Stebbins, 1996; Stebbins and Graham, 2004).

This body of work has identified three kinds of leisure volunteering. Casual volunteering is exemplified by 'cooking hot dogs at a church picnic or taking tickets for a performance by the local community theatre' (Stebbins, 2004: p. 5) while project-based volunteering is 'a short-term, reasonable complicated, one-off or occasional, though infrequent, creative undertaking' (ibid.: p. 7). This might, for example, involve participation in the organisation of a sporting or cultural event. Finally, volunteering as *serious* leisure involves 'the systematic pursuit of...a hobby ... or a volunteer activity sufficiently substantial and interesting in nature for the participants to find a (non-work) career therein acquiring and expressing a combination of its special skills, knowledge and experience' (ibid.: p. 5).

Serious leisure volunteering provides us with a third set of characteristics:

Motivations.   Motivations are seen as essentially intrinsic rather than extrinsic. Volunteers engage in serious leisure activities because of an enthusiasm for the specific form of involvement and a commitment to acquiring the knowledge and skills needed to practise it. For some, it will involve the use of 'free' time to create a substitute for the intrinsic rewards not available to them through mundane forms of employment. For others, it represents an opportunity to express other dimensions of their personality.

Areas of activity.   Leisure volunteers are typically thought to be involved in the fields of arts and culture and sports and recreation where they form a major proportion of the volunteering population. Activities include performance art such as theatre, music and dance; painting and sculpture; archaeology, local history and heritage; the full gamut of organised sport and recreations like rambling and non-competitive cycling.

Organisational context.   While much of this kind of voluntary action takes place in the kinds of voluntary associations we found in the world of the civil society perspective, leisure volunteering can be associated with quite large and complex organisations as well as small, community-based groups. Many of the local societies or clubs are also connected to wider structures at regional and national level: sports clubs, for example, work within structures and rules laid down by national governing bodies and rely on wider structures for arranging fixtures and providing officials as well as setting standards and providing support and training (Nichols, 2006).

Volunteer roles.   The 'classic' role for the leisure volunteer is as performer, practitioner or participant but there is a range of other functions to be undertaken. These include coaching, teaching or tutoring others; acting as directors, conductors or managers; officiating at matches and judging competitions; and carrying out administrative and support roles such as painting scenery, stewarding and 'front of house' duties. A significant minority of organisations working in these fields also have major capital assets – such as buildings, playing fields and special equipment – which

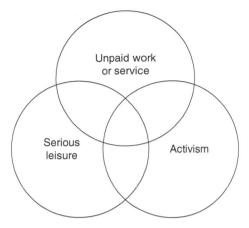

Figure 2.1 A three-perspective model of volunteering

require management and maintenance, and this is often carried out by volunteers.

A three-perspective model

Each of the three perspectives described above captures a part of the phenomenon of volunteering; we can easily identify examples of the different kinds of volunteering opportunity and volunteers which can be explained satisfactorily as volunteering as service; as activism; and as serious leisure. Separately, however, they do not adequately reflect the complexity of many volunteering experiences which combine more than one of these perspectives. If we take as a model from Billis (1993) the use of overlapping circles to identify ambiguities and hybrid forms, the result is Figure 2.1.

Alongside the unambiguous forms of volunteering as unpaid work or service, as activism and as leisure, we have identified four hybrid forms where either the nature of the organisation through which volunteering takes place or the combination of roles undertaken by the volunteer means that more than one perspective is required to understand the kind of volunteering involved.

- Volunteering which can be seen as a combination of unpaid work and activism;
- Volunteering which can be seen as a combination of activism and serious leisure;

- Volunteering which can be seen as a combination of serious leisure and unpaid work and
- Volunteering which can be seen as a combination of all three elements.

The values of volunteering

Our second approach to 'making sense' of the complex phenomenon of volunteering is based on an examination of the values that underpin it and the general principles that flow from them. Much of the literature deals with the values held by individuals and the influence of these on their propensity to volunteer (see, for example, Dekker and Halman, 2003), and we will discuss this relationship as part of our chapter on the motivation to volunteer (Chapter 10). In this section, however, we will be looking at values held at a collective level in our society and the ways in which they shape our attitudes to voluntary action. This discussion has been stimulated by and is informed by an important article by Kearney (2001/2007).

But what exactly do we mean by values? Dekker and Halman use Halman and de Moor's (1994) definition of 'deeply rooted dispositions guiding people to act and behave in a certain way' and describe them as 'an important attribute of culture' which 'includes what we think, how we act and what we own' (quoting Macionis and Plummer, 1998). There are four key sets of values of this kind which may have a significant impact on volunteering:

- The principle of *altruism* or *beneficence* is based on the moral imperative of compassion or care for other people;
- The idea of *solidarity* expresses a feeling of identification with a group or society and a responsibility to contribute to the well-being of the group and its other members;
- *Reciprocity* is the understanding that helping others may lead in some way and some time to being helped in turn when we are in need and
- The values of *equity* and *social justice* are based on the belief that inequality and injustice are morally and socially wrong and should be addressed or eliminated.

These values are underpinned in many cultures by religion. The imperatives of caring for other people – both within one's own community and beyond – is, for example, common to all major faith groups, while social justice is arguably at the heart of some religious beliefs but not others.

Another spectrum of cultural influence on the extent and nature of voluntarism in any society is the degree to which individual or collective forms of action are valued. At one end of the spectrum, the individual is expected to 'stand on his or her own two feet' and take full responsibility for his or her well-being. At the other end, society – through the institutions of the state – takes responsibility for the welfare of its members 'from the cradle to the grave'. Both extremes are unfruitful cultural environments for voluntary action. In between, we can find a great variety of different balances between individual responsibility (and freedom) on the one hand and collective provision on the other. In the plural societies of the 'developed' world, different value systems co-exist and provide the foundations for different forms of voluntary action.

A further useful way of looking at some of these differences has been provided by Billis's (1993) characterisation of the 'welfare ideologies' associated with different value positions. For Billis, the key question is 'who should be responsible for meeting the kinds of social need that cannot be met within the "informal world" of friends and family?' There are three broad answers to that question which define one's 'welfare ideology' and, we would argue, shape one's views about the nature and role of volunteering in our society. The first is that these needs should be met by the market – those in need should purchase services from for-profit firms – and the state and voluntary action should only be deployed where the market was unable to meet the needs of those who cannot afford to pay. The second is that the responsibility lies with the state and that social needs should be funded by taxation. And the third option is that the key role should be played by voluntary action supported by membership subscriptions and donations of money and time.

Kearney (2001/2007) has gone beyond this kind of discussion of the role of values in shaping volunteering and helping to explain the variety of forms it may take by seeking to draw out some general principles that can inform our understanding of voluntary action. He lists six of these.

1. *Volunteering is inclusive*: Kearney suggests that there is a 'right to volunteer' and that it can be exercised regardless of race, gender, religion, disability, age, sexual orientation and of the kinds of skills they bring to it.

2. *Volunteering is an act of free will or choice*: People volunteer 'in response to their own personal values and belief systems' (Kearney, 2001/2007: p. 6). The freedom to volunteer also involves the freedom *not* to get involved: 'just as a person may decide to volunteer he or she must also be able to refuse to do so' (ibid.). It also follows that 'the volunteer has the right to choose in what area he or she will participate and for what purpose' (ibid.). Volunteers are 'not biddable'; have the right to be 'mavericks'; and, do not have to 'volunteer for good'. Kearney quotes with approval Sir Kenneth Stowe's (2001) view that volunteering 'is essentially self-starting, inner-directed, and often angry ... So it is or it can be untidy, uncoordinated, awkward and irresponsible, even to the point of unacceptable law-breaking. That is the nature of the beast.'

3. *Volunteering is a two-way process*: On one level, this is a recognition of the view that volunteering is not a 'gift' to a less fortunate person but an exchange from which the volunteer also derives a benefit. This 'may include the satisfaction of responding to needs, the acquisition of new skills and experience, making social contact, and personal enjoyment' (p. 7). But Kearney also highlights the growing trend towards framing volunteering in reciprocal arrangements like local exchange trading schemes (LETS) and TimeBanks.

4. *Volunteers make a distinctive contribution*: They are not a substitute for paid staff or an alternative source of labour but complement and provided added value to the efforts and activities of employees. Both the distinctive nature of their activities and its value need to be recognised.

5. *Volunteering empowers*: Volunteers not only develop their skills and gain new knowledge but also gain the confidence to make an effective and creative contribution to their communities and to social and economic development.

6. *Volunteers make an impact*: '[V]olunteering involves grass-roots participation and ... has an economic, social, cultural and environmental impact, adding value to the work of the public, voluntary and private sectors' (ibid.).

These 'basic principles' which underpin volunteering not only provide us with some further evidence of the heterogeneity of voluntary action but also give us basic framework for defining what it is that its various manifestations have in common. They also lay down some markers to delineate the boundaries of what is and what is not volunteering, and it is to these issues of definition that we turn in the following section.

The question of definition

Cnaan et al. (1996) identified four dimensions that were common to a variety of definitions they found during a review of the volunteering literature: free choice, absence of remuneration, structure and intended beneficiaries. This is reflected in the formulation adopted by the UK Volunteering Forum in 1996 and quoted by Kearney (2001/2007):

> It is the commitment of time and energy for the benefit of society and the community and can take many forms. It is undertaken freely and by choice, without concern for financial gain. (p. 6)

Work by Cnaan and his colleagues (Cnaan and Amrofell, 1994; Cnaan et al., 1996; Handy et al., 2000) has led to the development and testing of the principle that public perception of who is a volunteer is related to the conception of the net cost of any given volunteering situation. This is calculated by measuring the total costs to the volunteer and setting against them the value of any benefits associated with the activity. They found that the higher the net cost, the higher the publicly perceived valuation of the volunteer (Handy et al., 2000). A follow-up study by Meijs et al. (2003) extended the enquiry to eight countries and found that the basic concept applied across a range of societies and that there was a consensus as to who could be counted as a definite volunteer. There was 'some variation ... regarding who is least likely to be considered as a volunteer' but 'remuneration and less free will have a definite impact on people's perception of who is a volunteer across all regions' (p. 32). However, there were differences of culture and context such as different views about the legitimacy of some of the 'perks' of volunteering.

While there is a measure of agreement about the core characteristics of volunteering, we do not have a single, simple, objective definition which enables us to draw a clear line between what is volunteering and what is not. Instead, we need to look more closely at the fuzziness of some of the boundaries.

Formal vs informal volunteering

The first of these is the question of structure. The Citizenship Surveys (undertaken in England and Wales in 2001, 2003, 2005 and 2007/2008) distinguish between three kinds of participation in community and voluntary activities:

1. *Civic participation*: defined as contact with an MP or other elected representative or a public official, attending a public meeting or

rally, taking part in a public demonstration or protest, or signing a petition;

2. *Informal volunteering*: defined as 'giving unpaid help as an individual to people who are not relatives' and

3. *Formal volunteering*: defined as 'giving unpaid help through groups, clubs or organisations to benefit other people or the environment [for example, the protection of wildlife or the improvement of public open spaces]'.

An increase in the numbers taking part in informal volunteering was the main element in the Home Office's achievement (in 2003) of its Public Service Agreement (PSA) target of increasing the numbers involved at least once a month in any of the three activities by 5 per cent by 2006 (Home Office, 2004). (Whether this claim is justified is, of course, a different matter; it all depends on which figures are chosen. Our analysis – see Chapter 4 – suggests that the trend more recently has been downward rather than rising.) It has also been suggested that informal rather than formal volunteering offers a more useful approach to increasing participation in voluntary action by people at risk of social exclusion (Williams, 2003a,b). It is, however, doubtful whether the public perception of volunteering would include individual acts of neighbourliness or citizenship. Similarly, some of the acts of civic participation as defined by the Home Office can be seen as activism but not volunteering.

Free choice vs coercion

A second fuzzy boundary divides free choice from coercion. Some forms of activity involve a level of coercion that clearly puts them into a category of non-voluntary unpaid work. These include some forms of employer-supported volunteering (Tschirhart, 2005), some forms of service learning by students in higher education (Paxton and Nash, 2002), community service and work experience by school students, and internships and other unpaid work experience activities which represent a necessary preparation for employment.

Other activities may involve moral coercion. Parents may not experience volunteering to help run services they want their children to benefit from as entirely uncoerced. Similarly, people holding office in a community organisation may not feel they have the option of resigning if there is no suitable successor in view.

Even in the field of volunteering as leisure, the idea of completely free choice has to be qualified: after all it 'normally includes the clear requirement of being in a particular place, at a specified time, to carry out an assigned function' (Stebbins, 2004: p. 4). Stebbins suggests that alongside coercion and choice, we need to discuss the concept of obligation. 'People are obligated when, even though not actually coerced by an external force, they do or refrain from doing something because they feel bound in this regard by promise, convention or circumstances' (ibid.: p. 7). Volunteering thus involves obligation, but this is typically outweighed by the rewards it brings and the option for the volunteer to exit from the activity at a convenient point in the future. In any case, it might well be an *agreeable* obligation rather than a disagreeable one. Moreover, compared with the demands of work and one's personal life, the obligation involved in volunteering can be seen as flexible.

For love or money?

The third dimension of Cnaan et al.'s (1996) framework – the absence of remuneration – is also problematic. While the conventional wisdom is that good practice in volunteer management means that volunteers should not be out-of-pocket as a result of their involvement but should not receive any other material reward, this is by no means universally applied. Blacksell and Phillips (1994) found that a significant proportion of volunteers in their study had received some kind of payment over and above the reimbursement of expenses. The ambiguity of this boundary has also been emphasised by the use of other kinds of material reward – such as birthday or Christmas gifts, free theatre tickets, parties, the use of comfortable hotels for board 'away days' and so on. These practices have to date been less common in Britain than in the United States, and have been seen as inappropriate by some volunteers (see, for example, Rochester and Hutchison, 2002; Tihanyi, 1991) and may also have legislative implications.

There have been a number of suggestions that payment should be made for some forms of volunteering including charity trusteeship and Housing Association board membership (Ashby and Ferman, 2003; Charity Commission, 2003) and community activity by local residents (Williams, 2004a). These have been met with the argument that any remuneration will undermine the 'gift relationship' which is the essence of volunteering or 'if a job needs to be done, people should be paid the going rate for doing it' (Forster, 2004: p. 38). 'Payment' of volunteers also raises legal issues with regards to minimum wage legislation. Suggestions that volunteering by students in higher education should be rewarded by the remission of tuition fees or the award of course credits (Ellis, 2003b) have also failed to gain support. Alongside the concern about undervaluing voluntary action and employing people on substandard wages the research evidence also suggests that material rewards are unlikely to motivate large numbers of people to volunteer or to ensure that they continue to give their time (Ellis, 2004; Locke et al., 2003).

Cui bono (to whose benefit)?

Finally, we need to explore the extent to which volunteering can be seen as benefiting other people or the environment as well as the volunteer and her or his family. It is widely accepted that the motivation to volunteer is usually a blend of self-interest and altruism (Stebbins, 2004). Some definitions raise the bar by requiring the activity to produce public goods or deliver public benefit (Dekker and Halman, 2003). This might lead to the exclusion of a great deal of 'volunteering as leisure' in clubs and associations which are seen as benefiting their members rather than delivering public benefit. However, many of these organisations can be seen as 'mixed benefactories' (Lohmann, 1992) which produce both member and public benefits (Rochester, 1997). A similar case can be made in respect of self-help or mutual aid groups as a specialised part of the associational world (Borkman, 1999).

Conclusion

This chapter set out to begin to provide a 'round-earth map' of volunteering in the hope of capturing the full scope and heterogeneity of voluntary action. We have approached this through three different mapping techniques. In the first section, we challenged the adequacy of the dominant paradigm of 'volunteering as service' by highlighting two alternative perspectives of 'volunteering as activism' and 'volunteering as leisure' and bringing the three approaches together in a diagram that helped us to sketch out the diversity of volunteering activities. Second, we looked at the values that helped to shape the extent and nature of volunteering in different cultures and societies and drew on Kearney's work to identify some basic principles that underpinned the idea of volunteering as a single – if multi-faceted – phenomenon. Finally, we used the work of Cnaan and his colleagues (1996) to explore the fuzzy boundaries of voluntary action. We believe these three conceptual frameworks have both justified our contention that volunteering is a complex phenomenon and helped provide a means of understanding the major landmarks that are needed for a complete map of the territory. In the next chapter, we will try to fill in more of the cartographical information by exploring typologies of the activities undertaken by volunteers and of the volunteers themselves.

3
Capturing the Diversity of Voluntary Action

Introduction

In this, the second of two chapters in which we attempt to capture the full picture of the range and diversity of volunteering, we will look at typologies of volunteering and attempts to distinguish between different kinds of volunteers. The three-perspective model introduced in Chapter 2 has already presented one typology of volunteering, but here we will review authoritative alternative approaches before turning our attention to some useful typologies of volunteers.

Typologies of volunteering: a global perspective

One way in which we can better understand the heterogeneity of volunteering in the United Kingdom is to use the global templates that were developed as part of the process of preparing for, implementing and reviewing the UN's IYV in 2001. In a paper prepared at the invitation of UN Volunteers and submitted to a Special Session of the UN's General Assembly, Davis Smith (2000) set out a framework for examining 'the different ways in which volunteering manifests itself in different regional and national contexts' (p. 9). This typology identified four distinctive 'types of volunteer activity, categorised according to their final outcome or final purpose' each of which 'occurs in all parts of the world' although 'the form each takes and the balance between the different types differs markedly from country to country' (ibid.: p. 11).

The four types of activity are as follows:

1. *Mutual aid or self-help*: It is probably the oldest form of voluntary action in which people with shared problems, challenges and conditions

work together to address or ameliorate them. This is sometimes described as voluntary action 'by us, for us'. In many parts of the world and especially in the developing countries of the South, mutual aid continues to provide 'the main system of social and economic support for the majority of the population' (ibid.: p. 12). While the industrialised economies of the North support welfare bureaucracies that meet many of the same needs, self-help continues to play a significant role in providing support and assistance to people in need, notably those who have a common medical problem.

2. *Philanthropy and service to others*: This is what most people in Britain would identify as volunteering; typically involving an organisation which recruits volunteers to provide some kind of service to one or more third parties. This is the kind of activity referred to in the previous chapter as forming 'the dominant paradigm'. While it may be a more prominent 'feature of developed societies, philanthropic volunteering can nevertheless be found in all parts of the world' (p. 12).

3. *Participation*: It is the involvement on a voluntary basis in the political or decision-making process at any level from participation in a users' forum to holding honorary office in a voluntary and community sector organisation. In the developing world, participation has been 'the watchword of development in recent years' (ibid.: p. 13) although theory has tended to run ahead of practice and the involvement of citizens in decision-making can be little more than tokenism. For the United Kingdom, the idea of participation helps to highlight the voluntary contribution made by so many in the field of governance – including the 350,000 school governors in England alone and the 900,000 charity trustees in England and Wales – which is rarely included in discussions about volunteering.

4. *Advocacy or campaigning*: It is the collective action aimed at securing or preventing change which includes campaigning against developments seen as damaging to the environment and campaigning for better services, for example, for people with HIV/AIDS. This kind of activity can be undertaken at a local, national or global level and can be controversial both in the causes pursued and the methods adopted by the volunteers involved. It can thus test the boundaries of the largely unspoken assumption that volunteering is a 'good thing'.

This global typology is a powerful tool in helping us to understand the variety of forms that volunteering takes on the worldwide stage. It is not, however, truly comprehensive; it does not take account of the 'volunteering as leisure' perspective we discussed in Chapter 2 and makes no reference to the very large numbers of volunteers active in the fields of sport and recreation and the arts and culture. This is no doubt because, like any such framework, the typology has been developed for a specific purpose which, in this case, is to highlight the social and economic benefits of volunteering and the contribution that it can make to social development. An alternative approach has been developed by Inglehart (2003) in the interests of measuring the changes in the scale and nature of voluntary action that might accompany the transition of countries into post-industrial 'knowledge societies'. Inglehart's focus is on civic participation in the form of 'membership and volunteering', and he distinguishes between three broad types of voluntary action (p. 63).

The first of these 'involves volunteering in environmental (or "Green") associations, peace movements, welfare activities for the old, the handicapped or the deprived, volunteering for health-related associations, and volunteer work associations concerned with aiding the development of poor countries or with human rights'. The second 'involves volunteering for political parties, local organizations concerned with poverty and unemployment, women's groups and labor unions'. The 'third dimension reflects volunteering in religious or church-linked associations, youth work, sports groups, professional associations and educational and cultural associations'. Together, the three 'types' provide a fairly comprehensive framework for capturing membership and volunteering but the rationale for the allocation of specific areas of activity to each of the categories is not apparent and it could be argued that they merely describe the fields of interest in which the volunteering takes place and not the types of activities being undertaken.

Another useful counter-balance is provided by Salamon and his colleagues (2003) whose global view of civil society highlights the importance of understanding that voluntary organisations are 'more than service providers'; they also perform 'a broader *expressive function*, providing the vehicles through which an enormous variety of other sentiments and impulses – artistic, religious, cultural, ethnic, social, recreational – also find expression' (p. 20).

A check-list of activities

Perhaps the most comprehensive of the attempts to develop a global typology of volunteering is another product of the UN's IYV 2001. This takes the form of a check-list of different kinds of volunteer activity which has been developed as part of a toolkit to assist people around the world to conduct comprehensive surveys of the extent and of nature of volunteering (Dingle, 2001). Below, we summarise the check-list.

Community activity which includes helping to bring in the harvest and other resources that are vital for the community, remove rubbish or debris from public areas or make improvements to them, organise a collective response to a problem affecting the community or draw public attention to a problem faced by the community;

Emergency response which involves such activities as helping to prepare for a natural disaster or eliminate its effects (e.g., building dykes or putting out fires), save victims of a disaster from immediate danger, provide comfort for victims of disaster or organise a response to a disaster;

Community peacekeeping which might involve helping organize members of the community to maintain order (e.g., patrolling public areas), taking part in direct action to investigate or prevent illegal or detrimental activity, undertaking training to equip you with the skills to protect your community from criminal activity, helping to resolve a dispute between groups or communities, or helping to set up or organise a conflict resolution programme or organisation;

Social assistance which includes helping to provide immediate assistance to people in need (such as food, shelter and health care for elderly and disabled people), helping to build structures to house or help people in need, or setting up or managing a programme or organisation to provide help for people in need;

Personal assistance which includes providing counselling, emotional support or advice to friends, colleagues and neighbours, or helping to provide food or other necessities of life for them;

Children and youth which involves helping to set up or manage programmes that tackle problems affecting young people such as delinquency, neglect and abuse, helping to provide services to children and young people, helping to set up or organise a day-care programme, or taking care of children while their parents or carers are working;

Human rights, advocacy and politics which involves contacting and organising people to advance their political interests such as encouraging people to vote or helping candidates, participating in direct action (such as a demonstration or march) support of a social or political cause, helping to elect a candidate for political office, helping to set up or manage elections, or setting up or managing a party or other political organisation;

Economic justice which involves helping to organise people to advance or protect their economic interests (e.g., setting up a union or a campaign about working conditions), or participating in direct action, such as a strike, to advance or protect the interests of working people;

Religious volunteering which includes helping to organise a special event to celebrate a religious holiday or as an act of worship, promoting religious faith or values, participate in direct action to bring attention to a matter of religious intolerance, helping to set up or manage a church or other religious body, or helping to organise a funeral;

Education which involves teaching or training others to acquire new skills, or helping to set up or manage a school or other educational institutions;

Health care which involves helping to disseminate information or organise a programme addressing health issues; helping to provide support services for health care institutions; providing health care or rehabilitation services; donating blood, bone marrow or organs; or setting up or managing a programme designed to provide heath care, treatment or heath education;

Environment which involves campaigning against threats to the environment or on behalf of endangered indigenous peoples;

Data collection which involves collecting specimens, reading scientific instruments, observing the weather for research or science, observing or interviewing people for research purposes, consulting archives and other documents for research purposes, or setting up or managing a programme or organisation designed to collect data for public information;

Promotion of knowledge which involves disseminating knowledge or professional skills by giving public lectures, writing or editing articles or serving on the board of a professional association; helping to organise a public event aimed at disseminating knowledge or professional skills; setting up or managing an organisation aimed at representing professional interests; facilitating communication within professions; and disseminating information about them;

Promotion of commerce which involves helping to improve or promote the production of goods, the exchange of goods and services and product safety, or setting up or managing a programme or organisation designed to promote these interests;

Law and legal services which involves providing legal advice or legal representation on a *pro bono* basis, helping to promote a general understanding of the law and legal rights, or setting up or managing a programme to provide legal advice and representation on a *pro bono* basis;

Culture which involves helping to plan, set up, advertise, manage, provide technical assistance at, maintain order at, and clean up after a cultural event for public entertainment; or acting, performing music, singing, dancing, reading poetry, lecturing or displaying one's works of art or crafts at a cultural event for public entertainment;

Recreation which includes helping to plan, set up, advertise, manage, provide technical assistance at, maintain order at, and clean up after a sporting or recreational event for public entertainment (such as a football match, chess tournament, animal show or festival), or taking part as a player, contestant, team member or participant in any of these events which were organised to save a public cause (such as raising funds and promoting peace, human rights or social justice) rather than purely for one's own enjoyment.

Different kinds of volunteers

Having looked at some of the ways in which we can distinguish between the different kinds of activities in which volunteers are engaged, we now turn our attention to typologies based on differences in the characteristics and attitudes of volunteers and the kind of involvement or relationship they have with the organisations through which they engage in voluntary action. We will look in turn at the increasingly important distinction between long-term and short-term volunteers, a typology that has been developed for volunteer managers, and distinctions based on the organisational context within which volunteering takes place.

Long-term and short-term volunteers

A key distinction that is increasingly made is between those whose volunteering is long-term and those who commit themselves to organisations or causes for shorter periods (Danson, 2003; Macduff, 2005).

The long-term volunteer is distinguished by a high level of dedication to a cause or organisation and a strong sense of affiliation with the organisation and the work of its volunteers. They are likely 'to have a strong emotional investment in their volunteer role and in the sense of personal worth and identity they gain from their participation' (Danson, 2003: p. 36). There are three ways in which long-term volunteers tend to be recruited. They may seek out the organisation as a means of pursuing an existing commitment to the cause (and thus recruit themselves), they may become increasingly connected with the organisation over time or they may be brought to the organisation 'because of a close connection with the existing circle of volunteers'. Long-term volunteers 'will tend to shape their own job, adapting their time and energies to whatever is needed to make the cause succeed' and are 'willing to do whatever type of work is required... although this may not be exciting or rewarding in itself'.

By contrast, the relatively new phenomenon of the *short-term volunteer* has an interest in the cause which falls well short of dedication. He or she does not 'usually view the organisation or their involvement as a central part of their life'. Short-term volunteers tend to be 'recruited through participation in a specific event, such as a weekend sports programme' or 'by forced choice – they are asked by a friend or employer to volunteer'. They are looking for 'a well-defined job of limited duration' and want to know from the start 'exactly what they are being asked to do and for how long they are committed to it'. They will tend to undertake only one kind of work and, while 'they may well volunteer throughout their life, they do not usually remain too long with any one organisation'.

Macduff (2005) has suggested that a better description of short-term volunteering is episodic – defined in her dictionary as 'made up of separate, especially loosely connected episodes; or limited in duration or significance to a particular episode, temporary, occurring, appearing or changing at irregular intervals, occasionally' (p. 50) – and has identified three different forms of it.

The *temporary episodic volunteer* offers a few hours or at most a day of his or her time on a one-off basis. He or she may 'pass out water bottles at a marathon, cook hamburgers at a party for homeless children, or arrive at a beach to clean refuse' (p. 50). This is a form of volunteering often found in the team challenges of employer-supported volunteering.

The *interim volunteer* is involved on a regular basis but for a limited period of time – less than six months. Examples might include a student on a work experience placement or the members of a time-limited task force.

The *occasional episodic volunteer* provides 'service at regular intervals for short periods of time' which may range from a month to a few hours 'but the manager of volunteers can count on this person returning year after year' (p. 51). An example from the United Kingdom might be the volunteer who solicits donations during Christian Aid week each year.

Macduff finds common ground with Hustinx (2001/2007) in describing these episodic forms as 'new volunteerism' by contrast with the older tradition of 'classic volunteering'. The Table 3.1 (taken from Hustinx, 2001/2007: p. 65) shows the different characteristics of the two models.

The contrast between the two models of volunteering is clearly related to the pithier distinction made by Evans and Saxton (2005:

Table 3.1   Two models of volunteerism: classic and new

	Classic volunteerism	New volunteerism
Culture	Identifies with traditional cultural norms	Individualization
Choice of organization	Based on: Traditional cultural identities Great loyalty Delegated leadership Solid structure	Based on: Personal interest Weak ties Decentralised structure Loose networks
Choice of field of action	Based on: Traditional cultural identities Inclusion and exclusion	Based on: Perception of new biographical similarities Taste for topical issues Dialogue between global and local
Choice of activity	Based on: Traditional cultural identities Needs of the organization Idealism	Based on: Balance between personal preference and organization's needs Cost/benefit analysis Pragmatic
Length and intensity of commitment	Long-term (unlimited in time) Regular Unconditional	Short-term (clearly limited in time) Irregular or erratic Conditional
Relationship with the beneficiary	Unilateral, 'altruistic', 'selfless'	Reciprocal

Source: Hustinx (2001/2007: p. 65)

p. 41) between the decreasing number of 'time-driven' volunteers and the growing number of 'cause-driven' volunteers; rather than treating volunteering as a means of filling their time, people are increasingly seeking specific experiences and rewards.

Concern about the implications of the newer attitude to volunteering has been highlighted by the popularity with Dutch organisations of the idea of 'revolving door' volunteers (Dekker and Halman, 2003). Researching the history of the London Voluntary Service Council, its Chief Executive came across a volunteer who had worked for the organisation for thirty years and commented 'I couldn't rely on getting anyone to stay for thirty *days* nowadays' (personal communication to the authors).

This is not to argue that long-term volunteering no longer happens; it is simply less frequent than before and cannot be taken as the norm it once was. But it is also important to distinguish between different levels of long-term commitment. A study of Jewish lay leaders (Harris and Rochester, 2001a) identified a minority of volunteers whose commitment to their organisations involved many hours a week over a period of a number of years. A similar division between 'an inner group of willing people' and other volunteers was found in religious congregations (Harris, 1998) and between the 'stalwarts' and the rest in sports volunteering (Nichols, 2006).

A typology for practitioners

A leading handbook for those who manage the work of volunteers (McCurley and Lynch, 1998) lists a number of 'new types of volunteers' which present new challenges for the organisations with which they are involved. These include the *episodic* volunteers identified by Macduff (2005) and which were discussed above. They are characterised here as 'volunteers who go from organisation to organisation getting involved in one-off events, then move on to other events in other organisations' (p. 16). Other specific types of volunteers highlighted by the authors are as follows:

Employer-supported volunteers: Employers are increasingly concerned to promote and encourage volunteering by their staff as part of their approach to corporate social responsibility; as a means of developing the experience and skills of their employees; and as a series of opportunities for team-building. Typically, teams of volunteers undertake practical tasks such as painting and decorating for a few hours at a time but there are also opportunities for organisations to access professional and technical skills such as accountancy and marketing while some senior managers serve as trustees and members of management committees.

Older volunteers: The pool of older people from which volunteers may be recruited is growing larger as people live longer or retire earlier. McCurley and Lynch suggest that 'retirees can be recruited to an unpaid or expenses-only second career, attracted into traditional volunteering opportunities, or volunteer in completely new ways – such as the University of the Third Age (U3A) where retired people run course and classes for retired people' (p. 15).

Professional volunteers: Professional associations like the Institute of Chartered Accountants and the Law Society have encouraged and facilitated volunteering by their members. Much – but not all – of this involves making their professional expertise available to voluntary organisations.

Transitional volunteers: Those who use 'volunteering as an activity to forge a path back into the community'. They include 'housewives re-entering the job market, those with emotional disturbances moving back into interaction with others, those with disabilities learning new skills' (p. 16).

Unemployed volunteers: Successive governments have looked to volunteering to provide a route into employment for jobless people. Attracting people from this group and making their involvement a success is, however, a challenge requiring new ideas and innovative approaches to meet the needs of people who may have low skills and little experience of work and working relationships.

More controversially, McCurley and Lynch add two further categories which identify other kinds of involvement with an organisation which would not be accepted by many as falling within the definition of volunteering. These are as follows:

Alternative sentencing volunteers: Community service as an alternative to prison sentences and as part of an 'intermediate treatment' regime for young offenders and those at risk is sometimes seen as a form of volunteering. But as Kearney (2001/2007) has pointed out, freedom of choice is absolutely central to the philosophy and practice of voluntary action.

Stipended volunteers: A similar phenomenon which can be regarded as quasi-volunteering is the practice, common in the United States, of rewarding so-called volunteers with money and benefits such as free tuition for higher education and college courses. The consensus in the United Kingdom remains, however, that volunteering should not involve any material reward which goes beyond the reimbursement of out-of-pocket expenses.

Other new kinds of volunteer

McCurley and Lynch's typology – like the discussion of the distinction between long-term and short-term volunteering – suggests that diversity is the product of the development of new types of volunteer. We will review the changing face of volunteering and the challenges involved in the newer forms it is taking in Chapter 8. For the present, we will try to complete this practical account of the variety of volunteer types by making brief reference to three further kinds of volunteer that have increased in prominence in the recent past.

1. *Transnational volunteers*: The movement of volunteers from one country to another is not new; there have been examples of cross-country voluntary action since the 19th century and, more recently, it has been the focus of well-known programmes organised by organisations such as Voluntary Service Overseas (VSO) in the United Kingdom, the Peace Corps in the United States and the UN Volunteers across the world. There has been, however, a 'recent dramatic increase' which has affected not only the scale of the activity but also the range of forms it takes (Davis Smith et al., 2005). Much of this increase has been fuelled by the growing practice of young people taking a 'gap year' as part of the transition from school to university or between courses. But transnational volunteering is not restricted to the young; organisations such as VSO recruit increasing numbers of experienced professionals rather than new graduates (Rochester and Hutchison, 2002), and the idea of a 'career break' has become commonplace.

2. *Virtual volunteers*: Much of the discussion about the impact on volunteering of a society which conducts many of its business and personal relationships by means of information and communications technology (ICT) rather than face-to-face has concentrated on the need to use the new media as a means of recruiting and retaining volunteers (Evans and Saxton, 2005). There is growing evidence that volunteering activity can itself be undertaken on a virtual basis. It offers an attractive option to those who are used to operating in a virtual world as well as an enhanced opportunity for some older people and those with long-term medical conditions who have problems with mobility. As well as enhancing the capacity of voluntary organisations 'on-line volunteering can be a positive side to "globalisation", happening at a very local personal level for people and organizations all over the world' (Cravens, 2006: p. 22).

3. *'Disaster' volunteers*: Preparing for and responding to natural disasters figured in the typology of volunteering presented above, and there are some well-known and long-established volunteer-involving organisations founded to assist in times of natural and political crisis such as the Red Cross and Red Crescent societies and Medecins Sans Frontieres. A more recent phenomenon, however, has been the very large numbers of spontaneous and unaffiliated volunteers who have come forward in response to major disasters such as the impact of the Tsunami in South Asia and the terrorist attacks on the World Trade Center in New York in 2001. In the immediate aftermath of the latter event, for example, 30,000 or more people converged on the city of New York to offer help (Sharon, 2004/2007). While this was a disaster on an unparalleled scale

and of an exceptional kind, we can expect similar spontaneous responses to other unexpected and tragic events and, as Sharon points out, our body of knowledge about this kind of volunteer is 'meagre'.

Organisational context

Finally, we can look at the different organisational contexts in which volunteering takes place and explore the extent to which they lead to different kinds of volunteering. Here, we shall draw on two strands in the work conducted at the London School of Economics and Political Science's (LSE) Centre for Voluntary Organisation in the 1990s – a study of the distinctive organisational challenges facing small voluntary agencies carried out by a team led by Rochester (1999/2007) and studies of local churches (Cameron, 1998; Harris, 1996).

The 'small agencies' study led to the identification of four distinctive kinds of volunteer involvement in small voluntary organisations (Rochester, 1999/2007):

1. *The service delivery model*: Here the lion's share of the operational work of the organisation is carried out by volunteers who are recruited to undertake pre-determined and specified tasks such as proving support to the victims of crime or mediating in disputes between neighbours. The role of the paid staff in agencies of this kind is essentially one of recruiting, training, deploying and supporting the work of these front-line workers.

2. *The support role model*: Unlike the service delivery model which is based on the assumption that it is appropriate for the main work of the agency to be undertaken by volunteers, the support role model is found in organisation where this responsibility has been given to paid staff. In order to maximise the time that staff can devote to these activities, volunteers are recruited to play a variety of support roles. They may, for example, act as receptionists, secretaries, administrators or bookkeepers.

3. *The member/activist model*: This is found in associations – organisations which lack paid staff. The members have come together to pursue a common interest or meet a shared need. Their goals are pursued and all of their operational and support activities are carried out by the members themselves and not delegated to a separate group of staff – paid or unpaid. The work is not shared equally, and clear distinctions can be made between passive and active members and between the majority of active members and a smaller inner group who undertake most of the work.

4. *The co-worker model*: Here the differences in role and distinctions of status between paid staff and volunteers are unclear and blurred. Like the support role model, it is found in agencies where the total activities of the organisation can only be covered if the work of its staff is supplemented by the contribution of volunteers. There is, however, an important difference; the division of labour is not straightforward. Tasks and responsibilities are allocated through a process of discussion and negotiation which take into account the skills and expertise of each person – staff and volunteers alike – as well as the amounts of time each of them is able to commit to the work.

Members and volunteers

Cameron has drawn on the research on local churches undertaken by herself (1998) and Harris (1996) to explore the conceptual differences between 'volunteers' and 'members'. 'Are the two sets of activists essentially the same or are there differences that have a significant impact on the way these groups are deployed in voluntary organisations?' (Cameron, 1999/2007: p. 53). Cameron identified five distinctions between volunteering in a service-providing organisation and volunteering in a membership association:

1. Members are more committed to the values of the organisation than volunteers. They tend to feel responsible for sustaining it and ensuring that its activities continue.
2. They have greater expectations that the organisation will take their views into account.
3. Members have a stronger sense of reciprocity than volunteers; they see their relationship with the organisation as an exchange in which their contribution helps to build up an organisation on which they themselves rely.
4. They have a better overview of the work of the organisation and will try to make helpful connections whether it is their 'job' to do so. They feel a sense of responsibility for the organisation as a whole rather than for their own activities.
5. Members distinguish less between their private and public roles than volunteers do.

A key explanation for these differences, according to Cameron, is that members operate in the unambiguous 'world' of associations (Billis, 1993) while volunteers are involved in ambiguous situations where the norms and rules of the associational world overlap with those of the world of bureaucracy which treats them as unpaid staff with defined roles and responsibilities. On the round-earth map of volunteering, both 'members' and 'volunteers' are volunteers, but the distinction between the two categories is a useful one.

Conclusion

In this chapter, we have explored a variety of attempts to distinguish between different types of voluntary activity and different kinds of volunteer. The proliferation of typologies is evidence of the complexity of the phenomenon that is volunteering and the range of perspectives brought to bear on it. These multiple points of view make the task of producing a 'round-earth map' of voluntary action extremely difficult, but we hope that this chapter, together with Chapter 2, provides the tools with which readers can produce their own guides to the terrain. We now turn our attention to another kind of mapping in which we draw on the current research data to provide a profile of volunteering in the United Kingdom and answer the question 'who does what'?

4
Profiling Voluntary Action: Who does what?

Introduction

How we define volunteering inevitably makes a difference to how we count how many people do it. Chapters 2 and 3 discussed the various definitions of volunteering and the diversity of activities captured therein. This chapter focuses on levels of volunteering and patterns of participation: exploring who volunteers and what volunteers do. In this endeavour, however, we are to some extent limited by the ways in which these definitions of volunteering have been built into the research questions which have been designed to measure it.

How you ask about volunteering makes a big difference to the number of people who say they volunteer (Hall, 2001; Lynn, 1997; Lyons et al., 1998). As Rooney et al. (2004: p. 648) put it 'when it comes to estimating... volunteering, methodology is destiny'. Even if the same definition of volunteering is used within a survey, different questions lead to different answers (Hurley et al., 2008). If a survey asks something along the lines of 'do you volunteer', in the United Kingdom, very broadly speaking, we tend to find that approximately 20 per cent of the population will say 'yes', as in the Northern Ireland survey by the Volunteer Development Agency discussed below. However, if we ask about participation in a range of organisations, and then about helping those organisations through a range of activities, which we have defined as volunteering but which respondents might not themselves recognise as such, then we find approximately 40 per cent of people volunteer. This is the approach taken in the Citizenship Surveys in England and Wales. If we give respondents multiple opportunities to reflect on their engagement in different organisations, groups and communities and whether they have taken part in these 'volunteering' activities, we get a higher figure still, as in *Helping Out,* a 2006/2007 national survey of volunteering and charitable giving in England (Low et al., 2007; see Lynn, 1997 and Rooney et al., 2004 for discussions on how longer, more detailed prompts lead to higher reported levels of volunteering).

In this chapter, we discuss the number of people engaged in volunteering and who these volunteers tend to be – their demographic and socio-economic characteristics. We also discuss the areas of social life to which volunteers contribute and the roles and functions they perform. This review depends heavily on the Citizenship Survey, which is a household survey of approximately 10,000 adults in England and Wales (plus a BME boost sample of approximately 5,000) conducted initially by the Home Office and more recently by the Department of Communities and Local Government every other year since 2001. We supplement the data from these surveys by drawing on several other smaller studies from each of the four home countries.

How many people volunteer?

Few surveys have been conducted to ascertain the levels of volunteering across the whole of the United Kingdom. The most recently available internationally comparable data come from the World Values Survey conducted in 1999–2001, which asked respondents whether they belonged to any one of 14 listed voluntary organisations and then asked for which of those they were currently doing 'unpaid work' (Musick and Wilson, 2008). This survey found that 43 per cent of the United Kingdom's population were volunteering, a reasonably high level of participation when compared with many other countries from around the world, although far from the highest (we discuss international comparisons of volunteering in Chapter 5).

A far more detailed, if not always comparable, picture is available within the individual home countries. If taken at face value, the data from individual countries discussed below suggest volunteering is considerably higher in some home countries than others. Again, however, it all depends on the comprehensiveness of the definitions used, on the questions asked and the way surveys are administered.

England

Three-quarters (73 per cent) of England's adult population volunteered in some way (including formal and informal volunteering) at least once in the year between April 2007 to March 2008. Half (48 per cent) did so on a regular (once a month) basis.

Informal volunteering (unpaid help between individuals other than family members) is more common in England (and across the United Kingdom) than formal volunteering (unpaid help within groups and organisations), although the scale of the difference between the two forms of participation is changing (see below). According to the 2007/2008 Citizenship Survey, 43 per cent of the adult population of England had volunteered formally at least once over the past 12 months, while 64 per cent had volunteered informally. These figures represent an estimated 17.7 million people getting involved in formal volunteering each year, each volunteering an average of 7.6 hours over a four-week period and so giving a combined annual population contribution of 1.75 billion hours, with an equivalent economic value of £22.7 billion.

Regular volunteering (at least once a month) is less common across both types, with 27 per cent of adults being regular formal volunteers and 35 per cent being regular informal volunteers.

Wales

Until recently, levels of volunteering in Wales have been analysed through the Citizenship Survey allowing direct comparisons with England. The sample size for Wales has, however, been small. In 2003, just over half (54 per cent) of Wales' adult population were found to have volunteered informally at least once in the previous 12 months. This compared to a figure of 63 per cent for England in the same year, and a figure for levels of volunteering in Wales in 2001 of 64 per cent. In terms of formal volunteering, the 2003 survey reported that 40 per cent of Wales' adult population had participated at least once in the past year, no change (1 per cent difference) on two years previous, and not significantly lower (2 per cent) than in England.

Scotland

In 2006, 32 per cent of Scotland's adult population volunteered formally. This equated to 1.3 million people who together gave the equivalent of 3.8 million 35-hour weeks, representing over 79,000 full-time equivalent jobs, with an economic value of £1.8 billion (Volunteer Development Scotland [VDS] Research Team, 2007). Levels of informal volunteering were significantly higher in the same year, with three-quarters (74 per cent) of the population (or 3.8 million people) having participated in informally volunteering over the course of the year. Nearly all (90 per cent) of those people who volunteered formally also volunteered informally (VDS Research Team, 2007).

The same survey was undertaken in 2005, when it found that 38 per cent of the adult population took part in formal volunteering (VDS, 2006). By way of contrast, however, the 2005 Scottish Household Survey found that 20 per cent of Scottish adults volunteered (Hurley et al., 2008). Although both used the same definition of volunteering, they asked different questions to ascertain levels of participation (see Hurley et al., 2008 for a discussion on the methods used). These findings neatly illustrate the impact that asking different questions about volunteering and/or using different methods can have on the results which are generated.

Northern Ireland

Levels of volunteering in Northern Ireland appear to be the lowest from the four countries. In 2007, 21 per cent of the adult population reported having volunteered formally in the past 12 months. This equated to 282,067 adults, and represented over £504 million to the economy, with each volunteer giving an average of 13.4 hours each month (Volunteer Development Agency, 2007). It should be noted, however, that some, if not much, of the apparent difference in levels of volunteering in Northern Ireland as opposed to the other home countries may be explained, in part at least, by the different methodological approaches of the studies done to establish these figures.

As with elsewhere in the United Kingdom, levels of informal volunteering were higher than formal volunteering in Northern Ireland. One-third (35 per cent) of the adult population had volunteered informally in the 12 months prior to interview in 2007. This equated to 470,111 individuals, each giving an average of 9 hours per month, with the equivalent economic value of £433 million. Among the informal volunteers, 31 per cent of those were also engaged in formal volunteering which suggests that a significant minority of people were involved in both types of voluntary action.

Trends over time

In terms of how levels of volunteering have changed over time in the United Kingdom, there is little longitudinal evidence currently available. What evidence we do have, however, would seem to suggest that after a short period of gentle growth leading up to the mid-2000s, volunteering is currently either static or on the decline, despite considerable levels of government investment (Chapter 7).

We do know quite a bit about volunteering in England since 2001, but earlier data are not comparable. Here we can see that levels of volunteering in 2007/2008 (73 per cent) were the same as they were in 2001 (74 per cent). Within this time period, levels of volunteering peaked in 2005 at 76 per cent but then dipped back down again in the following two years (CLG, 2008).

Again, within these figures there are variations according to how we define volunteering. Levels of formal volunteering, which has received a great deal of government attention (see Chapter 7), have risen from 39 to 43 per cent, while levels of informal volunteering, which has received less interest from government, have dipped from 67 to 64 per cent. The regularity of volunteering also makes a difference, with less change apparent in regular (once a month) volunteering. Twenty-seven per cent of the adult population had been regular formal volunteers in 2001 with no change in 2007, although the figure did rise to 29 per cent in 2005. For informal volunteering, 34 per cent had been regular participants in 2001 with an insignificant change to 35 per cent in 2007, although again there was a slight rise to 37 per cent in 2005. Reporting on these slightly different figures or combination of figures can, therefore, give a more or less optimistic picture about the trends in levels of volunteering in England.

Levels of volunteering appear to be dropping faster in the other home countries than they do in England. In Scotland, for example, formal volunteering apparently fell from 43 per cent in 2004 to 38 per cent in 2005 and to 32 per cent in 2006; meanwhile, informal volunteering fell from 81 per cent in 2003 to 74 per cent in 2006 (VDS Research Team, 2007). In Northern Ireland, formal volunteering fell from 29 per cent in 2001 to 21 per cent in 2007, although this was still higher than the 18 per cent who volunteered in 1995 (Volunteer Development Agency, 2007). At the same time, the average number of hours volunteered had also declined in Northern Ireland from 15 a month in 2001 to 13.4 a month in 2007. Fewer people were volunteering and those that were volunteering were giving less time. Levels of informal volunteering appear to have dropped even more rapidly – going from 65 per cent in 2001 (or 56 per cent in 1995) to 35 per cent in 2007. Here, however, the average number of hours volunteered had increased, with informal volunteers in 2007 giving an average of 9 hours per month compared to 8 hours per month in 2001 (ibid.).

Who volunteers?

Propensity to volunteer is not equal across the United Kingdom's adult population. Some people are considerably more likely to volunteer than others. In this chapter, we do not attempt to explain why this might be the case; we concentrate instead on describing the patterns across key socio-demographic groups.

Gender

The long-held perception that women volunteer more than men is borne out by the evidence, although the difference is not as marked as is perhaps often assumed, and men volunteer more than women for certain activities (see below). In England, for example, 29 per cent of women were regular formal volunteers in 2007/2008 compared to 25 per cent of men (CLG, 2008). The differences were greater for regular informal volunteering, with figures of 39 per cent and 31 per cent, respectively.

Age

Volunteering varies by age, but the relationship is complex. Broadly speaking, the youngest and oldest age groups are least likely to volunteer, but when we look at the detail the pattern is less clear cut. Looking again at data from England, those aged 20 to 34 and 75 and over were least likely to take part in regular formal volunteering, while 16 to 24 year olds were more likely than other age groups to take part in regular informal volunteering (see Table 4.1). Similar patterns for formal volunteering are found in Scotland (Hurley et al., 2008), while in Northern Ireland those aged between 35 and 49 and between 16 and 24 are most likely to volunteer (Volunteer Development Agency, 2007).

Table 4.1 Volunteering in England, by age

	Formal volunteering		Informal volunteering		
	At least once a month (%)	At least once a year (%)	At least once a month (%)	At least once a year (%)	*Base*
16–19	28	48	41	67	*308*
20–24	20	35	42	67	*419*
25–34	22	40	36	68	*1319*
35–49	29	50	37	70	*2449*
50–64	29	44	31	62	*2084*
65–74	31	41	35	60	*1148*
75+	24	31	28	49	*1072*
All	27	43	35	64	*8804*

Source: Citizenship Survey 2007/2008

Ethnic origin

Our knowledge of volunteering among people from different ethnic groups has increased over recent years, challenging a number of previous and inaccurate assumptions and stereotypes. People from White and non-White backgrounds in Scotland have been found to be equally likely to volunteer (VDS Research Team, 2007). Similarly, in England, people from Black, White and mixed race groups have been found to take part in regular, formal volunteering at similar levels, but Asian and Chinese people were found to be less likely to be regular formal volunteers (see Table 4.2). In terms of informal volunteering, people of mixed race origin were found to have the highest rates of regular participation (42 per cent), followed by Black people (38 per cent) and White people (35 per cent).

These overall figures, however, mask considerable differences in volunteering within ethnic groups. For example, among Asian groups in England, while 22 per cent of people with an Indian background were regular formal volunteers in 2007/2008, this figure was 16 per cent for Pakistani people and 15 per cent for Bangladeshi people (see Table 4.2).

Being born outside the United Kingdom seems to have a significant impact on the likelihood of volunteering and may explain much of the

Table 4.2   Volunteering in England, by ethnicity

	Formal volunteering – At least once a month (%)	Informal volunteering – At least once a month (%)	*Base*
White	28	35	*8036*
Minority ethnic groups	22	32	*5493*
All Asian	19	28	*2745*
Indian	22	28	*1361*
Pakistani	16	29	*812*
Bangladeshi	15	24	*292*
All Black	27	38	*1672*
Caribbean	27	39	*808*
African	26	36	*818*
Mixed	27	42	*479*
Chinese/Other	16	27	*597*
All	27	35	*8804*

Source: Citizenship Survey 2007/2008

apparent difference between ethnic groups (Kitchen et al., 2006a). The 2005 Citizenship Survey, for example, found no significant differences in participation in formal volunteering among Black, White and Asian people born inside the United Kingdom (ibid.). Equally, other studies of volunteering in England have suggested that if we consider all formal volunteering, rather than just regular volunteering, there is no significant difference between different ethnic groups (Low et al., 2007).

Religion

Religion makes a difference to volunteering. Being actively religious has a particularly significant influence on the propensity to volunteer (Low et al., 2007). Being actively religious seems to be particularly influential on volunteering among White people and Black people (Kitchen et al., 2006a). There are also differences across different religious groups, although different surveys seem to suggest that different groups are most or least likely to volunteer. *Helping Out*, for example, found that Hindu respondents reported highest levels of formal volunteering (Low et al., 2007), while the 2005 Citizenship Survey found that Christians had higher levels of formal volunteering (Kitchen et al., 2006a). A study in Northern Ireland found that Catholics were slightly more likely to volunteer than Protestants (Volunteer Development Agency, 2007).

Employment, education and socio-economic status

Whether someone is employed and the nature of their employment affects their likelihood of volunteering. Studies in the United Kingdom have consistently found that those who are unemployed are less likely to volunteer than those who are working (Hurley et al., 2008; Low et al., 2007; Volunteer Development Agency, 2007). Again, however, there are considerable nuances. While being employed/working increases the likelihood of volunteering, there is a cut-off point. Those who are self-employed and those who are employed part-time have generally been found to be more likely to volunteer than those who are employed full-time. As Table 4.3 indicates, among those who are not working, the 2006/2007 *Helping Out* survey found that those who were looking after the home had higher levels of volunteering than those who were unemployed but looking for work, and those who were retired or sick and disabled (Low et al., 2007).

People's socio-economic status and their income also affects propensity to volunteer. Both are positively correlated with formal volunteering (Hurley et al., 2008; Volunteer Development Agency, 2007). For example, the 2005 Citizenship Survey found that 59 per cent of those in

Table 4.3 Formal volunteering in England, by employment status

	Employee (%)	Self-employed (%)	Not working (%)	Reason for not working				All (%)
				Unemployed/ looking for work (%)	Looking after home (%)	Sick or disabled (%)	Retired (%)	
All formal volunteers	62	60	55	57	65	34	55	59
Regular formal volunteers	38	36	40	35	42	17	42	39
Occasional or one-off formal volunteers	24	24	15	22	23	17	12	20
Non-volunteers	38	40	45	43	35	66	45	41
Base	*1100*	*165*	*887*	*51*	*109*	*117*	*551*	*2155*

Source: Helping Out 2006/2007

higher managerial and professional occupations volunteered (formally, at least once in the past 12 months), compared to 26 per cent of those in routine occupations (Kitchen et al., 2006a).

Full-time students are more likely to volunteer than the population as a whole (Kitchen et al., 2006a), and those who have a formal qualification are far more likely to volunteer than those who do not. Indeed, the higher the level of qualification the more likely you are to volunteer. For example, while 26 per cent of those who had no qualifications volunteered (formally, at least once in the last year), and 47 per cent of those whose highest qualification was GCSEs at grades A-C volunteered, this rose to 61 per cent among those who had a degree or higher qualification (Kitchen et al., 2006a). Increasing levels of volunteering among those who have no educational qualifications has become a key government target in England.

Disability

Disabled people and/or those with a Long-Term Limiting Illness (LLI) are less likely to volunteer than the population as a whole, although the differences are greater for formal volunteering than for informal volunteering. For example, the 2007/2008 Citizenship Survey found that in England 22 per cent of people with a disability or LLI regularly took part in formal volunteering compared to 27 per cent of all adults. With regards to informal volunteering, the figures were 33 per cent compared to 35 per cent. Removing barriers to disabled people and so increasing levels of volunteering has received considerable government attention in recent years (see Chapter 7).

Family structure

People's participation in volunteering changes throughout their life cycles. Married people in Scotland are, for example, more likely to volunteer than those who are divorced or single (VDS, 2007). Having children also makes a difference. Generally speaking, people who have dependent children are more likely to volunteer than those who do not, although there are nuances, particularly related to the age of the children and the types of volunteering being considered. The 2005 Citizenship Survey found that while 42 per cent of those with no dependent children had (formally) volunteered at least once in the past 12 months, this rose to 45 per cent amongst those whose youngest child was aged between 0 and 4, and then peaked at 61 per cent amongst those whose youngest child was aged 5 to 9, dropping back down to 45 per cent for those whose youngest child was aged 16 to 18 (Kitchen et al., 2006a).

We are most likely to volunteer when our children are of primary and secondary school age.

Geographical variations

Where you live within the United Kingdom also affects the likelihood of your volunteering. Alongside the national differences discussed in the sections above, there are differences within countries. People living in the northeast of England, for example, have been found to be less likely to volunteer than those living in England as a whole (Kitchen et al., 2006a) while those in the north of Scotland have been found to be more likely to volunteer than those in the west, east or south (VDS Research Team, 2007).

The 'type' of area also makes a difference. Rural areas have been found to be 'richer' in volunteering than urban areas (see Yates and Jochum, 2003 for a discussion of rural voluntary action). Deprived areas tend to have lower rates of volunteering than affluent areas. The 2003 Citizenship Survey, for example, found that the areas of England ranked as the 10 per cent least deprived had volunteering rates of 52 per cent, compared to 31 per cent in the 10 per cent most deprived areas. This is less true, however, for informal volunteering than it is for formal volunteering (Kitchen et al., 2006a; see Williams, 2003a,b, 2004b for discussion on the different formats of volunteering found in affluent and deprived communities). Similarly, areas with the highest density of minority ethnic populations have been found to have the lowest rates of volunteering. Fifty per cent of people volunteered in the 10 per cent of areas with the lowest minority ethnic density, compared to 34 per cent in the 10 per cent of areas with the highest minority ethnic density (Home Office, 2004).

The Citizenship Survey uses the ACORN classification system in order to explore geographical variations in volunteering. This system classifies areas in 17 groups, according to various Census characteristics. In 2003, levels of volunteering were found to be highest in 'Affluent Greys, Rural Communities' (62 per cent), followed by 'Wealthy Achievers, Suburban Areas' (53 per cent). The lowest levels of volunteering were found in areas classified as 'Council Estate Residents, High Unemployment' (27 per cent) and 'Multi-Ethnic Low Income Areas' (28 per cent) (Home Office, 2004).

Liking where you live also seems to make a difference to whether you volunteer. Data from the 2003 Citizenship Survey data showed that 45 per cent of people who reported that they enjoyed living in their neighbourhood volunteered compared to 30 per cent of those who did not. Those who trusted their neighbours, or at least other people who lived in their neighbourhood, were also more likely to volunteer: almost half (49 per cent) of the people who felt that many people in their neighbourhood could be trusted volunteered compared to one-quarter (27 per cent) of those who felt none could be trusted.

What do volunteers do?

'Formal' volunteers

Volunteers are involved in a wide range of organisations from across the voluntary and community, public and even private sector. While 82 per cent of volunteers in England helped an organisation in the voluntary and community sector; 28 per cent did so in the public sector and 14 per cent reported helping a private sector organisation (Kitchen et al., 2006a). The sectors are, however, self-reported. The accuracy of some of this reporting is thrown into doubt by a closer look at the detail of the responses to the survey.

Many volunteers help more than one organisation. Over half (59 per cent) of respondents to the latest national survey of volunteering in England volunteered for more than one organisation, with 36 per cent volunteering for three or more (Low et al., 2007). Interestingly, data from England suggest that volunteers tended to be getting involved in a greater number of organisations. In 1997, 47 per cent volunteered in one organisation while 29 per cent volunteered for three or more. In Northern Ireland, however, the opposite seems to be true, with 75 per cent of volunteers in 2007 being involved in a single organisation compared to 59 per cent in 1995.

In terms of the fields of interest served by these organisations, sports, education, children and religion are consistently found to be amongst those most commonly supported by volunteers. In England, for example, the 2007 *Helping Out* study found that 31 per cent of volunteers (or 18 per cent of the population) volunteered in educational organisations, 24 per cent in religious organisations, 22 per cent in sports and exercise, 22 per cent in disability and 18 per cent in organisations that focused on children and young people (Low et al., 2007). Meanwhile, in Northern Ireland, sports and exercise-based organisations have been found to be the most common field for volunteers (15 per cent), followed by children's education/schools (12 per cent), youth/children's activities (12 per cent) and then religion (10 per cent) (Volunteer Development Agency, 2007).

Different groups of volunteers, however, tend to volunteer for different types of organisations. Women in England, for example, are more likely than men to volunteer in education, in health/disability organisations and in those involved in overseas aid/disaster relief. Men, however, are more likely to volunteer in sports organisations (Low et al., 2007). This is also true in Scotland, where men are also more likely than women to support environmental organisations (Hurley et al., 2008). Age also makes a difference to the types of organisations volunteers support. For example, older people (aged 55 plus) in England are more likely to volunteer in religious organisations than younger people (Low et al., 2007), while young people in Northern Ireland were more likely to volunteer in sports organisations (Volunteer Development Agency, 2007). People from BME groups in England were more likely to volunteer in religious organisations than White people: 20 per cent of White volunteers, for example, helped in religious organisations compared to 49 per cent of Asian volunteers.

In terms of what volunteers actually do for organisations, raising or handling money is the most common activity, followed by organising or helping to run an event and then being a committee members or helping to run a group. *Helping Out*, for example, found that 65 per cent of volunteers (or 38 per cent of the adult population) in England were involved in raising/handling money; while 50 per cent of volunteers helped with organising or running an event and 28 per cent were committee members (Low et al., 2007).

Again, however, there are differences in the activities undertaken by volunteers according to their backgrounds, although generally raising and handling money and organising or helping to run events are the two most common forms of volunteering across all socio-economic groups (ibid.). Women in England were more likely than men to get involved in organising or running an event; while men were more likely to be involved in transport-related activities. Men in Scotland were more likely than women to be involved in committee work (Hurley et al., 2008). Age also makes a difference to participation in committees. In *Helping Out*, 32 per cent of young volunteers (aged 16–24) were committee members, compared to 19 per cent of 25 to 34 year olds, 30 per cent of 45 to 64 year olds and 37 per cent of volunteers aged 65 and over. White people were also more likely to be committee members than were volunteers from BME groups, while Black people were more likely to be involved with visiting people than any other ethnic group. Socio-economic status also influences the kinds of activity undertaken with people in management positions more likely than others to be

Table 4.4 Activities undertaken, by informal volunteers

	At least once a month (%)	At least once in the last year (%)
Giving advice	52	45
Looking after property or pet	37	39
Transporting or escorting someone	38	31
Babysitting, caring for children	35	31
Keeping in touch with someone	38	28
Writing letters, filling in forms	30	25
Doing shopping, collecting pension	33	25
Cooking, cleaning, laundry	26	20
Decorating, home improvement	17	16
Representing someone	11	8
Sitting with someone, providing personal care	8	6
Any other activities	6	5
Base	*3109*	*5608*

Source: Citizenship Survey 2007/2008

involved in organising and running events and serving as committee members (Low et al., 2007).

Informal volunteering

The most common activities undertaken by informal volunteers are giving advice (45 per cent of informal volunteers in England did this at least once a year in 2007/2008), looking after a pet or property (39 per cent) and transporting or escorting (31 per cent) (see Table 4.4). These lists are, however, inevitably limited by the options included in a survey.

Bringing it all together

It is difficult to sum up in a sentence or two the patterns of volunteering across the United Kingdom. Levels of volunteering appear to be highest in England and lowest in Northern Ireland. At best, they appear to have been static over the past decade and, at worst, they seem to be declining. Some of these differences, however, are explained by the use of different research methodologies in different countries and within countries over time.

There are considerable differences in volunteering according to socio-demographic and geographical characteristics. Whether these socio-demographic variations in levels of volunteering add up to an explanation of why some people volunteer more than others is questionable. When added together, factors including age, sex, economic status, annual household income, urban/rural classification, ethnic group, index of deprivation and illness/disability were found by one study to only account for 8 per cent of the variance in volunteering in Scotland (Hurley et al., 2008). In other words, demographic characteristics are quite a poor predictor of whether someone will volunteer; other factors influence the propensity to volunteer.

5
UK Volunteering in International Perspective

Introduction

The increased interest in volunteering from policy-makers, as noted in Chapter 1, has not been restricted to the United Kingdom. Volunteering has histories in the United States and in parts of Europe, but its importance and the attention it is receiving is increasing everywhere. The 2001 UN IYV saw 126 countries set up volunteering committees to draw attention to the work of volunteers and the four aims of the year – promotion, recognition, facilitation and networking – were intended to enhance the profile of volunteering with governments and citizens everywhere (IVR, 2002).

The previous chapter suggested that rates of participation in volunteering in the United Kingdom are quite healthy. But how do they compare with other countries? Do other countries have a similar profile, or does the United Kingdom have many more, or significantly fewer, volunteers? What are the different ways in which volunteering is viewed by people and supported by policy? This chapter takes a selective look at volunteering as an international phenomenon and asks whether it is possible for countries to benchmark themselves against one another, something policy-makers seem very keen to do. It begins by discussing some methodological issues with data collection and considers the relative benefits of data collected in international and national surveys.

The chapter then looks at some of the data available from a selection of surveys before examining several theories that scholars have used to attempt to explain differences. It is through the application of these theories that we begin to understand that participation is the result of complex historical forces and that similar rates are not necessarily the result of comparable driving forces. In particular, the chapter makes

use of data from the Johns Hopkins Comparative Nonprofit Sector programme and discusses how this has contributed to the development of
theories which explain the existence, size and nature of volunteering in
different countries.

Comparing volunteering internationally

Chapter 4 argued that the definition used, the questions asked and the
methodology employed to survey volunteering could all influence the
results obtained. A close look at published figures in a slew of different UK surveys shows just how difficult it is to get a clear idea of who
does what. Compare, for example, the 56 per cent of people participating about once a month or more frequently in voluntary and community activities obtained by the Home Office in 2001 (Krishnamurthy
et al., 2001) with the 1997 national survey of volunteering figure of
48 per cent volunteering at least once during the previous year, and
with 29 per cent being regular volunteers (that is, taking part at least
once a month). Figures for the United Kingdom are given in more detail
in Chapter 4, but this example does illustrate the care that should be
taken when quoting figures.

These problems are multiplied as soon as we try to compare surveys
from different countries and try to draw comparisons internationally.
Looking across eight surveys (four of which were country-specific, and
four cross-national) Lyons et al. (1998) noted that a range of definitions and techniques were used and that surveys were underpinned by
different assumptions. To begin with, the surveys had some important
technical differences – sample sizes and methods of sampling varied,
as did the ways in which non-respondents were handled within the
results. Another source of difference between the surveys is the question of who should be asked to respond: some set a lower age limit
of 18 while some asked the questions to anyone aged 15 and above.
Another difference was whether the survey was stand alone or part of
a larger survey; that is, did the survey just ask about volunteering, or
were volunteering questions contained within a survey asking about
other subjects?

The surveys also differed in scope. All but one of the eight tried to
establish the field of volunteering; that is, they asked what areas people volunteered in – sports, education, health and so on. Some used
prompts suggesting fields to jog memories of where volunteering took
place and some did not. Several, but not all, surveys asked about types
of voluntary work. Where volunteers were asked about the work they

did, some surveys asked volunteers to report only on the organisation they did most of their volunteering for while one asked volunteers to report on up to three organisations and another for up to six organisations with which they were involved. Some surveys asked explicitly about formal volunteering, some about both formal and informal and some were unclear about the distinction.

These technical issues in themselves can cause problems when we try to compare volunteering rates reported from different surveys, but there are more fundamental problems. These are the differences which Lyons et al. refer to as '[M]ore fatal to reliable comparisons' concerning '[T]he way the activities that are the object of study were defined and how questions designed to elicit the data were framed and put' (Lyons et al., 1998: pp. 48–49). Put simply, the surveys differed over how they defined volunteering; the definitions used ranged across 'voluntary activity', 'unpaid activity', 'unpaid voluntary work', 'giving time freely (without pay)' or 'volunteer work'. Lyons and his colleagues emphasise the problems terminology can cause by drawing on the work of Lynn (1997) who showed that terms such as 'voluntary work' triggered a narrower range of activities in peoples' minds than 'voluntary activity' and recommended that the word 'volunteer' should not be used in surveys.

But we should also be aware that, as Lyons et al. point out, these differences are not just differences in methodologies, but '... reflect unconscious differences in defining the object of study; differences that are influenced to varying degrees by one or other of the two rather different paradigms that shape research onto the third sector' (1997: p. 52). We have met these paradigms before in Chapter 2 as we tried to map the field of volunteer study and understanding. They are the 'non-profit paradigm' characterised by framing the subject in economic, legalistic and management terms; and the 'civil society paradigm' which emphasises participation and social capital and within which clubs, societies, self-help and membership in general are of more interest.

Looking at it from this perspective, we can learn a great deal from surveys, but we must interpret their findings with caution – are surveys measuring a common understanding of what a volunteer is, and are we interpreting rates correctly, or do similar rates hide a very different volunteering landscape? After reviewing some surveys, we will look at how the similarities and differences have been interpreted, and how the two paradigm distinction can help us to grasp how volunteering is conceptualised in different countries.

International volunteering rates

Comparative surveys

The eight surveys which Lyons et al. (1998) compared included four that were specifically international in focus. They noted that, while comparing country-specific surveys almost inherently presented methodological problems, surveys that set out to collect data across countries were able to overcome many of the issues by standardising questions, methodologies and so on. However, because of the expense involved, there are very few of these.

Research for *A New Civic Europe* which was undertaken by the IVR in the mid-1990s is an example of a project that set out to gather together researchers across Europe to use a common methodology to enable comparisons on volunteering and volunteering issues (Gaskin and Davis Smith, 1995). Although the figures from this survey are somewhat out of date, they do provide a suitable anchor point from which to start exploring comparisons. This study has also identified a number of insights as to why differences were observed which remain valid, and we shall review these below as we seek to explain differences.

Table 5.1 sets out some key findings from this report. Because these figures are from 1995, it is important to note here is that figures are given for Great Britain, which makes them difficult to compare with other volunteering surveys which are UK-focussed, and also that figures for Germany report volunteering in the East and the West before

Table 5.1   Volunteers as a percentage of the adult population in Europe in 1995, by sex

	Men (%)	Women (%)	All (%)
Belgium	27	35	32
Bulgaria	21	18	19
Denmark	29	27	28
Germany	18	17	18
Great Britain	31	36	34
Ireland	28	24	25
Netherlands	42	34	38
Slovenia	12	12	12
Sweden	38	32	36

Source: Adapted from Anheier and Salmon's use of Gaskin and Davis Smith (1995) study

unification. Given the vintage of the data, perhaps the most interesting point here is not the absolute figures, but how the countries measure relative to each other: the largest percentage of volunteers is found in the Netherlands, followed by Sweden and then Great Britain.

Looking further afield than Europe, Musick and Wilson (2008) draw on data from the World Value Survey (WVS) using four surveys conducted between 1991 and 2001. This may appear somewhat dated, but again we are able to compare rates from a survey which employs the same methodology across countries. It is the relative rates that are of interest, and these are shown in Table 5.1.

The authors note some 'troubling' differences when they juxtapose these results against other sources for each country. They note, for example, that the figure for Canada from the WVS is much higher than that from a Canadian survey of volunteering from 2000, and similarly inflated figures from the WVS can be seen for, among others, the United States, the United Kingdom and Argentina (Musick and Wilson, 2008). This could be attributable to the sort of issues Lyons et al. highlighted; for example, respondents to the WVS were asked whether they belonged to any organisation and were shown a list of voluntary organisations and activities which included 'social welfare services for elderly, handicapped or deprived people', 'religious or church organizations', 'education, arts, music or cultural activities' and 'local community action on issues like poverty, employment, housing, racial equality'. They were then asked whether they currently did any unpaid voluntary work for the organisation. The very next question completely changed focus by asking respondents to say who they would not like as neighbours including for example 'people of a different race', 'heavy drinkers', 'emotionally unstable people' and 'immigrants/foreign workers' (http://www.worldvaluessurvey. org/). Asking questions about volunteering when the context changes so rapidly could affect the results. Nevertheless, Musick and Wilson (2008) use the WVS survey figures relative to each other – they are assuming that, even if the survey gives an inflated figure, all figures will be inflated more or less evenly.

Keeping in mind that care must be taken in reading across surveys, the WVS and New Civic Europe figures show that there is an approximate relative order – the UK figures are somewhere about the top of the list, the Netherlands show strong participation figures as does Sweden, while, by and large, the countries of Eastern Europe show lower rates. The United States comes near the top, but the position of some of the other countries such as China and Uganda require further explanation.

A third key source is The Johns Hopkins Comparative Nonprofit Sector Project. This is a huge undertaking under the leadership of Lester Salamon (see the project web site at http://www.jhu.edu/~cnp/) which has built up successive waves of country data and, at time of writing, had collected surveys from over 40 countries. The project focuses on the third sector as a whole rather than just volunteering and attempts to scope the size and shape of the sector in each country. As part of the ongoing analysis, Salamon and Sokolowski (2001) compared volunteering across 24 countries. Their report took as its key measure the total of *Full-Time Equivalent Volunteers* as a percentage of non-agricultural employment, so we cannot attempt to compare rates with other surveys. However, again, Sweden was ranked top of the countries surveyed with a total number of full-time equivalent volunteers which represented 8 per cent of the non-agricultural paid workforce. It was followed by the Netherlands (7.5 per cent), France (5.2 per cent), the United Kingdom (4.9 per cent), the United States (4.6 per cent), Finland (3.5 per cent), Germany (3.3 per cent) and Australia (3.2 per cent). The bottom five (from the bottom up) were Mexico (0.2 per cent), Hungary (0.3 per cent), Brazil (0.3 per cent), Slovakia (0.4 per cent) and Peru (0. 5 per cent). It should be noted, however, that the project had to use a variety of sources and, although the authors were confident that they presented an accurate picture, they felt the need to qualify their results by saying 'We thus believe that we were able to capture most volunteer input in every target country' (Salamon and Sokolowski, 2001: p. 5).

The comparative surveys give us a chance to see volunteering rates relative to each other because these surveys are carried out with a view to minimising methodological differences. At the time of writing, work is underway with Lester Salamon at the Johns Hopkins University and the International Labour Organization (ILO) to design a module on volunteering that can become part of labour force surveys (see http://www.jhu.edu/~ccss/volunteering/index.html), by measuring the work of volunteers using standardised questions in labour force and household surveys. Comparable figures across countries are on the horizon. In the meantime, it needs to be stressed again that comparing volunteer rates needs to be undertaken with care. As we have seen, Musick and Wilson (2008) allowed for the fact that the WVS seemed to inflate figures, but for their purposes they assumed all the surveys gave figures greater than those conducted within countries. It is to the evidence provided by single country surveys that we now turn.

Country surveys

The difficulty of which figures to use is borne out if we look for figures from individual surveys. For example, Wieloch (2007) reviews a variety of sources on volunteering in the Netherlands and notes that the *Giving in the Netherlands* survey for 2004 (which includes questions directed at the population over 18 years of age and asks if they have performed any work separate from paid work, for the benefit of others and for which they did not receive a salary) showed that 41 per cent of the population had volunteered. By contrast, the CV (Cultural Change) study – which asked people aged 16 and above about volunteering for associations and institutions for more than one hour a week – reported that 25 per cent of the population engaged in regular volunteering of this kind. Despite the differences, nevertheless, these figures do suggest that the participation rate for the Netherlands is quite high.

Similarly, the high rates for Sweden appear to be confirmed; 'the Population Survey from 2005 showed that an exceptionally large number of Swedes engage in voluntary work, namely around 50 per cent of the population. Only in the United States, Norway and Holland are people as active as in Sweden' (Granholm, 2007: p. 11). There is a lack of official figures for Spain, but those that are available suggest that between 10 per cent and 15 per cent of the population volunteer (Olabuenaga, 2001 cited in Casals, 2005) which is again in line with Musick and Wilson's analysis of the WVS. Data from Belgium seem to confirm, as Musick and Wilson suspected, that the figures within the WVS are inflated. Figures from 1999 based on statistics produced by the University of Liege indicate that volunteering is more likely to be around a fifth of the population (Wade et al., 2004). These figures are clearly much lower than either those reported by the WVS or Gaskin and Davis Smith (1995) which both suggest that Belgium has a volunteer rate comparable to those of the United Kingdom and the Netherlands.

In Germany, a national survey from 2004 indicated that 36 per cent of Germans devoted some time to volunteering (Wiedermann, 2004), showing a significant increase from the figures found by Gaskin and Davis Smith (1995). This, however, may be accounted for, as suggested above, by the fact that the figures from *A New Civic Europe* for Germany involved separate figures from the old East and West Germany. The need to explain these figures has prompted the suggestion that the former communist regimes would show lower levels of volunteering. We will explore this further below, but it does seem that countries of the former Eastern Bloc do report lower rates of participation. In Lithuania, for example, there are no official statistics on volunteering, but a 1998 survey on the third sector and volunteering indicated that 9 per cent of Lithuanians volunteered to work with a non-governmental organisation (NGO) (Zaltauskas, undated). It should be noted, however, that this study did not include religious organisations – another example of the problems of trying to look internationally when some surveys include or exclude particular forms of voluntary action. Data for Slovakia emphasise the problems of comparing figures with rates of volunteering reported as between 39 per cent and 46 per cent, or a '...more realistic' 13 per cent (according the analysis of the Focus Agency from 2004) depending on the methodology used and the way in which the questions were formulated (Mraková and Vlaicová, undated). Certainly the 13 per cent chimes more with Salamon and Sokolowski's study which showed that FTE volunteers as a percentage of non-agricultural employment accounted for just 0.4 per cent (2001: p. 6). In Poland, volunteering rates increased from 10 per cent of the population in 2001 to 18.3 per cent in 2004, an impressive increase which, it has been suggested, was due to a change in the perception of voluntary activity by Poles; a greater awareness of voluntarism had replaced the idea of compulsory work of a collective nature (Samolyk, 2005).

The United States presents another interesting case; Haddad (2006) begins her investigation into comparative volunteering by asserting that in comparative studies, '[t]he United States is always at or near the top of the pack... This is true whether the studies examine participation using survey data such as the WVSs or whether they look at the size of and participation in non-profit organizations such as the Comparative Nonprofit Sector Project' (Haddad, 2006: p. 1220). But is this true? The findings of the WVS outlined by Musick and Wilson above, provide a participation figure of 60 per cent plus, while Salamon and Sokolowski (2001: p. 6) rank the United States fifth in their table based on full-time equivalent volunteer rates as a percentage of non-agricultural employment. But the United States abounds with surveys. AARP – the non-profit organisation for the over 50s in the United States – looked at the giving of time and money by those aged 45 and above and, in order to situate volunteering in a wider perspective, made reference to two surveys, one by the United Way and one by Civic Ventures, which put volunteering at 34 per cent and volunteering and/or community service at 59 per cent (Kutner and Love, 2003). Time series data from the Bureau of Labor Statistics of the U.S. Department of Labor, however, tell a different story. They show a figure for 2007 of 26.2 per cent, which represented a slight decrease over the previous year. In 2003, 2004 and 2005, it was 28.8 per cent, while in 2006, there was a slight dip with

26.7 per cent of the population reporting having volunteered at least once in the previous year (Department of Labor, 2008).

Canada, by contrast, although appearing to have a lower rate on the WVS, reports an impressive 45 per cent of the population aged 15 and above volunteering their time in an organisation (Hall et al., 2005). Neither Australia nor New Zealand appear in the list of WVS data used by Musick and Wilson and shown in Table 5.2, but, as we saw above, Australia does feature in the comparative list of volunteering in Salamon and Sokolowski's study. With 3.2 per cent full-time equivalent volunteers, Australia was ahead of the average for the 24 countries studied and ranked just below Germany (Salamon and Sokolowski, 2001: p. 6). Figures available for 2006 indicate 34 per cent of Australians volunteer. Meanwhile in New Zealand, volunteering is measured in the Census of Population and Dwellings and therefore covers everybody in New Zealand. The survey asks everybody aged 15 and above about unpaid work. Results are categorised as unpaid work that 'occurs within own household', 'unpaid work outside own household' and 'other voluntary work'. The first category involves cooking, cleaning, gardening, looking after child from own household and looking after a member of own household who is ill or has a disability. Unsurprisingly the rates are high. Unpaid work outside own household includes looking after a child, someone who is ill or has a disability but does not live in own household. Other voluntary work is 'other Helping or voluntary work for or through any organisation, group or marae' (a marae is a distinctive Maori form of voluntary action). This figure is 15.4 per cent

Table 5.2 Rate of volunteering reported from World Value Survey, by country

0–10%	Russia, Serbia, Turkey
11–20%	Japan, Latvia, Lithuania, Ukraine, Montenegro, Northern Ireland, Poland, Portugal, Spain
21–30%	Austria, Argentina, Bosnia, Croatia, France, Italy, Luxembourg, Slovenia
31–40%	Belgium, Czech Republic, Denmark, Finland, Iceland, India, Ireland, Mexico, Moldova, Macedonia, Singapore
41–50%	Algeria, Canada, Chile, Korea, Netherlands, Peru, Puerto Rico, United Kingdom
51–60%	Albania, Philippines, South Africa, Sweden
Over 60%	Bangladesh, China, Tanzania, Vietnam, Zimbabwe, Uganda, United States

Source: Musick and Wilson (2008: p. 34)

and, because it is based on a census rather than a sample survey, we should see this as one of the most comprehensive results we have (http://www.stats.govt.nz/NR/rdonlyres/8783B6EF-B8A4-419C-89D4-DF52664F809F/0/quickstatsaboutunpaidwork.pdf). But we still have questions: what constitutes unpaid work outside one's own home? Is there a clear demarcation between caring and volunteering? Or should some of that be counted as volunteering if we want to compare figures across countries?

Explaining the differences

Cross-national comparisons have a very limited utility if they are used only to construct league tables of volunteer rates. The challenge is to explain the differences. One explanation barely needs repeating – differences are down to methodology. We can, however, overcome these differences if we look at international surveys that use the same methods in each country studied. Indeed, this was the solution chosen by Musick and Wilson (2008) when they examined WVS data while accepting that data from each country within the WVS might not correspond with other national surveys. As a basis for trying to unpick what might cause differences, the WVS provided them with results from a consistent form of survey. They begin by noting that explanations could be found in 'compositional' or 'contextual' factors (Musick and Wilson, 2008: p. 342).

Compositional factors would explain differences in terms of the people of a country and their characteristics. For example, we know that people who continue in education for longer will volunteer more. We also know that people in managerial and professional jobs are more likely to volunteer. Could we then explain volunteer rate differences in terms of countries that have more people educated to a higher level, or a larger middle class? In fact, looking across education, employment and age, Musick and Wilson (2008) do not find sufficient explanatory power in any of these to help us understand the differences in the WVS.

Contextual factors include experience with democracy, political regimes, welfare states and economic development (Musick and Wilson, 2008: pp. 246–353). We have touched on some of these already; we noted, for example, that former communist countries seemed to have lower rates of volunteering. This might be explained by the suppression of the growth of civil society organisations under communism. Without a thriving civil society, there is far less 'space' for volunteering. Added to that, volunteering was something else that was state controlled, something else people were told to do (for example, see Davis Smith, 2001 for an explanation of Lenin's enforced volunteering or 'subbotnik'). As those countries emerged from communism, people had to shed the negative connotations of enforced volunteering and 'learn' how to associate. Surveys suggest that it is in the countries where democracy has developed most rapidly that volunteering has grown quickest (Jukenevicius and Savicka, 2003, cited in Musick and Wilson, 2008). Alternatively, Musick and Wilson (2008) review analysis that tries to explain volunteering by looking at the extent to which countries have developed welfare states. Some scholars have suggested that those with strong welfare states have less need for volunteers, but this argument falls down when it also appears that strong welfare states encourage volunteering, for example in the Netherlands.

Social origins theory

Social origins theory has been developed as an attempt to delve more deeply into historical developments, to look at why a strong welfare state may or may not have developed, what this means for voluntary organisations and in turn why it is that this has sometimes been associated with more volunteers and sometimes with fewer.

The theory begins with a quest to explain why the non-profit sector exists at all. Salamon and Anheier (1998) begin by asserting that, before comparative data from the project were available to start testing models, theory building on the sector was hampered: 'With no real possibility to subject such theories to systematic test, the only real constraint on their development has been surface plausibility, the ability to formulate a logical "story" explaining how the theory *might* work' (1998: p. 214 – italics in original). It is through looking at government/ market failure, supply-side theory, trust theory, welfare state theory and interdependence theory that the authors find that single-factor explanations are found wanting (further discussion can be found in Anheier, 2005 and Salamon and Anheier, 1998).

Single-factor theories, such as government failure, or even interdependence can treat voluntary provision as if it were a simple choice of which sector should deliver what services or functions. By extension, similar arguments can explain volunteering (see Anheier and Salamon, 1999). Social origins theory draws on the work of Esping-Andersen (1990) who used a social origins approach to explain the complexities of the modern welfare state. Salamon and Anheier (1998) build on this approach to analyse the historical struggles between class relationships

Government social spending	Economic non-profit sector size	
	Low ⟹ High	
Low	Statist	Liberal
⇓	*Japan*	*United States*
		United Kingdom
High	Social Democratic	Corporatist
	Sweden	*Germany*
		France

Figure 5.1   Non-profit sector regime types
Source: Anheier and Salamon, 1999

and patterns of state–society relationships and extend the theory to the third sector and volunteering.

Their work leads them to a four-regimes model which can be seen in Figure 5.1. Each of these regimes is associated with a particular configuration of third sector organisations and volunteering which are discussed below.

Liberal: A liberal regime is one in which middle classes are in the ascendance without significant opposition either from traditional landed elites or the working class. The result is that government does not extend its remit into further welfare protection, and there is a preference for voluntary solutions. The example here is the United States where a distrust of extending the role of government and historically weak working-class organisation mean that welfare provision was left to third sector organisations and volunteers.

Social democratic: This is where the state sponsors and delivers social welfare with little room for the third sector. This model is exemplified by the Scandinavian countries and is argued to be a result of working-class political parties having the influence and power to ensure welfare benefits are delivered as a right by the state.

Corporatist: In this regime, the state is strong but makes an alliance with non-profits. The example of Germany is one in which history shows a state concerned about radical demands from below which has partnered with churches and ruling classes to enable the development of state-sponsored welfare. In the case of Germany, many institutions delivering welfare are church-based, non-profit organisations.

Statist: The state remains in control of welfare. Business and economic elites drive the exercise of power while the state traditionally has little lobbying from outside forces that remain deferential. The example given is Japan where welfare spending is low but this does not mean a corresponding growth in the third sector.

To take the United Kingdom for example, this model explains the relatively high rate of volunteering with reference to history: the ruling classes have tried to minimise the role of the state in providing welfare, and the working classes were never strong enough to insist that it should be a government role. As a result, the United Kingdom has a long history of voluntary provision. What is more, even the advent of the welfare state could not undo the long-established tradition of voluntary provision – volunteers did not disappear even when the state took over more welfare roles.

As a model, social origins theory has its faults; critics argue that it is hampered by focussing mainly on the sector rather than volunteering and on the economic impact of the sector which limits its usefulness. But, given the difficulties of heterogeneity within and across voluntary sectors, any model developed would struggle to explain volunteering across the globe. There are many anomalies to address, but social origins theory provides a light to shine on those anomalies to help explain them. Social origins theory, for example, locates Sweden as having high government spending but a relatively small non-profit sector when all our other data suggest Sweden has a large number of volunteers. In fact, Anheier and Salamon note this too. Their answer is that volunteering in Sweden is characterised by membership within associations which are active in sport and recreation, advocacy and hobbies rather than by involvement in a third sector which has a significant role in delivering welfare. To offer a plausible explanation, we need to interrogate the Swedish example further. In particular, we may want to have in the forefront of our minds the paradigm distinctions Lyons drew our attention to – the Third Sector Comparative project and social origins theory study are rooted in a 'Third Sector' perspective rather than the 'civil society' perspective. The higher rates in some countries may also be the result of an approach to measuring that is concerned with the delivery of social welfare rather than one which is mainly concerned with associational activity.

We are thus arguing that the Swedish example shows that it is possible to explain how a country appears to have a small voluntary sector but can have many volunteers. What therefore may seem surprising – the fact that Sweden has a higher volunteer rate than the United Kingdom – becomes understandable when we realise that volunteers are found in a different part of society and carrying out different tasks. The apparent anomaly can be explained when we look more closely at the nature of Swedish society. This understanding is underlined by a further study from the comparative project when the authors rank countries by the size of their voluntary sector. There is a recognisable pattern: the Netherlands is at the top; the United Kingdom is fifth; and Eastern European countries are near the bottom. The really interesting data, though, are found in the percentages of the workforce who are volunteers. For example, the Netherlands has 14.4 per cent of its active workforce working in the civil society sector of whom 37.1 per cent are volunteers, whereas Sweden has 7.1 per cent of its workforce in the sector of whom 75.9 per cent are volunteers (Salamon et al., 2003). We can explain this from the social origins perspective – Sweden has a smaller sector but with a lot of volunteers which, as we have seen, can be explained by the membership of associations.

The project has also added another dimension to the analysis by looking at volunteering as it contributes to service or expressive functions. The service function speaks for itself while the expressive function includes volunteering for artistic, recreational, cultural expression and religious expression; 'Opera companies, symphonies, soccer clubs, churches, synagogues, fraternal societies, book clubs and girl scouts are just some of the manifestations of this expressive function' (Salamon et al., 2003: pp. 20–21). Sweden rates highly on volunteers' involvement in this expressive function but not on the service function. This is entirely consistent with social origins theory which argues the welfare sector is small because strong historic demand for the state to guarantee welfare; there are relatively few volunteers in welfare, and they are mostly to be found in sports club membership.

Conclusions

This chapter has looked at rates of volunteering internationally and has provided examples of levels of participation in volunteering in a selection of countries. It has, however, also argued that comparisons are of limited use unless we know exactly what is being measured. Above all, it is essential to try to understand what these rates mean with reference to the 'volunteering history' of the country.

The chapter points to several theories and frameworks to explain differences, and focuses on social origins theory. This theory is not complete but offers a way of drawing in a range of explanations to show how volunteering is positioned within countries. Like any theory, it needs to be critiqued, refined and expanded. Haddad (2006), for example, explores why the United States usually figures near the top of participation lists while Japan languishes near the bottom. She adds to the theory by arguing it is important to consider the 'embeddedness' of volunteering organisations. She argues that volunteering in Japan takes place in organisations that are 'embedded' within the state and that the Third Sector Comparative project does not pick up on volunteers in small associations – such as parent–teacher groups, neighbourhood groups – that have a very close relationship with the state. Haddad frames the argument in the values that each country has historically exhibited. In Japan, people, by and large, think government is the right place to solve issues, and so people participate in organisations that have a strong relationship with the state. This is in contrast to the United States which, as we have seen, has a strong participation in associations outside the state.

Finally, this understanding can also help us recognise why volunteering receives the support it does. Where volunteering can be explained in terms of welfare states, then it is little surprise that focus on developing volunteering is couched in these terms. In the United Kingdom, therefore, education and welfare accounts for the majority of volunteering involvement. As Chapter 7 shows, the development of volunteering from a policy perspective is very much linked to this predominance. An alternative approach has been suggested by Williams (2003a) who has argued that there is a need to give more attention to supporting and developing the huge amount of informal work that goes on in deprived areas. From this point of view, formal volunteering can be seen as the arena of the more affluent. Surveys that focus on formal volunteering will report that people with higher education are more likely to get involved, and our explanations of volunteer rates will lead us to argue that the way to develop volunteering will be to draw more people into formal volunteering. How we define and count volunteering will have a significant impact on how we support volunteering.

Theory needs to be continually refined. This chapter has suggested that we can choose from a range of frameworks and hypothesise to analyse the relative development of volunteering across countries. We have chosen to look at social origins theory – but can it help us go forward? Just as Esping-Andersen (1990) provided the foundation on which the social origins approach was built, so others may have the key to further developments. Bonoli et al. (2004) agree with Esping-Andersen that the configuration of welfare states in any one country is a product of a balance of forces. However, they argue that welfare states are undergoing a process of retrenchment, and that the relationships that have explained how welfare states have come to be in the past will be different in the future. Social origins theory may help cast a light on how we have arrived at the particular form of volunteering we have in particular countries, but we need to constantly revisit our understanding if we are to help map the future of voluntary action.

6
A Changing Society

In this chapter, we review the changes that have taken place, and are taking place, in our society in order to provide a better understanding of the context in which voluntary action takes place today. We will look in turn at demographic trends, the changing relationship between the individual and society and contemporary values and mores. In the second part of the chapter, we will draw out some of the key implications of these changes for the future of volunteering and the practices of volunteer-involving organisations.

The changing demographics of the United Kingdom

An ageing population

In common with other Western industrialised countries and Japan (but unlike the developing countries of the South where there has been an upsurge in the numbers of young people) Britain has experienced a very significant increase in the proportion of older people in its population (Murphy, 2005). The average (median) age rose from 34.1 years in 1971 to 38.4 in 2003 (Cook and Martin, 2005), and Britain is expected to become the third country in the world (after Japan and Italy) to reach an average age of more than 40 in the near future (Carnegie UK Trust, 2007). This is 'primarily the result of fewer babies being born and people living longer' (Cook and Martin, 2005: p. 4). Fertility rates fell during the 1960s and 1970s and again in the 1990s as women tended to delay childbearing until later in their lives and to have fewer children while an increasing number of them remained childless (ibid.). Life expectancy in the United Kingdom has risen from 76 years for men and 81 years for women in 1981 to 80 and 83, respectively, in 2007 and is on course to reach 84 and 87, respectively, by 2025 (Carnegie

UK Trust, 2007). Between 1981 and 2003, the numbers of people aged 65 or over rose by 28 per cent while those under 16 fell by 18 per cent (Hughes, 2009). The trend is set to continue: it has been estimated that the number of people aged over 50 will rise by 5.5 millions – from 18.3 to 23.8 millions – between 2005 and 2023 (Evans and Saxton, 2005) and that, by 2025, there will be more over 60s than under 25s (Carnegie UK Trust, 2007).

The composition of households

The number of households in Great Britain has increased much faster than the population has grown. Between 1971 and 2003, the population grew by 6 per cent while the number of households rose by almost one-third. There is a marked trend towards smaller household sizes with an increase in the number of people who live alone and a decrease in the size of many families. Single-person households represented less than 20 per cent of the total in 1971 but nearly 30 per cent in 2003 (Cook and Martin, 2005). While many of those living alone are older people (Evans and Saxton, 2005), the biggest increase has been among those who are below the age of eligibility for a state pension – from 6 per cent of all households in 1971 to 14 per cent in 2003. This is partly explained by the increasing rates of divorce and separation which have led to more men in particular living alone (Cook and Martin, 2005). Between 1960 and 1998 the divorce rate more than doubled (Evans and Saxton, 2005), and today 40 per cent of marriages end in breakdown (Carnegie UK Trust, 2007). However, the figures for single households could be even higher: the number of young adults living at home with their parents in England has also risen – to 58 per cent of young men (aged 20–24) and 39 per cent of young women of the same age (Cook and Martin, 2005).

Marriage has become less of a norm with the proportion of 'married couple households' falling from 70 per cent in 1971 to an expected figure of less than 40 per cent in 2021 (Evans and Saxton, 2005) while 41 per cent of births in the United Kingdom occurred outside of marriage in 2003 (Cook and Martin, 2005). The number of 'cohabiting couple households' is rising – from virtually nil in 1971 to an expected figure of more than 10 per cent in 2021 (Evans and Saxton, 2005). At the same time, the proportion of dependent children living in families headed by a couple fell from 92 per cent to 77 per cent between 1972 and 2004 while the proportion of children who live in one-parent families has tripled over the same period to almost a quarter.

Overall, the nature of the family unit has been transformed into what Evans and Saxton (2005: p. 16) have called the 'any way up' family:

> Half a century ago a child was typically a part of a broad family unit made up of grandparents and parents as well as a number of uncles, aunts, cousins and siblings. As people began to live longer and have fewer children, the family has become 'taller' (with children increasingly likely to know their great grandparents) but 'narrower' – less children means less uncles, aunts, cousins and siblings. It doesn't stop there. The more 'vertical' family structure has become increasingly complicated because of the increase in divorce and remarriage and decrease in marriage...The widespread fracturing and restructuring of the family unit has resulted in some very complex and disjointed family arrangements.

Patterns of employment

Patterns of employment have also changed radically over the past three or four decades. In the first place, we spend less of our lifetime engaged in paid work as the result of the increase in life expectancy noted above and of the longer periods spent by a greater proportion of the population in full-time education. Increasing numbers of young people have extended their education to degree level. By 2003, one in six of the adult population were graduates (Hughes, 2009) and in 2002 nearly 3 million people were beginning their tertiary education, an increase of 2 millions in the 26 years since 1976. The present government has set a target for participation in higher education of 50 per cent of young adults. In 2001, only 5.4 per cent of 16 to 24 year olds had no qualifications compared with 56 per cent of those aged over 65 (Evans and Saxton, 2005). While the age at which people become eligible for the old age pension is being raised, the number of years spent at work rather than in education or in retirement is significantly lower for the great majority of the population.

The second major change is to the gender balance. The overall UK employment rate (the proportion of people of working age who are in paid employment) has changed little, ranging from 68 to 76 per cent over the past thirty years. This conceals, however, important changes and diverging trends in the rates of employment for men and for women. In 1971, the gap between the genders was 35 percentage points with 92 per cent of men and 56 per cent of women in work. Since then, the gap has narrowed dramatically as the rate for men fell to 79 per cent and the proportion of women in employment rose to 70 per cent, a gap of just 9 percentage points. While much of the increase in women's involvement in the labour market has taken the form of part-time work, there has also been a smaller rise in the full-time employment of women (Cook and Martin, 2005).

The growth of part-time work by women has contributed to a third significant development of employment patterns – the growing flexibility of working conditions. The notion of a 'job for life' and the commitment to a career which were key facets of the experience of employment thirty years ago have little, if any, currency in the 21st century along with the norm of a 35- or 40-hour week. The proportion of people working 'flexibly' – that is, part-time, in a job share or working from home – has risen from 47 per cent in 1994 to 57 per cent ten years later. An increasing number of people are following the example of young people taking gap years by arranging career breaks which give them space to follow other interests (Carnegie UK Trust, 2007).

These experiences are not, however, universal; a significant proportion of those in certain kinds of employment remain 'time poor'. Eighty-one per cent of male and 50 per cent of female managers, higher officials and professionals worked longer than 45 hours in a typical week (Hughes, 2009). British workers continue to work the longest hours in Europe, and a 'long-hours culture' has led to the workforce contributing 36 million hours of unpaid overtime in a year, while one in three do not take up their full holiday entitlement for fear of the backlog that would greet them on their return (TUC, 2009).

Growing wealth and inequality

Britain has become a richer society during the past two or three decades and, until the collapse of confidence in the banks and the world's financial systems in the autumn of 2008, its wealth was expected to continue to grow. Between 1971 and 2004 – and despite three important 'blips' in the mid-1970s, the early 1980s and the early 1990s – the volume measure of United Kingdom's Gross Domestic Product doubled. Household disposable income – 'the amount that people in private households have available in their pockets to spend or save' (Cook and Martin, 2005: p. 2) – grew even faster over the same period by one and a third (ibid.). Similarly, figures presented by Evans and Saxton (2005) for the period 1986–2003 demonstrate that there have been significant increases in real personal income (after housing costs) for all levels of British society. Further evidence of increased wealth is provided by data from Social Trends (Hughes, 2009) which show that the amount spent on less essential items – such as communication, travel abroad, recreation and culture – has risen much faster over the past 35 years than spending on essentials like food, housing, water and fuel.

This growing wealth has not, however, been equally shared, and the gap between the richest and the poorest has widened and is likely to widen further. It is estimated that by 2010, the United Kingdom's richest 10 per cent will own 30 per cent of total household income (up from 24 per cent in 1996) while the bottom 10 per cent will have the same share – 3 per cent – as they owned in 1996 (Carnegie UK Trust, 2007). While most of the population have shared in the growing wealth of British society, a sizeable minority remain locked in poverty; 17 per cent of households in 2001–2003 earned less than 60 per cent of median disposable income (Hughes, 2009). The 'social groups who are more likely than others to be living on low incomes...include those in lone-parent families, the unemployed, children – especially those in workless households, pensioners, and people from minority ethnic groups, particularly those of Pakistani or Bangladeshi origin' (Cook and Martin, 2005: p. 2).

The individual and society

The changing nature of community

The importance and strength of the ties that historically bound people together in communities based on location have decreased significantly. Modern patterns of employment and the increased mobility brought about by almost universal car ownership mean that people cannot rely on finding work in or near the place where they live and do not depend on local shops and facilities. Settled communities in the large cities have been dispersed by redevelopment and slum clearance from the 1930s onwards, a trend that has accelerated in the later years of the last century. In addition, the opening up of higher education to almost half of the population has led to ever-higher levels of social and geographical mobility. The process and its results have been graphically summarised in an unpublished paper prepared for the Commission on the Future of Volunteering (Zimmeck, 2007: p. 4):

> Even though more people than ever are physically packed together in cities, they are becoming more rather than less isolated socially. There are a number of reasons for this – moves from place to place in pursuit of education, jobs, homes, new lives, with families and friends left behind; retreat into the sanctuaries of their homes; preferences for 'keeping themselves to themselves', passive recreation in front of the TV and 'virtual' socialising over the web. Many people no longer

live in a place where they know people and are known by people but in a place where they are unknown and prefer to stay that way, with no nostalgic desire to borrow the proverbial cup of sugar from their neighbours. Paradoxically, people's isolation increases their need to make connections but undermines their ability to do so.

The communities in which people live and work are also increasingly characterised by a diversity of cultures and faiths. The proportion of the population made up of minority ethnic communities has risen from 6.0 per cent of the UK population to 7.9 per cent in 2001. In some inner city areas, people from minority ethnic communities comprise more than half of the population (Carnegie UK Trust, 2007).

This combination of factors raises questions of identity: 'few people see themselves as simply "British" or "English" but have more complex and fluid senses of identity based on factors including education level, ethnicity, religion and even a "virtual" persona' (ibid.: p. 17).

Loss of trust in the political process

The second salient feature of the changing relationship between the individual and society is the growing lack of trust in and disengagement from the conventional political system. Participation in general elections has fallen steeply since 1992 (Power Inquiry, 2006) while two of the three lowest turnouts ever were recorded in the last ten years (Carnegie UK Trust, 2007). The membership of political parties has been in precipitous decline since 1964 (Power Inquiry, 2006) and fell by half between 1980 and 2000 (Carnegie UK Trust, 2007) while active participation in them has declined even more dramatically. There has also been a fall in the numbers of those involved in local community, neighbourhood and citizens' groups (Home Office, 2002; Low et al., 2007) and 'a perceived erosion of the role and status of elected volunteer representatives in parish councils and local authorities, due to tighter control by central government and, in the case of local authorities, by the introduction of a two-tier system of cabinets of paid councillors and rumps of volunteer councillors. These changes have left some volunteer councillors feeling excluded and undervalued' (Zimmeck, 2007: p. 8).

But this is only part of the story. Alongside the decline of interest in the conventional political process, there has been an increase in the numbers of people involved in single issue politics (Carnegie UK Trust, 2007) through 'new types of campaigning and in new areas of activity – for example, the Countryside Alliance, the anti-war movement, the Make Poverty History campaign, the Green movement' (Zimmeck,

2007: p. 8). The Power Inquiry into Britain's Democracy also found that the appearance of apathy created by such indicators as the numbers involved in elections and political parties was misleading. It cited an abundance of research evidence that very large numbers of British citizens were engaged in community and charity work outside of politics while involvement in pressure group politics such as taking part in campaigns and demonstrations; joining consumer boycotts or signing petitions had been growing significantly over a number of years; and there was increasing participation, through the Internet and its blogs and discussion forums, in debates about political and social issues.

The Power report argued that disengagement from the formal political process was a response to dissatisfaction with the systems and structures for political decision-making. It called for major shifts in political practice to reflect the need for more flexibility and responsiveness in the system and for citizens to be able to exercise a more direct and focused influence on the decisions that concern them. Imaginative ways in which people could be involved in decision-making are discussed in the *Involve* report on *People and Participation* (2005). These included Appreciative Inquiry, Citizens' Juries, Citizens' Panels, Consensus Conferences, Deliberative Meetings of Citizens (Democs) and Planning for Real.

The importance of connecting the newer forms of political engagement into the mainstream of the political process is underlined by the Carnegie Inquiry's concern about the way in which 'lines are drawn between the rights of the individual and the security of the state' (Carnegie UK Trust, 2007: p. 28). On a global scale, much of the legislation introduced since 2001 'has had the effect of curtailing the ability of activists to speak and demonstrate' (ibid.). In the United Kingdom, this has included the introduction of restrictions on the right to demonstrate in the vicinity of parliament. This has been accompanied by the increasing regulation of civil society associations and other public organisations. However, the ability of activists to challenge the use of state power has been enhanced by the incorporation of the European Convention of Human Rights to British Law (Carnegie UK Trust, 2007).

A virtual society

The third and almost certainly the most significant change in the way in which people interact and conduct relationships with others is the arrival of ICT 'as a new way of life' (Evans and Saxton, 2005: p. 18). There has been a very rapid growth in the proportion of households with access to the Internet, from 10 per cent in 1996/1997 to 45 per cent in 2002/2003 and 65 per cent – or 16 million households – in 2008. Today, moreover, 56 per cent of households have a broadband connection – up from 51 per cent in 2007. Access to the Internet has become more equally spread across the genders and age groups but is unequal across occupational groups with 80 per cent of the highest group (the ABs) 'wired up' compared to only 29 per cent of the lowest group (the DEs) (Evans and Saxton, 2005; Office of National Statistics, 2008). There has been a similarly dramatic increase in mobile phone ownership from 16 per cent of the population in 1996/1997 to 45 per cent in 2002/2003 (Hughes, 2009) and 77 per cent in 2005 (Evans and Saxton, 2005). Ownership is spread across the entire age range; nearly half of children aged 8 to 11 owned a mobile phone in 2008 and so did around 30 per cent of men and nearly 20 per cent of women aged 80 or over in 2002 (Office of National Statistics, 2008).

The rise of 'pervasive personal technology' (Carnegie UK Trust, 2007: p. 27) has transformed the way in which people access knowledge, communicate with one another and, through websites like Facebook, establish and maintain social relationships. Its influence is continuing to grow: 'in the 2000s, we are heading into a new era of ubiquity, where the "users" of the Internet will be counted in billions and where humans may become the minority as generators and receivers of traffic' (ibid.: p. 19). In addition, the trend looks set to continue: 'technology continues to double its processing capacity for a given price every eighteen months'. The Carnegie Inquiry (Carnegie UK Trust, 2007) also highlighted a qualitative change in which people have gone beyond the use of the new media as consumers to become media producers, creating blogs at the rate of one every three seconds worldwide.

The impact has been especially strong on younger people. According to the Carnegie UK Trust (2007: p. 19), 'the average youth spends 23 hours a week online and 67 per cent of youngsters say they would be "lost" without their PC'. A whole generation has grown up with the new technology: 'they have spent their whole lives surrounded by and using computers, videogames, digital music players, video cams, cell phones, and all the other toys and tools of the digital age' (Prensky, 2001: p. 1). Arguing that 'today's students *think and process information fundamentally differently from their predecessors*' and from those who teach them, Prensky has called them 'digital natives'. They are, he argues, ' "native speakers" of the digital language of computers, video games and the Internet' unlike people of earlier generations who have not been born into the digital world but have learned to adapt to it and can thus be seen as 'digital immigrants'. While the terminology and the underlying assumptions of this view have been challenged (Bennett et al., 2008) as an over-reaction brought about by an academic form of 'moral panic', it is clear that many younger people have a significantly different experience of the new media and use them in very different ways.

The 'civil society' dimension

Another useful perspective on the relationship between the individual and society has been provided by the Carnegie Trust's *Inquiry into the Future of Civil Society in the UK and Ireland*. Its report on *The Shape of Civil Society to Come* (Carnegie UK Trust, 2007) identifies two dimensions on which to assess changes in the shape and nature of civil society – the sphere of social activity which is independent of the state and outside the market. It looks in turn at civil society as associational life and as arenas for public deliberation.

The key changes relating to the associational dimension of civil society include the growing involvement of voluntary and community sector organisations in the delivery of public services which has brought with it demands on them for increased effectiveness and 'professionalism' and 'the importation of models and practices from the business and/or public sector' (p. 9). These developments have brought with them concerns on the one hand that increasing reliance on government funding will erode independence and autonomy and on the other that the size and role of the sector will grow at the cost of its 'fundamental characteristics and distinctiveness' (ibid.).

Arenas for public deliberation – the second of these dimensions – are defined by Carnegie as 'formal and informal "spaces" that enable individuals and associations with diverse and potentially opposing views to come together to debate the means and ends of civil society' (p. 14). The development of new technology 'has opened up infinite possibilities' for the creation of virtual forums across wide geographical areas and 'the potential for expanding the public arena is potentially endless' (ibid.). This does not represent a panacea, however. The Carnegie report is concerned that the kinds of relationship engendered by technology, unlike those developed face-to-face, may not generate trust and social capital and questions the ability of civil society associations to make use of the new media. It is even less optimistic about other arenas for public deliberation. Newspapers, radio and television have become commodities rather than tools for public discourse while there is growing concern about the availability and quality of public open spaces – especially in deprived urban areas.

Contemporary values and mores

Individualism

There is a widespread perception that the decline of traditional family, neighbourhood and community ties in British society has been accompanied by a rising tide of individualism famously captured by Margaret Thatcher's slogan, quoted by the Carnegie report (Carnegie UK Trust, 2007: p. 25) that 'there is no such thing as society'. One symptom of this is the number of people who holidayed alone which rose from 9.6 millions in 1995 to 15.4 millions ten years later. More tellingly, 'the majority of UK citizens now believe that the best route to raising standards for everyone is to "look after ourselves" rather than "look after the community's interests"' (ibid.: p. 17). However, the Carnegie Inquiry found that other evidence suggested 'perhaps that this trend towards individualism had reached its apogee' (p. 25) as people felt the need for engagement as they pursued a well-being agenda and were freer to get involved by the shift to more flexible working arrangements.

Consumerism and choice

Rising individualism has been accompanied and fuelled by the growth of consumerism and the agenda of choice. As much of the population has enjoyed greater spending power and the cost of consumer goods has fallen in real terms, people have increasingly defined themselves as consumers. The range of choices available to them has increased dramatically. Some of this increase is market driven; in the 2000s, the average out-of-town Tesco supermarket offered a range of 40,000 products as against a mere 5,000 in the 1980s (Evans and Saxton, 2005). Some of this increased range of goods and services is the result of technological change, including a choice of 900 television channels (rather than the four available in 1990) and 600 different Internet service providers (ibid.). Some is the consequence of deregulation which has given us the choice of 22 gas and 16 electricity suppliers (ibid.). Furthermore, successive Conservative and New Labour administrations have adopted the rhetoric and practices of the commercial sector and sought to apply them to the work of government and the delivery of public services (Deakin, 2001).

Aspirations

There is growing evidence that the aspirations of UK citizens are 'high and rising' (Evans and Saxton, 2005: p. 19) and extend beyond the material rewards of wealth and consumption. Evans and Saxton suggest that we may be 'witnessing the evolution of the status of leisure from that of luxury to necessity' (ibid.) and quote figures to support that claim:

> The average person currently spends 27 hours on leisure activities a week (two thirds of these hours are spent in front of the television). The typical UK citizen claims that they socialise 110 times a year, eat out or have take-out 65 times a year, go out 65 times a year, play sport 45 times a year and partake in cultural activities 10 times a year.

The Carnegie Inquiry found that the 'rise of the well-being agenda' had been a 'deep and persistent trend over the last decade or more' (Carnegie UK Trust, 2007: p. 25) and its report suggested that 'many of the requirements necessary to achieve well-being cannot be achieved through consumption; for example, the need for better quality public spaces, better social connections within one's local community, and so on' (ibid.). It also underlined the importance of non-material well-being by reporting that 'over 80 per cent of consumers consider family, friends and education/knowledge a source of pride, compared to 57 per cent for wealth' (p. 17).

Contemporary aspirations are often associated with the generation born between 1946 and 1962 and known widely as the 'baby-boomers'. They are seen to have experienced unprecedented affluence and personal freedom, and they are better educated than their forebears. As a result, they expect more and are more demanding. And their significance goes beyond their own numbers: 'the baby boomers laid the foundations for the values and experiences that many younger people now take for granted' (Evans and Saxton, 2005: p. 29).

Religion and secularisation

Overall, the trend over the past 40 years or more has been towards secularisation, the process through which religious belief and observance has declined, and religious organisations have lost many of their adherents and much of their influence with other social institutions (Torry, 2005). In 2000, 60 per cent of the population claimed to belong to a specific religion with 55 per cent being Christian. However, half of all adults aged 18 and over who belonged to a religion had never attended a religious service (Matheson and Babb, 2002). However, inward migration and the establishment of significant BME communities – especially in Britain's cities – has led to greater religious and cultural diversity while the importance of faith-based organisations in civil society has been increasingly recognized in the development and implementation of social policy.

Regulation and risk

During the last twenty years of the 20th century and into the present one, the conviction has grown that the world in which we live is beset by danger and that it is a major government responsibility to reduce to a minimum the many risks to which the population is exposed (Rochester, 2001). According to Gaskin (2005: p. 42), 'economic, social and cultural changes have destroyed collective belief systems and individual responsibility, replacing it with a sense of vulnerability and a tendency to blame others when things go wrong'. Risk aversion has also played its role in the loss of areas for public deliberation: 'health and safety legislation, security legislation and increasingly stringent insurance regulations all, to an extent, stifle spontaneity' while the regulations governing private or 'quasi-public' spaces 'can impede legitimate organised and/or spontaneous activity' (Carnegie UK Trust, 2007: p. 14).

Implications for volunteering

This combination of 'demographic, economic, social, cultural and political change, which are already under way' will alter the climate in which volunteering takes place. And 'the final outcome for volunteering will be determined by the magnitude and interplay of these changes and by the ingenuity, adaptability and hard work with which people, organisations, communities and governments respond to them' (Zimmeck, 2007: p. 4). To conclude this chapter, we will look at some of the challenges and opportunities volunteering is likely to face as a result of the changing context and discuss some possible responses to them. These challenges are returned to and expanded upon in several other chapters.

The first set of challenges concern, on the one hand, the future composition of the volunteering population, and on the other hand, the ways in which people become involved in voluntary action. Recent employment trends have significantly reduced both the numbers of women who are not part of the labour market and the length of time they remain outside it. The long-term impact on volunteering is likely to be considerable as the supply of people from the section of the population that has historically provided large numbers of volunteers overall, and many of the most committed of them in particular, begins to dry up. However, the growing numbers of the 'active retired' are a potentially rich source of replacements and a variety of initiatives have provided evidence that older people have a major contribution to make to volunteering, if targeted efforts were made to recruit and support them (Rochester and Hutchison, 2002).

A basket of other trends – the weakening of traditional family ties, the loss of a sense of community based on location, secularisation, the professionalisation of voluntary and community sector organisations and the reduction in the number of 'public spaces' – all tend to undermine the institutions and networks through which many people found their ways into volunteering. There are, however, some countervailing trends. First, the individual communities which constitute the mosaic of cultural and religious diversity which is a feature of contemporary British society are very successful incubators of voluntary action within the immediate community. Second, the longer periods of time spent in full-time education by a growing proportion of the population means that colleges and universities have the potential to engage large numbers of younger people as volunteers. Third, the workplace has become a significant organisational context for the involvement of employees in volunteering.

The greatest opportunity and the most daunting challenge appear to be presented by the new technologies of the virtual society. The experience to date of 'virtual volunteering' will be discussed in Chapter 8. For the moment, we will simply note that the potential of the Internet to provide the conditions in which voluntary action by the individual and the group can be stimulated and undertaken may well be enormous but that the 'digital immigrants' who lead and manage volunteer-involving organisations and the volunteering infrastructure are yet to engage fully with the challenge of realising it. At the same time, they will need to take account of the reduction in the importance and frequency of face-to-face communication which has been the key traditional route into volunteering.

The literature has also highlighted three different – and perhaps more profound – kinds of challenge for voluntary action which arise from the changes in our society. The first of these is the need to address continuing poverty in an otherwise affluent society. A 'strong theme' identified in the consultations carried out for the Carnegie Inquiry was the idea of the '80/20' society in which 'most people were comfortably off, but a bottom tier found themselves in very different economic circumstances' (Carnegie UK Trust, 2007: p. 24). The challenge was for the associations of civil society to become 'more than a vehicle for the

80 percent' and 'engage with and legitimately articulate the views of the most marginalised' (ibid.). The second broad challenge involves revitalising the political process: can voluntary action provide the means of reconnecting the vital green sprouts of single issue campaigning with the more conventional apparatus of government and politics to address the perceived 'democratic deficit'? Third, what kind of role can volunteering play in strengthening social cohesion in general and knitting together communities which are fragmented by religious and cultural differences?

We can distinguish two broad approaches to engaging with this agenda of issues for volunteering thrown up by our changing society. One can be characterised as 'going with the flow'. It starts from the belief that volunteer-involving organisations need to adapt their practices to reflect and take account of the changes which have been and are still taking place in their environment. This approach is exemplified by Evans and Saxton of the think-tank, nfpSynergy, whose report 'on the changing face of volunteering in the 21st Century' was commissioned by the Scout Association (Evans and Saxton, 2005). Their recommendations are essentially about better marketing: the image of volunteering needs to be renewed; different sales approaches need to be tailored to different segments of the market – such as the baby-boomer generation, students and other young people, and employee volunteers; and those recruiting volunteers could learn a great deal from the ways in which fund-raising teams went about their work. Above all, they call for the 'productisation of volunteering' which involves transforming the 'average volunteering request, where the amount of time required is unspecified the benefits are unclear, the duration is usually indefinite and how the organisation will use the time is unmentioned' (p. 48) into something much more like a commercial sales pitch:

> Forgive us for saying so, but McDonalds can teach charities a thing or two about productisation. Not for them a menu without prices, a meal with an ill-defined portion size, or a restaurant waiting time that is unclear and unpredictable. The price is set, the contents are clear and the waiting time is (allegedly) low.

The nfpSynergy strategy is clearly located in the dominant non-profit paradigm of volunteering we discussed in Chapter 2 and, as such, is an option for a significant proportion of volunteer-involving organisations but an inappropriate or inadequate response for many others. An alternative, more inclusive approach would look rather different. It would, of course, take account of the competing pressures on people's time and seek to achieve a better match between volunteering opportunities and potential volunteers' availability as well as making the activity inherently desirable – 'something interesting, challenging and meaningful, not just the boring bits that others would rather not do' (Zimmeck, 2007: p. 7). It would also seek to develop better – more coordinated and more inclusive – ways of making the connections between potential volunteers and organisations offering opportunities to volunteer. At the same time, it would not look for a better image so much as a better *vision* of volunteering, one that would be 'bigger, shaggier and more inclusive' and that would recognise the 'diversity, quirkiness and sheer humanity' of volunteers (ibid.).

Such an approach would, however, need to go beyond changing the perceptions and the practices of volunteer-involving organisations and the specialist infrastructure bodies and look to challenge the status quo in the wider environment. On one level, this would entail concerted action to overcome or find a way past the increasing numbers of obstacles in the way of engagement in voluntary action and civil society which would include mitigating the excesses of bureaucracy. On another – more important – level, it would involve expressing and actively promoting some key values at the expense of other societal norms. It would mean, for example, promoting solidarity and cooperation rather than individualism; the pursuit of well-being rather than material wealth and consumption; and engagement in society as a citizen rather than as a consumer.

7
Government and Volunteering: Towards a history of policy and practice

Meta Zimmeck

Introduction

It is a happy thought that 'volunteering has never had it so good' in terms of government's interest and support (Commission on the Future of Volunteering, 2008: p. 3), but this hopeful message skates over a more complex historical reality. Since the 1960s, government has promoted volunteering to a greater or lesser extent through a wide variety of different policies and programmes. Sometimes these were based on party-political agendas, sometimes on expediency and sometimes on serendipity. Sometimes these were generated within government and sometimes in response to external pressures. Sometimes these were effective and sometimes not. This means that the history of government's approaches to volunteering since the 1960s is not a narrative of linear progress – from obscurity to apotheosis, from periphery to core, from zero to sixty. Rather it is a narrative of changes of emphasis and scale, twists and turns, fits and starts, ups and downs, two steps forward and one step back.

Before 1997, government's interest in volunteering was intermittent and its approach, in Kendall's useful typology (Kendall, 2005), was mainly vertical, as individual central government departments took steps from time to time to secure through volunteering assistance in the delivery of public services in the policy areas for which they were responsible (Sheard, 1992). It was only with the Make a Difference Campaign of John Major's Conservative Government in 1994–1997, shortly before the arrival of New Labour, that government experimented with a more holistic and broadly based approach. Since 1997, under New Labour,

84

government's interest has been more sustained, and its approach has been more horizontal, shaped not by departments' individual needs but by policies determined at the political centre (by No.10, H.M. Treasury and the Home Office/Cabinet Office) and rolled out across (and in some cases over) departments and other government bodies. Moreover, since 1997, government has been, in Kendall's words, 'hyper-active' and has created a vast array of events, initiatives and programmes; reviews, consultations and commissions; pilots and demonstration projects; machinery of government changes and new organisational vehicles; and exemplars and champions.

Making sense of the multifarious activities of the central government departments tasked with 'leading' on volunteering; the devolved administrations that put their own stamp on policies on volunteering conceived in London and implemented them in their own way (since funding for most programmes was England-only); other central government departments that incorporated volunteering in the delivery of their own programmes; and other parts of government (local authorities, the National Health Service, fire authorities and police authorities) that incorporated volunteering in the delivery of their services is not an easy task.

In this chapter, we do not – and cannot – aim at comprehensiveness. We focus on developments in England and note developments in the devolved administrations; at regional level; and at local authority level, where appropriate. We focus on the main characteristics of government's approach to volunteering and some of its most important or iconic activities, and we indicate where changes have occurred over time. In particular, we explore changes along the following four axes:

1. *The reasons that government gave for supporting volunteering:* Reasons range from its being a 'good thing' in and of itself to its contributing to some other policy end *(inherent value vs instrumental value)*
2. *The parts of volunteering that government supported:* Choices range from all volunteering – all sorts of activities by all sorts of people in all sorts of fields of endeavour – to some volunteering – some activities, such as mentoring, by some people, such as young people or people from BME groups, in some fields of endeavour, such as health or sports *(holistic vs targeted support)*
3. *The way that government operationalised its interest in volunteering:* Methods range from helping the institutions of volunteering, infrastructure bodies and volunteer-involving organisations, to carry out their work to the best advantage to running specific initiatives in key

policy areas and/or creating bespoke organisational vehicles to do so *(enabling vs doing role).*

4. *The measures that government used to evaluate its progress in promoting volunteering:* Measures range from accepting on trust and without quantification that volunteering makes a valuable contribution to society to setting quantified targets for both process and outputs *(trust vs quantified measures).*

In this chapter, we explore what government did before 1997 and then what it has done since then under the two New Labour governments of Tony Blair and Gordon Brown. We describe some of the most important developments under each of the four axes set out above and look for continuities and discontinuities. We hope that this chapter will be a first step to gaining a better understanding of the development of government's policy and practice in promoting and supporting volunteering.

Government and volunteering before 1997

By the 1960s, the glory days of the welfare state were over. It had become clear that demand for public services always exceeded supply, costs were at the limits of affordability and, in any case, there were cracks, gaps and bumps in existing provision. As a result, government began to take a keen interest in ways of improving the reach, quality and value for money of its services and thus came to see volunteers, with their 'spontaneity, adaptability and freshness of approach' (Home Office, 1967: p. 3) and, most importantly, their willing hands as a means to an end. As time went by, however, government developed a more nuanced approach to volunteering. It came to see that volunteers were essential to democratic society and worthy of 'admiration and respect' in their own right (Home Office, 1978: p. 31). It came to see that volunteers ought to be representative of an increasingly diverse society. It came to see that volunteers needed proper organisation, management and support in order to be effective. Finally – from the 1980s onwards, when it committed substantial funding to employment programmes that included volunteering – it came to see that its support for volunteers should not only be determined by its main policy aims but also provide value for money. The great and divisive Efficiency Scrutiny of 1990, which took place in the last days of Margaret Thatcher's Conservative Government, recognised both the inherent and the instrumental value of volunteering when it recommended giving preference to voluntary organisations that involved volunteers because volunteering 'is a desirable activity in its own right, and ... a very cost effective way of providing desirable services' (Home Office, 1990: p. 18).

There are a number of milestones in government's approach to volunteering before 1997.

As the department responsible for prisons and probation, the Home Office carried out a number of inquiries into the potential contribution that volunteers might make to improving the quality of life of offenders and ex-offenders and reducing their propensity to return to crime, and it decided that it should involve volunteers and deploy them to the best advantage. For example, in 1967 the Reading Committee recommended more systematic involvement of volunteers in the probation service. It aimed to re-integrate ex-offenders into society by strengthening their relationships with their families, helping them to find work and accommodation and giving them a stake in the ordinary life of their communities, and it looked to volunteers as 'representatives of the public' to play an important part in this endeavour. It recommended that there should be proper procedures in place for recruiting volunteers (locally, not nationally, determined and administered), preparing (not training) them for their duties, paying their travel and subsistence expenses and training probation officers to involve and manage them. It also noted that volunteers were from 'a limited group of individuals, many of them drawn from the middle classes', and recommended opening up recruitment to the working classes: 'The original question "which age groups or which social classes are most suitable for the recruitment of volunteers?" may become "what are the methods of recruitment most suitable for different age groups and social classes?"' (Home Office, 1967: pp. 1, 5, 32, 38–43).

Commissioned jointly by the Home Office, the Department of Education and Science, the Ministry of Housing and Local Government and the Department of Health, the Seebohm Committee, which reported in 1968, proposed a radical re-engineering of local authorities' delivery of community-based social services and allocated to volunteers an important role in this new setting. It aimed to orient social services towards the 'well-being of the whole of the community and not only of social casualties' and to give communities a sense of ownership of these services. It looked to volunteers – informal ('good neighbours') and formal, involved directly through social services departments or indirectly through those 'vigorous outward-looking voluntary organisations' that worked to them – to play an important three-fold role as providers of services, 'citizen participants' in planning for services and campaigners for improvement of services. It made the point that the delivery of social services required 'large numbers of volunteers to complement the teams of professional workers' and that there was a 'large untapped supply of such people' who ought to be mobilised (Committee on Local Authority and Allied Personal Social Services, 1968: pp. 147, 151–153; Glasby, 2005).

A year later, the Aves Committee, commissioned jointly by the National Council of Social Service and the National Institute for Social Work Training (outside government but close to it), seconded the Seebohm Committee's affirmation of the 'essential' contribution of volunteers to the provision of community-based personal social services and of their supporting role, 'to extend and improve a service, by adding something to what is already being done, or by opening up new possibilities'. It carried out an audit and found that many local authorities and four central government departments (the Ministry of Health/Department of Health and Social Security, in hospitals; the Home Office, in probation and childcare services; the Ministry of Social Security, in war pensions administration; and the Department of Education and Science, in youth services, special educational services, schools and playgroups) had a positive view of volunteering and involved volunteers in their activities. It concluded, however, that they had given 'comparatively little thought' to what they were doing and that their involvement of volunteers was, in consequence, unnecessarily narrow in scope, casually organised and inadequately resourced. In order to put volunteering on a more satisfactory footing, it set out a programme of action (the basis for volunteering infrastructure bodies' campaigning for the next 40 years) that included clarification of volunteers' roles and objectives, including setting boundaries between their roles and those of paid workers; 'widening the fields' of recruitment to include volunteers from 'all sections of society' and, in particular, older people; management of volunteers by trained specialist organisers; provision of appropriate training for volunteers; payment of volunteers' travelling and out-of-pocket expenses; use of mass media for developing interest in and providing information about volunteering; and establishment of a comprehensive network of volunteer centres financed by local authorities and an independent national infrastructure body or 'Volunteer Foundation' financed by central government (Aves, 1969: pp. 53–57, 183, 190, 195–198).

The economic crises of the late 1970s and 1980s prompted government to promote volunteering more actively in order to lighten the load on public services. In 1977, Jim Callaghan's Labour Government launched the National Good Neighbour Campaign which encouraged volunteers to look after their elderly and disabled neighbours and thus reduce demand on health and social services. The Thatcher Government established a number of programmes – including the Urban Programme (Department of the Environment) and the Community Enterprise Programme (later rolled up into the Community Programme; Manpower Services Commission) – to combat unemployment and urban decay, and these involved voluntary and community organisations and, through them, volunteers, in their delivery. In 1981, as an experiment it allocated some funding in the Community Enterprise Programme to supporting volunteering directly – by employing unemployed people as volunteer organisers (Elliott, Lomas and Riddell, 1984; Gay and Hatch, 1983).

The next year, government established two programmes that supported volunteering directly. In the first, Opportunities for Volunteering (Department of Health and Social Security), it aimed 'to enable unemployed people to participate in voluntary work in the health and/ or social services fields', but it was fairly open in its approach. It used a broad definition of 'unemployed people' (those of working age but not in full-time employment) and 'voluntary work' (both informal and formal volunteering). It was also open to volunteers who were not unemployed. It promoted benefits to volunteers as well as 'output of relevance to health or personal social services'. This programme has continued and is thus the most durable of government's programmes for volunteering, although its funding of £6.7 million in 2006/2007 represents a decline in real terms on that of its early years (£3.6 million in 1982/1983 and £5.6 million in 1988/1989). In the second, the Voluntary Projects Programme (Manpower Services Commission) had a narrower focus. It used a strict definition of eligibility and was only open to volunteers who were unemployed. It provided volunteers with opportunities and training geared to improving their chances of obtaining employment. It viewed volunteering as an 'exit option' (Department of Health and Social Security, 1984; Home Office, 1988, 1990; Mocroft, 1984; Sheard, 1992).

In 1994, the Major Government launched the Make a Difference Campaign, the most ambitious and innovative programme to encourage and support volunteering before 1997 and, perhaps, since. For the first time, government planned coordinated implementation of a jointly agreed policy for volunteering in all four nations of the United Kingdom. For the first time, it used methods of consultation and policy formation which now seem familiar but which were then novel and exciting: appointment of the Make a Difference Team, an independent working group of 'representatives of organisations which have a strong interest in volunteering' from the private, public, and voluntary and community sectors and from all four nations (later translated into an advisory body, the Volunteering Partnership) and tasking it with carrying out an extensive consultation (reference groups with 130 members and a postal consultation with over 300 responses) and formulation of a strategy that would take volunteering 'into the next century'. For the first time, it approached volunteering primarily as a 'vehicle for participating in and contributing to society' rather than as a vehicle for delivering public services, and when it, inevitably, dealt with the delivery of public services, it focused on how volunteering could improve the quality of life of service users. For the first time, it targeted all volunteers and all those who might become volunteers in the future, across all types of activities, all fields of endeavour and the remits of all government bodies, and in order to ensure the equitable distribution of the pleasures and benefits of volunteering, it made a strong case for breaking down 'barriers of class, wealth and race'. For the first time, it made a 'collective commitment' to working across the private, public and voluntary and community sectors. Finally, for the first time, it produced an action plan, which it declared to be 'no bureaucratic exercise', for implementing its strategy across central government departments.

The Make a Difference strategy, based on 81 recommendations of the Make a Difference Team, supported nine objectives: encouraging more people to participate in volunteering, 'especially from those groups in the population whose potential is insufficiently tapped'; making it easier for people to participate; involving volunteers more purposively and imaginatively in society, 'whether through informal or formal volunteering or through the informal response of each community to its own agendas'; encouraging the more effective use of volunteers' contributions for the benefit of volunteers and of those helped by their efforts; improving the organisation and infrastructure of volunteering; communicating 'the importance, effectiveness and value of volunteering'; securing 'greater recognition for the contribution of volunteers to society'; constructing and communicating more positive images of volunteers and volunteering; and mobilising more people to volunteer. In the end, government did not commit sufficient resources to deliver all it had promised – only around £3 million out of an estimated £41 million needed. It did use its resources sensibly: a media campaign to promote volunteering, a national telephone helpline to publicise opportunities for volunteering, employer-supported volunteering in government departments; and funding for volunteer centres. Its most important product was not what it did but what it thought, a comprehensive, holistic and volunteer-centred blueprint for action (Davis Smith, 2001; Home Office, 1995; Make a Difference Team, 1995; Wardell, Lishman and Whalley, 1997).

Government and volunteering since 1997

It is commonly assumed that New Labour's arrival in 1997 signalled a new departure in government's approach to volunteering. After all New Labour's *raison d'etre* was that it was 'new' – that it had broken with its own heritage and the legacy of its immediate predecessors in government and that it was moving forward by leaps and bounds or, in New Labour speak, 'step-changes'. This is not necessarily the case, since its approach shows continuities as well as discontinuities with what went before and has deviated from its original course in the years since 1997. New Labour has demonstrated continuities with the past in the way it has valued volunteering for instrumental rather than inherent reasons. However, it has also demonstrated discontinuities with the past in the way it has determined cross-governmental policies from the political centre (a vertical rather than horizontal approach) and the extent to which it has singled out particular types of volunteers, used centralised command and control methods of policy formation and implementation rather than allowing departments to harness volunteering to their own priorities and set targets backed up by standardised measures for monitoring progress rather than merely aiming for value for money.

Overview

Since 1997, government has been 'hyperactive' in terms of its approach to volunteering – in fact, busier in 12 years than its predecessors had been in the previous 40. Under New Labour government, activities have fallen into a number of different categories:

Creating a positive climate for volunteering by

- incorporating performance measures on volunteering in central government departments' Public Service Agreements (PSAs) and in local authorities' Local Area Agreements (LAAs); these testified to the designation of volunteering as an important and therefore measurable part of government's social and community policies;
- funding volunteering programmes and projects; these were mostly sponsored by the lead department for volunteering (Home Office/ Cabinet Office in England, Department for Social Development

in Northern Ireland; Development Department in Scotland and Voluntary Sector Unit in Wales) and included the Active Community Demonstration Projects (ACDPs), Beacon Councils, BME Twinning Initiative (BMETI), Experience Corps, GoldStar Volunteering and Mentoring Exemplar Programme, Home Office Older Volunteers Initiative (HOOVI), Mentoring/Mentoring and Befriending Programmes, Millennium Volunteers, ONE20/TimeBank, Opportunities for Volunteering, Strategic Grants Programme, v, Volunteer Brokerage Scheme for Unemployed People (just announced) and Volunteering for All. All of these programmes and projects included elements of promotion of volunteering as a positive activity, the recruitment of particular groups of volunteers and the dissemination/celebration of good practice. Most were England-only or, if more widely implemented, operated to different timetables and with different funding bases. For example, the devolved administrations continued Millennium Volunteers after it had been replaced by v in England;

- backing high-level promotional campaigns such as the Queen's Award for Voluntary Service, the UN's IYV 2001 and the Year of the Volunteer 2005; all of these aimed to attract media coverage and raise the profile of volunteering;
- appointing Baroness Neuberger, chair of the Commission on the Future of Volunteering, as the Prime Minister's special advisor on volunteering for England.

Rationalising and improving the capacity of the volunteering infrastructure by

- providing strategic funding for infrastructure bodies such as VE (created by the merger of the National Centre for Volunteer, Volunteer Development England and the Consortium on Opportunities for Volunteering in 2004), Volunteer Development Agency Northern Ireland, VDS, and Wales Council for Voluntary Action. (Wales is the only nation that does not have a separate national volunteering infrastructure body.);
- providing new forms of infrastructure support through ChangeUp/ Capacitybuilders in England; this included a network of local and regional partnerships and the establishment of the Volunteering Hub, one of six hubs (first phase) and the Modernising Volunteering Workstream, one of nine workstreams of National Support Services (second phase) and involved coordinating and modernising infrastructure from the local up to the national level;

- supporting locally based volunteer centres (on an *ad hoc* basis in England and a systematic basis in the devolved administrations);
- supporting IT projects to make it easier to volunteer (Do-It website).

Incorporating good practice, where possible, in its relationships with volunteers, whether its staff or its clients by

- promoting employer-supported schemes for volunteering for public servants;
- giving sympathetic treatment to clients who wish to volunteer – for example, benefits claimants, patients and tenants.

Policy context and rationale for supporting volunteering

Government's policies and programmes to promote and support volunteering have developed in the context of its overall policy framework and spending priorities, and, contrary to the view that volunteering has 'never had it so good', it would appear that volunteering had it best late on under the Conservatives, at least in principle, and early on under New Labour and has steadily lost ground to other policy priorities since then.

Like previous governments, New Labour has been interested in volunteering mainly for instrumental reasons, but its approach has included something old and something new. Like previous governments, it turned to volunteering as part of its efforts to reform the delivery of public services through streamlining, outsourcing, pursuing efficiency gains, and involving the community in provision, planning and campaigning for improvements in a changing menu of 'key services' such as criminal justice, education, health and social care and recently, in the unfolding economic crisis, in employment. But unlike previous governments, it also turned to volunteering as part of its efforts to forge 'civil renewal', a more democratic, inclusive and cohesive society, by 'building the capacity of both individuals and groups within communities... [and] enabling local people to develop their own solutions to the issues which most affect them' (Home Office, 2003: p. 4).

However, these two agendas were responses to different problematics, used different conceptual frameworks, had different organisational and ministerial power bases and competed for resources. Since 1997, New Labour has made two significant strategic shifts. First of all, while it gave these two agendas roughly equal attention in its early days, it has come to prioritise the civil renewal agenda, in the light of actual and anticipated civil disturbances and the shadow of 9/11 and the Iraq War, although the spectre of mass unemployment and a general election likely to be fought on its track record of public service reform may prompt some rebalancing. Second, within its public service delivery agenda, having initially viewed volunteering as the most important component of its 'active community' strategy, it now views volunteering as one of the lesser components of its 'third sector' strategy. Initially, it was interested in the activities of individuals, but it is now more interested in collective activities – by 'communities' and community/third sector organisations and is strangely fascinated by social enterprises. In cases where it is interested in people's activities as individuals, initially it was interested in their activities as volunteers, but it is now more interested in their activities as 'citizens' and their non-electoral participation in democratic process.

A comparison of New Labour's spending reviews in 2000 and 2007 demonstrates these strategic shifts.

New Labour's Spending Review 2000 included a 'cross-cutting review on the active community', which was all about volunteering and followed in the footsteps of the Make a Difference Campaign. It aimed 'to develop a strategy for increasing voluntary and community activity in all sectors of society' and to identify the best methods of implementation. It laid out three reasons for supporting volunteering – 'helping to deliver quality services', 'achieving more active, engaged communities' and 'contributing to the personal development, self-esteem and well-being of volunteers themselves'. It reviewed support for major volunteering and community support programmes in order to identify the most effective and work out the reasons why they were effective; considered how local infrastructure and systems might be improved in order to inform people about opportunities for volunteering or community support; developed costed models for creating and filling volunteering opportunities (with emphasis on those for older people); outlined work with departments and other government bodies to ensure 'more proactive use of volunteers in delivering services'; reviewed central and local support for organisations that promoted or supported volunteering or community activity, including the media and the private sector; and developed a publicity strategy to 'raise public and corporate awareness' (Home Office, 2000).

New Labour's Comprehensive Spending Review 2007, three spending review cycles later, included a review of 'the future role of the third sector in social and economic regeneration', in which volunteering and volunteers played a very small role indeed. It anticipated that this and other contributing reviews would enable it to respond to 'world' issues such as demographic change, globalisation, economic competition, poverty, pressure on natural resources and climate change. In particular, having carried out a wide-ranging consultation of stakeholders, it outlined a framework for partnership working between the third sector and government: 'enabling voice and campaigning' so that 'third sector organisations are able to play a growing role in civic society, better engage with decision makers and are never hindered from speaking out and representing their members, users and communities'; 'strengthening communities' so that third sector organisations are able to 'foster greater shared action between different sections of the community and work with Local Government, public services and others to promote understanding and relationships across society'; 'transforming public services' so that third sector organisations are able to contribute to the design, development and delivery of services; and 'encouraging social enterprise' so that third sector organisations can 'diversify their income streams' and become more sustainable. It made reference in passing to 'volunteering and mentoring' (treated as distinct activities) and the need to 'build a culture of volunteering', but it focused on volunteers as a resource for third sector organisations' working in partnership with government to deliver public services and to build communities and on getting volunteers young through the inclusion of volunteering in the citizenship curriculum, promotion of volunteering by young people and support for mentoring of young people (H.M. Treasury and Cabinet Office, 2007).

The trajectory of New Labour's overarching targets, PSAs, set out in successive spending reviews, tells a similar tale.

In SR1998, the first year in which government produced performance targets, the relevant target was 'increasing the quantity and quality of people's involvement in their community and ensuring fulfilment on the vision of the Giving Age'.

In SR2000, the target (Home Office PSA13) was 'make substantial progress by 2004 towards one million more people being actively involved in their communities', and it was accompanied by a technical note that defined 'actively involved in their communities' with reference to informal and formal volunteering and 'substantial progress' as 500,000 or more people aged 16 and over between 2001 and 2003.

In SR2002, the target (Home Office PSA8) was 'increase voluntary and community sector activity, including increasing community participation, by 5 percent by 2006' and it had two limbs, 'increasing the contribution of the voluntary and community sector to the delivery of public

services' and 'increasing the involvement of people to their community'. It was accompanied by a technical note that defined 'community
involvement' as 'participating at least once a month in the last year in
any of three core activities – civic participation, informal volunteering
and formal volunteering' – and '5 percent' as 931,655 people aged 16
and over between 2001 and 2005/2006.

In SR2004, the target (Home Office PSA6) was 'increase community
engagement, especially amongst those at greatest risk of social exclusion'; and it had two limbs, 'increasing voluntary activity by individuals
at risk of social exclusion' and 'increasing the voluntary and community
sector contribution to delivering public services'. It was accompanied by
a technical note that defined 'voluntary activity' as informal volunteering and formal volunteering and 'people at risk of social exclusion' as
those with no qualifications, people from minority ethnic groups and
people with disabilities and set the measure as an increase (unquanti-
fied) in voluntary activity by those in socially excluded groups between
2003/2004 and 2007/2008.

In SR2007, the target (H.M. Treasury/Department for Communities
and Local Government PSA21) was 'build more cohesive, empowered
and active communities', and it had six indicators – the 'percentage of
people who believe that people from different backgrounds get on well
together in their local area', the 'percentage of people who have meaningful interactions on a regular basis with people from different ethnic or religious backgrounds', the 'percentage of people who feel that
they belong to their neighbourhood', the 'percentage of people who
feel they can influence decisions affecting their local area', a 'thriving
third sector', and the 'percentage of people who participate in culture
and sport'. It was accompanied by a technical note that defined, *inter
alia*, Indicator 5, a 'thriving third sector' by reference to the percentage of people who engage in formal volunteering on a regular basis (at
least once a month), 'the number of full-time equivalent staff employed
within the sector' and the measure as an overall 6 per cent increase of
the two components in index form.

The Office of the Deputy Prime Minister/Department for Communities
and Local Government included an indicator for volunteering, 'an
increase in the number of people recorded as or reporting that they
have engaged in formal volunteering on an average of at least two hours
per week over the past year', in its set of 35 indicators to be used in
monitoring performance by Local Strategic Partnerships. This indicator was optional in Rounds 1 and 2 but mandatory in Round 3. This
indicator was not particularly apt, as it did not harmonise with the

national indicator used in the Home Office Citizenship Surveys; and, by concentrating on more intense and regular volunteering, it set the bar very high, caused widespread confusion and made measurement difficult, if not impossible. As part of SR2007, H.M. Treasury and the Department for Communities and Local Government recently revised the system for monitoring performance and issued a set of 198 national indicators, some mandatory and some discretionary, from which each Local Strategic Partnership must create a portfolio of up to 35 priority targets/improvement targets. National Indicator 6, which is mandatory, is 'participation in regular volunteering', defined as 'the proportion of individuals undertaking regular (once a month) formal volunteering'. It now matches the national indicator used in the Citizenship Surveys (Cabinet Office, 2008; Office of the Deputy Prime Minister, 2006).

Thus, since 1998, government has moved from viewing volunteering – both informal and formal – as the critical component of community involvement across all sectors to viewing formal volunteering as an increasingly minor element of a thriving voluntary and community/third sector. It has also moved from viewing the third sector as valuable in its own right to viewing parts of the third sector as valuable in proportion to their ability to deliver government's particular (and evolving) agenda – social inclusion, social cohesion, provision of public services and future Olympians.

Segmentation of support for volunteering

Before 1997, government differentiated among volunteers in accordance with the fields in which they were active (which corresponded to departments' remits), but it did not differentiate among volunteers according to the types of activities they engaged in and only fairly late in the day differentiated according to their demographic characteristics – for example, their employment status (Opportunities for Volunteering and Voluntary Projects Programmes). The Major Government's Make a Difference Campaign took an unusually broad and holistic view of volunteering – all sorts of activities by all sorts of people in all sorts of fields of endeavour, and it also aimed to make volunteering an equal opportunity activity by removing 'barriers of class, wealth and race'. While New Labour initially echoed this comprehensive and egalitarian view, its approach differed from those of its predecessors in two important respects.

In the first place, New Labour has differentiated among volunteers in terms of the types of activities it supported and has had a predilection for anything 'modern' or high tech. In particular, in response to the personal interest of both Labour prime ministers, from 1999 it has supported mentoring and, when research findings indicated, befriending as well in the Active Community Demonstration Projects, Mentoring/ Mentoring and Befriending Programmes, Big Brothers/Big Sisters and GoldStar Volunteering and Mentoring Exemplar Programme. It has done so far more generously than it has supported the national and local volunteering infrastructure, which catered to a much larger clientele.

In the second place, New Labour has differentiated among volunteers in terms of their demographic characteristics. While previous governments noted that volunteers should be recruited from a broader range of social groups in order to improve their effectiveness, they were primarily concerned with social class, the seeming domination of volunteering by middle-class people, and only secondarily concerned with the under-representation of, *inter alia*, older people, younger people, disabled people, unemployed people and people from ethnic minority communities. Unlike previous governments, however, New Labour has focused on 'special' groups that played a role in its wider civil renewal agenda and in its early days provided programmes in support of volunteering by older people (HOOVI, Experience Corps) and people from ethnic minority communities (BMETI). In particular, from 1999 onwards, it has provided programmes in support of volunteering by young people – Millennium Volunteers and v. It has allocated £117 million over three years to v, the bulk of available resources for volunteering, despite the fact that young people were not designated as an under-represented group under SR2004 and despite the fact that they have high rates of participation in volunteering. In response to the economic crisis, it has recently announced a new programme, the Volunteer Brokerage Scheme for Unemployed People (a modern revival of Opportunities for Volunteering and the Volunteering Projects Programme) in support of volunteering by 40,000 unemployed, mainly young, people, in order to help them get back to work (Cabinet Office, 2009).

New forms of policy formation and implementation

Before 1997, government used fairly straightforward methods for implementing its policies. On the one hand, it administered its programmes diréctly and, less usually, indirectly by commissioning volunteer-involving organisations to act as agents (for example, the organisations and consortia of organisations that distributed funding for Opportunities for Volunteering). On the other hand, it supported the activities of the national infrastructure bodies for volunteering, with which it worked closely, and the nascent network of volunteer centres.

New Labour, however, has played a more active, interventionist and innovative role. As noted above, it centralised the formation of policy on volunteering in No.10, H.M. Treasury and lead departments such as the Home Office/Cabinet Office in England rather than in individual departments. It also incorporated the formation of policy on volunteering in its wider cyclical process – spending reviews, targets, action plans, cross-cutting programmes and initiatives. Initially, it managed many of its programmes directly and, when it devolved management to external organisations, instead of working through existing organisations (and former partners) it created new eccentrically named organisations such as Experience Corps, ChangeUp/Capacitybuilders and v. It also created new vehicles for mediating its relationship with the voluntary and community/third sector and volunteering.

New Labour's first new vehicle was the Compact, which is symbolically important as a manifestation of its corporatist aspirations. Drawing on the recommendations of the independent Deakin Commission in 1996, New Labour entered into the Compact, an agreement between government and the voluntary and community sector based on 'shared vision and principles' – signed in England, Scotland and Wales in 1998 and in Northern Ireland in 2001, which had supplementary Codes of Good Practice to cover various areas of special interest such as volunteering (published in England in 2001 and revised in 2005). The Compact set out a number of undertakings by government, the voluntary and community sector and government and the voluntary and community sector jointly. Government's undertakings included consulting the sector 'so that proposed legislation or regulation, guidance and policies take account of the ways they may affect volunteers and volunteering activities'; working to reduce barriers to volunteering caused by existing legislation, regulation and policies, recognising that, when applying for funding, voluntary and community organisations should be able to include as legitimate overheads the costs of involving volunteers; recognising the independence of volunteering infrastructure bodies; and adopting policies to ensure that volunteering infrastructure bodies 'develop realistic sustainable long-term funding' (Home Office, 2005: p. 2). These undertakings are indications of intent and are not legally binding and were not accompanied by agreed measures to monitor progress, so that it is difficult to ascertain the extent to which they have been implemented.

New Labour's second new vehicle was ChangeUp/Capacitybuilders with its various 'hubs'/'workstreams', established in 2004/2005 to provide subject-based infrastructure support to 'frontline' organisations that delivered public services. Itself an arm's length vehicle, ChangeUp/ Capacitybuilders kept the infrastructure bodies that managed the hubs/ workstreams at arm's length, a somewhat elaborate double-distancing. Government's arrangements at national level for volunteering under ChangeUp/Capacitybuilders were contentious and illustrative of its increasingly narrow and instrumental approach to volunteering and its infrastructure. VE managed the Volunteering Hub, which shadowed its core functions, at the cost of additional layers of governance and management. The Hub's brief was functional: to modernise volunteering infrastructure 'to achieve effective, efficient and sustainable England-wide coverage'; to support development of volunteer management by disseminating information and good practice and improving access to training; to deal with emerging issues of volunteering and risk management; and to involve the volunteering infrastructure 'in the process of creating a strategic approach to the development of volunteering' (Volunteering Hub, 2006: pp. 1–2). It performed well and was judged to have performed well in the Durning Review, which assessed the performance of all six hubs and recommended that VE should directly take over the work of the Hub (Durning, 2006). However, in its reorganisation of Capacitybuilders, government wrote the Volunteering Hub out of the script but then, following acrimonious public debate, wrote it back in as one of nine workstreams (albeit in the second tier of the less-well-funded) and tasked it, rather more instrumentally, with 'addressing the broader needs of third sector organisations in engaging its current and potential unpaid workforce [that is, volunteers], including activism, trusteeship, encouraging diversity and diversifying opportunities for involvement (including through ICT)' (Capacitybuilders, 2007: p. 12).

Measures for setting targets and evaluating progress

Before 1997, government attempted to ensure that its approach to volunteering was effective and provided value for money, although it recognised that doing so was not a straightforward task and that much would have to be taken on trust. The Thatcher Government's Efficiency Scrutiny rattled its sabre but, in the absence of agreed and quantifiable measures and the wherewithal to gather the necessary information, it acted more as an incitement to than a guarantee of good behaviour.

Unlike previous governments, however, New Labour, as noted above, has had an abiding fascination with targets and measures and hence with research. On the one hand, it has never been able to resist a big round number – for example, 'one million more people being actively involved in their communities'; 250,000 older people involved in

volunteering by the Experience Corps, 750,000 volunteering opportunities created for young people by v, 40,000 unemployed people to
be helped back to work by the Volunteer Brokerage Scheme. On the
other hand, it has resourced a programme of high-quality quanti-
tative research in support, *inter alia*, of its volunteering policies and
programmes – the Citizenship Surveys (from 2001), the State of the
Sector Panel (2003/2004 to 2005/2006) and the National Survey of
Volunteering and Charitable Giving (Low et al., 2007). However, it has
been hampered in getting the best out of its monitoring and evaluation
by its failure in many cases to ensure that the necessary measures were
embedded in the management of the programme and that funding for
research was available from the start; its lack of patience in allowing
programmes and initiatives to bed in, work through teething problems
and eventually deliver and its tendency to scrap or revise targets or
replace existing programmes with new programmes; and its unwilling-
ness to use monitoring information that shows that progress is slower
and less straightforward than previously announced.

Conclusion

In this chapter, we have set out what we believe are the main lines of
development of government's approach to volunteering over the last half
century. In particular, we have described along four axes continuities
and discontinuities between the approach of New Labour and its predecessors and some of the main shifts in New Labour's own approach since
1997. The first axis is government's reasons for supporting volunteering
(inherent vs instrumental value), and we have found that while all governments are naturally instrumental, some, including New Labour, are
more determinedly instrumental than others. The second is the parts
of volunteering that government supports (holistic vs targeted), and
we have found that New Labour, unlike its predecessors, has been particularly vigorous in supporting certain types of activities – mentoring
and befriending – and certain kinds of volunteers – young people – to
an extent not warranted by its own targets and monitoring information. The third is the way government operationalises its interest in
volunteering (enabling vs doing), and we have found that New Labour,
while as keen as its predecessors on direct management in its early years
has shifted to an enabling role thereafter, but, unlike its predecessors,
has not worked through existing infrastructure bodies and partnership mechanisms but instead has created novel forms. The fourth is
the measures government uses to evaluate progress in implementing

its programmes (trust vs quantified measures), and we have found that, unlike its predecessors, New Labour has adopted a range of quantified targets and measures for evaluation, but it has either not used them at all (Compact) or not used them to best advantage (PSAs).

Our analysis is not particularly subtle and has been hampered by the sketchiness of available information about the development of various policies and programmes, particularly before 1997 but also afterwards. We hope that it will be the starting point for future exploration rather than the last word.

8
The Changing Face of Volunteering: Current and future trends

Introduction

After reviewing the ways in which the context within which volunteering takes place has been transformed by societal changes (in Chapter 6) and the development of public and social policy (in Chapter 7), we now turn our attention to the ways in which volunteering itself is changing. We will begin by taking a closer look at the phenomenon of short-term or episodic volunteering which was introduced in Chapter 3 and discussing the growing diversity of the activities undertaken by volunteers, as 'the brain volunteer' begins to supplant 'the brawn volunteer' (Evans and Saxton, 2005: p. 44). We will then review two areas in which the numbers of volunteers have been growing rapidly (although it remains to be seen if these trends will survive the recession of the winter of 2008–2009) – volunteering which is promoted and supported by employers on the one hand and transnational volunteering on the other. The scale of virtual volunteering is also expected to increase dramatically, and this will provide a new set of challenges for volunteer-involving organisations which we discuss next. The chapter will then look at trends in the field of participation and engagement – where unprecedented numbers of people have been mobilised in support of two very different causes, the Countryside Alliance and the coalition against the war in Iraq – before concluding by reviewing the rediscovery and repackaging of mutual aid under the banner of timebanking.

Episodic volunteers

In Chapter 3, we highlighted the distinction that has been increasingly made between short-term or episodic volunteering – which is widely regarded as a rapidly growing phenomenon – and the kind of longer-term involvement with an organisation or cause which is generally seen as an older form of volunteering which is becoming less common. To recapitulate, the distinction between these two kinds of engagement has been captured neatly (by Evans and Saxton, 2005: p. 45) as the difference between episodic 'cause-driven' and longer-term 'time-driven' volunteers. Historically, long-term volunteers tended to have 'time on their hands' which they were prepared to put at the disposal of an organisation or cause. Typically, this came to involve high levels of commitment to the cause and affiliation to the organisation and the work of its volunteers. Long-term volunteers also tended to adapt their contribution to the work of the organisation in response to changing needs and demands. By contrast, episodic or short-term volunteering is just one of a number of ways in which people choose to use their leisure time; it is a commitment which is clearly limited in its scope and the length of time involved; and it is expected to be intrinsically rewarding.

There is a widespread consensus among commentators, volunteer managers and researchers that episodic volunteering is a growing phenomenon (Handy et al., 2006), and it has been hailed as one of the three major waves of the future for volunteering, together with employer-supported and virtual volunteering (ibid.). It is not a new phenomenon: in the United Kingdom, data from the 1981 and 1991 national surveys of volunteering (Field and Hedges, 1984; Lynn and Davis Smith, 1991) suggest that, for many people, the experience of voluntary action was limited to shaking a collection box once a year while Macduff (2005: p. 49) had noted reports from 'managers of volunteer programs that more volunteers were declining long-term positions in favour of short-term assignments' in the 1980s. Evidence from surveys has increasingly supported her view that there were 'changes in the way people were volunteering in westernized countries' (ibid.). Using data from a survey conducted by the Independent Sector in 2001, Weber (2003) found that 31 per cent of volunteers in the United States were involved sporadically, at specific times of the year or as a one-off. Handy et al. quote data from an AARP survey from 2000 which found that 47 per cent of people aged 50 to 59 volunteered mostly for episodic special projects.

Episodic volunteers do not, however, form a homogeneous group. Macduff (2004) distinguishes between the *temporary* or one-off volunteer who will commit a few hours or, at most, a day to the work on a single occasion; the *interim* volunteer who may be involved on a regular basis but for a strictly limited period of time; and the *occasional* episodic volunteer who makes him or herself available for short periods of time at regular intervals. A somewhat different set of categories emerged from the first empirical study to focus solely on episodic volunteers. This looked at a single community in Canada which hosted a series of summer festivals and local events which depended heavily on the work of short-term volunteers (Handy et al., 2006). The first of the subgroups identified by the researchers was made up of 'people who, in addition to the episodic volunteering they do at the summer festivals, are also engaged in long-term, regular, committed volunteering within the same or other organisations' (p. 33). These they termed 'Long-term Committed Volunteers'. The second sub-group – 'Habitual Episodic Volunteers' – consisted of 'individuals that local volunteer coordinators call "circuit volunteers", who volunteer for multiple episodic opportunities (three or more) throughout the year' (ibid.). Finally, individuals who volunteer for two or fewer episodes in a year form a third subgroup the researchers call 'Genuine Episodic Volunteers' (ibid.).

Handy and her colleagues set out to test four hypotheses about the different levels of commitment exhibited by the three different kinds of volunteer. The assumption was that Long-term Committed Volunteers would score more highly than the Habitual Episodic Volunteers who, in turn, would rank higher than the Genuine Episodic Volunteers in terms of the amount of time they had devoted to volunteering; the extent to which their motivations were more or less altruistic or less self-serving; the degree of their interest in tangible rewards associated with the events; and the likelihood that they had made donations to charity. One of these hypotheses was supported; one was rejected; and two were supported in part. The authors conclude that 'the fact that not all our hypotheses were supported raises the possibility that some of the current understandings of episodic volunteering in the literature need re-evaluation' (p. 42). More specifically, they report that the episodic volunteers they studied, contrary to the common belief that these represent a new breed of volunteers who pick and choose the tasks they will carry out and are unwilling to invest in training, were 'well able to be directed, as shown by their ability to sustain so many festivals and events ... year after year' and that 'they do attend orientation and training sessions, they come to their shifts on time and they carry out tasks assigned by the organisers' (ibid.). Suggestions that managing episodic volunteers needed a whole new model may, they add, be premature 'without a rigorous study of the types and nature of episodic volunteering in various organisations and sectors' (p. 43).

That is not to say, however, that growing numbers of episodic volunteers will not bring challenges for volunteer managers. Much depends on the mix of different styles of volunteering found in each organisation. Some, like those studied by Handy and her colleagues, are heavily reliant on episodic volunteers. At the other end of the spectrum, we can still find agencies whose volunteer body is almost exclusively made up of the long-term and the committed. But 'a mixture of volunteering styles' is an increasingly common feature of many organisations and, to further complicate the issue, individual volunteers may mix their own personal 'cocktail' of different kinds of engagement (Macduff, 2004: p. 55). Clearly, the different styles of volunteering may well require different arrangements for recruitment, induction and training and support and supervision. In addition, this is more than a variation between the needs of long-term versus those of short-term volunteers; 'attention needs to be paid to each specific group (of episodic volunteers) so that its members can be recruited and retained for future events' (Handy et al., 2006: p. 43). While Handy et al. (p. 42) found evidence to 'support Macduff's ... assertion that "supervision of short-term volunteers can be done quite effectively by long-term volunteers"', the number and variety of episodic volunteers will also tend to require additional management capacity.

More specifically, the growing emphasis on short-term volunteering will demand greater creativity in designing opportunities for involvement on the one hand and more detailed specification of roles and responsibilities on the other. Finally, it is possible that the different forms of engagement identified by Handy and her colleagues might be steps in a 'progression in volunteering experiences' in which 'initial experiences ... help people to "test the water" and that if their involvement results in a positive experience, they are more willing to increase their involvement in volunteering' (pp. 41–42). If this observation is confirmed by further research, then promoting that progression could become another facet of volunteer management.

The rise of the episodic volunteer has been a major factor in the increasing diversity of opportunities for involvement. It has also been driven by the growing numbers of 'knowledge volunteers' identified 20 years ago by Drucker – people in managerial or professional positions who are looking for similar challenges and responsibilities in their voluntary work to those that apply to their paid work (Davis Smith, 1996). Evans and Saxton have identified a similar trend which they call 'the rise of the brain volunteer and the demise of the brawn volunteer'. They argue that 'volunteering experiences where people are simply asked to do the drudgery that paid staff will not do will be increasingly untenable' as volunteers expect more from their involvement (p. 44). This does not mean, however, that volunteering as a more or less mundane chore has been relegated to the past; many of Handy et al.'s episodic volunteers were operating on this level and, as we shall see, teams of corporate volunteers are happy to redecorate community buildings and clear woodland and other open spaces.

Employer-supported volunteering

The second growth area for volunteering which has been flagged up by practitioners and researchers both in the United Kingdom and across the world involves the engagement of employees in volunteering with the encouragement and support of their employers. This aspect of voluntary action has acquired enthusiastic support from people in government, in business and in the voluntary sector and has spawned a large number of specialist development agencies or brokers. At the same time, however 'considerable scepticism persists in certain sections of the voluntary and community sector as well as within the middle management of even those companies with the largest volunteering programmes' (Brewis, 2006: p. 13). This is due in part to a lack of rigorous research (One important exception is Brewis, 2006) which in turn has been influenced by the difficulties of measuring the impact of employee volunteering initiatives (Rochester and Thomas, 2006).

A recent definition suggests that 'an employee volunteer program consists of the formal and informal policies and practices that employers use to encourage and help employees to volunteer in community service activities. The program is sanctioned by the employing organization' (Tschirhart, 2005: pp. 14–15). Such a scheme can take a variety of forms. There are a number of different arrangements for managing the programme within the employing body and in its relationship with the external world; a wide range of different kinds of volunteering activities; and different kinds of incentives and support for the employees who take part.

At one end of the spectrum of institutional arrangements, the scheme 'may be limited to asking employees to fill out forms if they are using company time for volunteer activities and to report their volunteer hours and activities so that they can be acknowledged by the employer' (Tschirhart, 2005: p. 16). At the other end, companies may employ designated staff to identify opportunities for volunteering by other employees, actively recruit volunteers from the workforce and support and supervise their involvement in volunteering. In many cases, these activities may be located in a department of the company which has the wider responsibility of implementing its programme of corporate social responsibility or community involvement, of which volunteering is often seen to be a component. These arrangements may or may not involve one or more collaborative arrangements with volunteer-involving organisations or with an intermediary or broker such as Business in the Community or a local volunteer centre.

The kinds of volunteering activities in which employees might be engaged are similarly diverse. Volunteer-involving organisations with which employee volunteers work vary greatly in size (from large 'household name' charities to small community-based groups), function (such as service delivery; information and advice; advocacy or campaigning; mutual aid; or community development) and cause (such as children; older people; refugee and migrant groups; or the environment). The variety of roles played by volunteers covers the full gamut from one-off team challenge activities clearing older people's overgrown gardens or repainting a community centre to long-term mentoring of school children or membership of a voluntary agency's board of trustees (Rochester and Thomas, 2006).

There are three principal ways in which employers may encourage and support volunteering by their employees. They may give staff time off work for volunteer activities; this might take the form of 'informally allowing staff time to leave early to volunteer, operating a flexi-time policy for volunteering, or granting a certain number of hours or days a year for volunteering' (Brewis, 2006: p. 14). The second means of supporting volunteering is brokerage: the employer may find volunteering opportunities for its staff, arranging team challenges or seconding an employee to a voluntary agency (Brewis, 2006). Third, companies provide incentives for involvement by including volunteering activities in personal development plans and taking account of them as part of their appraisal of employee performance (Rochester and Thomas, 2006).

The heterogeneous character of employer-supported volunteering is reflected in the proliferation of brokers and brokerage arrangements (national generalist bodies like Business in the Community, Community Service Volunteers (CSV) and REACH; national specialist brokers like Arts and Business; local generalist schemes such as the East London Business Alliance and a growing number of volunteer centres; and national and local for-profit consultancies). Moreover, the employers themselves are diverse: while employer-supported volunteering is generally associated with the corporate sector, it is not confined to the for-profit world. The Corporate Citizenship Company has, for instance, begun to work with some large charities and non-profit organisations and employer-supported volunteering is quite common in local authorities (Rochester and Thomas, 2006).

Apart from its diversity, this large and rapidly growing arena for volunteering has thrown up a number of challenges and issues for practitioners and researchers. The first of these is the extent to which many of the activities taking place under the banner of employer-supported volunteering can be accepted as 'voluntary'. This question has at least three dimensions. In the first place, employees may feel under pressure to participate in company volunteering programmes especially where this may be seen as part of their professional development programme and taken into account as part of their performance appraisal; in these circumstances, failure to take part might damage – or be thought to carry the risk of harming – their prospects of promotion and salary increases. The second test of how voluntary the employee's participation might be hinges on whether the employer or the employee chooses the specific cause or organisation to be assisted. And, third, much depends on whether or to what extent the activity takes place in work time; it can be seen as more or less 'voluntary' according to how much it takes place in the employee's own time (Tirschart, 2005).

The degree of choice afforded to the employee is likely to be governed by the company's overall approach. Brewis (2006) distinguishes between programmes which are 'top-down' or employer-led and those which are 'bottom-up' or employee-led. The choice of approach will in turn reflect the extent to which the programme is seen as meeting the needs of the company, those of its employees and those of the community (or one or more voluntary sector organisations). Employers may expect employer-supported volunteering to make a contribution to the achievement of corporate objectives, better team-working, improved staff recruitment and retention, and a higher profile or enhanced reputation. The potential benefits for employee volunteers include the opportunity to gain experience and develop new kinds of knowledge, understanding and skills. Volunteer-involving organisations, in turn, can tap into a new source of volunteers who often bring with them specific kinds of expertise such as marketing and financial management. Corporate volunteering schemes are often regarded as 'win-win' situations but, in practice, the matching or reconciliation of the interests of the three key components of the programme – which overlap but may not coincide – represents a significant organisational challenge, and this may help explain the growing numbers of 'broker' agencies whose function is to do just that.

International volunteering

Another burgeoning area of voluntary activity involves the movement of volunteers from one country to another. This is by no means a new phenomenon; there have been examples of cross-national volunteering since the 19th century and, more recently, it has become the focus of fairly high-profile programmes delivered by organisations such as VSO in the United Kingdom; the Peace Corps in the United States; and the UN Volunteers transnationally. Much of this activity has been focused on young adults and overseas volunteering has been promoted as an alternative to – and a replacement for – military service (Brewis, 2008). In the recent past, the increasingly common practice of young people taking a 'gap year' as part of the transition from school to university or between courses has increased the opportunities for volunteering overseas and spawned a minor industry dedicated to providing them. A review of the phenomenon undertaken for the then Department for Education and Skills (Jones, 2004) estimated that 'upwards of 800 organisations' were offering 350,000 placements in 200 countries (p. 15).

While overseas volunteering by young people has contributed to the 'recent dramatic increase of activity' (Davis Smith et al., 2005: p. 63) in this area, transnational volunteering is by no means the sole preserve of this age group. VSO, for example, has recruited increasing numbers of experienced professionals rather than young graduates (Rochester and Hutchison, 2002); the 'career break' has emerged alongside the gap year as an opportunity for volunteering; and, as we noted in Chapter 6, there are more 'early retired' people looking for new interests. VSO recorded an increase of 59 per cent in the numbers seeking volunteering opportunities between 1999 and 2000 and a rise of 17 per cent in the number of volunteers sent overseas (Thomas, 2001 quoted in Davis Smith et al., 2005).

At the same time, there have been significant developments in the number and kinds of form taken by cross-national volunteering. On a global level, Davis Smith and his colleagues (2005: p. 64) list five ways in which its characteristics can vary: 'geographical scale; function; direction; level of government involvement; and time scale'. In terms of geographical scale, the key distinction is between international volunteering which involves sending people from the home country to other countries and transnational programmes which involve an exchange of volunteers between two or more countries. Function can be defined in terms of 'a development continuum from emergency relief work...through filling skill shortages in the host country on a short-term basis...to sustainable development and conservation work' (ibid.). The third dimension – direction – is based on whether the volunteers are moving from the industrialised countries of the North to the developing countries of the South or between countries in the South or even from the South to the North. Next, the level of government involvement can range from schemes which are entirely government-led to those which are solely the function of voluntary agencies. Finally, the length of time involved may vary from short-term visits for a day or a week to longer-term engagement over a year or two.

There is some evidence that the nature of international volunteering is changing: away from the traditional flow of volunteers from North to South to movement within the countries of the South; along the 'development continuum' from emergency relief to more sustainable projects; and from short-term visits to longer-term activities. In addition, in common with volunteering more generally, the underlying ethos has changed from a one-sided gift relationship to one based on mutual benefit an exchange. However, 'these more positive changes within cross-national volunteering have to some extent been undermined by the growth of "volunteer tourism" or "volunteer vacations"' (Davis Smith et al., 2005: p. 68). International volunteering is increasingly promoted as a cheap way to travel and experience another culture and as a form of personal or career development. These opportunities may last no more that one to four weeks and the volunteer is often expected to meet the full cost of their trip.

These divergent trends highlight the key issue of international volunteering – who benefits from the activity and in what ways? From the earliest days, there have been concerns about the value of the contribution of international volunteers to the host organisations and the communities they serve. It has come a long way from the naivety of some of its initial manifestations based on the assumption that developing countries were 'in need' and that this situation could be addressed by the efforts of enthusiastic but unskilled young people. Carefully selected volunteers with the right experience and skills have been able to make valuable contributions to communities in other countries. There remains, however, a concern that their activities may reinforce rather than challenge a status quo based on inequality and dependence. The benefits to the volunteers themselves may include the acquisition of hard and soft skills and greater cultural awareness, but there is evidence that many of them did not feel able to use what they had learned when they returned to work in their home country (Thomas, 2001). The difficulties of readjustment experienced by long-term volunteers on their return to the United Kingdom, moreover, led to the formation of a mutual support organisation called Returned Volunteer Action (Davis Smith et al., 2005).

Virtual volunteers

The third and last of the areas of voluntary action which is expected to continue to grow in size and importance is 'virtual' or 'online' volunteering – 'the application of information and communications technology to the process of volunteering' (Murray and Harrison, 2005: p. 32). As we noted in Chapter 6, the ownership and use of computers and mobile phones has become an increasingly normal part of everyday life while a whole generation has grown up surrounded by the new technology. It is inevitable that this significant change in the way we access and process information and communicate with one another will have a major impact on volunteering.

Historically, the whole process of volunteering – identifying the kind of activity and the organisation with which to become involved on the one hand and actually carrying out the work on the other – has, with a few exceptions, involved a series of face-to-face interactions. The advent of ICT now offers an alternative route. 'It is now possible to locate potential volunteer positions on the World Wide Web, interact with the manager of volunteers to go through the selection process and actually carry out the work itself at a distance using ICT' (Murray and Harrison, 2005: p. 32). Writing in 2004, Murray and Harrison described virtual volunteering as 'not yet ... in large-scale use' (p. 33), and volunteer-involving organisations appear to have been quicker to adopt the new technology as a means of attracting and recruiting volunteers than to exploit its possibilities for enabling people to undertake volunteering itself on a virtual basis. A recent international study, however, concluded that online volunteers provided organisations with enhanced capacity and was a positive manifestation 'of "globalization", happening at a very local, personal level for people and organizations all over the world' (Cravens, 2006: p. 22). The potential for this form of voluntary action is underlined by the claim made that the online encyclopaedia composed and edited by more than a million volunteers may make the Wikipedia Foundation the world's largest non-profit effort (Chronicle of Philanthropy, 2006).

Virtual volunteering began more than thirty years ago; the first major example was Project Gutenberg whose online volunteers made classic books available in digital versions (Cravens, 2006). It 'began to become more widespread among mission-based organizations in the mid 1990s' (p. 16) and grew rapidly with the 21st century although it remains the case that there is 'no data...on exactly how many online volunteers exist nor how many organizations are involving them' (ibid.). We can, however, confidently predict that the numbers will grow dramatically in the near future both globally and in the United Kingdom.

Unsurprisingly, many virtual volunteers are engaged in activities which are specific to the use of the new technology: the two most common types of work performed according to the data reviewed by Murray and Harrison (2005) were desktop publishing and designing or maintaining websites. However, they also found that online volunteers were involved in a range of more generic activities including research, fund-raising, direct service delivery, policy development and training. Cravens (2006) includes the belief that 'online volunteers engage primarily in technology-related tasks' as one of the 12 'most common myths' about online volunteering. She points out that more than 50 per cent of volunteer assignments posted to the UN's Online Volunteering Service are 'non-tech-specific', and they include 'advising on business plans, human resources development, fund-raising and press relations, researching topics, and facilitating online discussions' (www.coyotecom.com/volunteer/ovmyths).

In addition to reflecting the way in which people increasingly interact in the 21st century, virtual volunteering has a number of advantages over face-to-face involvement. It enables people to volunteer without leaving their home or work place; it is particularly helpful for people with disabilities and those who have problems with mobility or travel; and it can allow volunteers to help specific organisations or causes despite the absence of on-site opportunities in their locality. It may also provide someone who is already involved with a organisation with the opportunity to contribute to its work in other ways.

It does not, however, provide volunteer-involving organisations with a 'magic bullet' which will solve the problems they encounter in attracting and recruiting volunteers and providing them with appropriate and satisfying opportunities for volunteering. Online recruitment can reach more people but may have a lower success rate: a recent survey for Volunteer Centre Tower Hamlets showed that 38 per cent of the volunteer centre's clients who had face-to-face contact became active volunteers as a result compared to a figure of 17 per cent for those who used the online facility (Donahue, 2007). Nor does online volunteering attract large numbers of people who would not get involved on a face-to-face basis. The great majority of virtual volunteers also volunteer in face-to-face settings while the idea that 'online volunteering is great for people who don't have time to volunteer' is 'probably the biggest and most annoying myth out there' according to Cravens (www.coyotecom. com/volunteer/ovmyths).

From volunteering to activism?

Transnational volunteering at its best taps into a rich vein of enthusiasm and commitment on the part of young people in particular (but not exclusive to them). With the help of the new technologies which have underpinned virtual volunteering, organisations have increasingly been able to tap into that reservoir of concern and mobilise large numbers of people in support of a range of causes. Young people have signed up in large numbers to the student campaigning organisation *People and Planet* and formed much of the constituency of campaigns like *Make Poverty History*. Although *People and Planet* was established as long ago as 1969 (under the name of Third World First), it has experienced remarkable growth during the early years of the 21st century. In 2007, Joel Joffe, a distinguished former chair of OXFAM, summed up its recent development and its appeal to young people:

> Over the last three years People and Planet has become an extraordinary organisation which attracts student volunteers on a scale unmatched within the UK charity and campaign sector. More than any other youth organisation it is encouraging the emerging generation to see themselves as global citizens with a responsibility for taking action on global problems of poverty and the environment. (www.peopleandplanet.org/aboutus/whatotherssay)

At the time of writing (late 2008), the organisation's website claimed that there were student-run People and Planet groups at 59 of the United Kingdom's universities and colleges of higher education and a further 75 groups in schools and further education colleges.

The *Make Poverty History* campaign was a much broader based coalition of voluntary organisations, religious bodies, campaigning groups and individual celebrities from Britain and Ireland which came together to take the opportunity offered by the United Kingdom's presidency of the EU and of the G8 summit meeting which was held at Gleneagles in June 2005 to increase awareness of global poverty and press governments to take action to relieve it. At the height of the campaign, it succeeded in mobilising an estimated 225,000 people to join a march through Edinburgh (www.makepovertyhistory.org/2005). This figure had, however, already been surpassed by two other massive displays of public concern and interest for two very different issues of the early years of the 21st century. In September 2002, some 400,000 supporters of the *Countryside Alliance* took part in its 'Liberty and Livelihood March' in London to protest about the general lack of understanding and concern shown by the government for the needs and concerns of those who lived and worked in the country and, more specifically, against the legislation it had brought forward to ban hunting with dogs (Branigan, 2002). This massive show of opinion was, however, dwarfed just months later by 'UK's biggest ever demonstration' when hundreds of thousands of people took to the streets to voice their opposition to the war in Iraq. The actual numbers taking part in the three-and-a-half mile long march are disputed; the organisers – the *Stop the War Coalition* with the *Campaign for Nuclear Disarmament* and the *Muslim Association of Britain* – claimed a total of 2 million participants against a police estimate of 750,000 (BBC News, 2003). Whatever the exact number was, it is clear that large numbers of people are getting involved in direct campaigning and activism.

Timebanking

The idea of the timebanking was developed in the United States by Edgar Cahn and introduced to Britain in the late 1990s. Ten years on, there are 109 active time banks in the United Kingdom with a further 48 in development, according to Timebank UK, the national umbrella charity linking and supporting time banks across the country (www.timebank.org.uk). Almost 8,000 people actively participate in these schemes which have, it is estimated, clocked up an aggregate of more than 600,000 hours of unpaid work since the 1990s. The initial 'person-to-person' or 'P2P' idea was simple: each hour of volunteering time given by an individual was 'banked' to build up a deposit on which he or she could draw to receive services donated by other members of the scheme. Essentially, it is an exchange of 'time credits' facilitated by a 'time broker'. In the interests of simplicity, each hour of time given received has an equal value, no matter what service is being provided: '1 hour of time = 1 time credit, whether you are a surgeon or an unemployed single mother' (Ryan-Collins et al., 2008: p. 7). Timebanking is based on two principles: 'it recognises that everyone, even those defined as disadvantaged or vulnerable, has something worthwhile to contribute' and it 'values relationships that are forged through giving and receiving' (ibid.).

Timebank UK makes large claims for the success of this approach: these include, 'inspiring and connecting a new generation of people to volunteer in their communities and enabling charitable organisations and businesses to develop innovative and effective volunteer recruitment programmes' and 'creating new ways for people to get involved' as well as 'transforming the image of volunteering to reflect its vital role in a healthy society and the dynamic effect it can have on the lives of volunteers' (www.timebank.org.uk). A review of the work of the Timebank network in its early years (Seyfang, 2001) provided some support for these claims, finding that they were beginning to achieve their objectives of 'building social capital and promoting community self-help through mutual volunteering, targeting socially excluded groups' – although the scale of these achievements was modest at this early stage – and that they had 'great potential to transform volunteering for the twenty-first century' (p. 30).

The P2P model remains the dominant form of timebanking in England and no fewer than ten new funded schemes were established in August and September 2008 (Ryan-Collins et al., 2008). Since 2001, however, the movement has developed in a variety of other ways: 'Timebanking is a dynamic tool, not a static one. New ways of using timebanking are constantly emerging' (p. 14). These newer manifestations can be grouped into two approaches. The first of these – Person to Agency or P2A – applies timebanking principles to the relationship between individuals and organisations. Here, people can earn time credits in return for making a contribution to the work of a public or third sector agency and use them to obtain access to 'community-based activities, trips, services and events' (ibid.: p. 17). The second comparatively new approach – Agency2Agency – involves transactions between organisations which can enable the agencies involved to draw on physical and human assets and resources which they do not themselves command without having to acquire additional funding.

The development of the timebanking model beyond the original individual-to-individual or neighbour-to-neighbour framework begins to take it beyond the boundaries of volunteering and thus beyond the scope of this book. While time credits are tax exempt, they nonetheless represent a form of tangible or material reward which casts some doubt over the status of timebanking as volunteering. Given that the P2P model is an exchange of mutual benefit to the individuals concerned, it can be seen as a reshaping of the long-standing mutual aid strand in volunteering albeit with a concern for measurement that some my feel is contrary to the spirit of that tradition. The Person to Agency arrangement, however, is fairly straightforward case of payment in kind for services rendered; it is not an incidental reward that follows from involvement as a volunteer but central to the transaction. As such, it hovers on or outside the boundary of volunteering. Finally, the relationship between organisations rather than individuals which characterises the third stream of timebanking clearly belongs to a territory which is separate to volunteering.

While timebanking represents an important and interesting set of alternatives to the orthodox cash economy and it can make a contribution to the future of volunteering, there remain doubts about the extent to which it is capable of living up to its claims to transform the scale and nature of volunteering in the 21st century.

Conclusion

This rapid survey of some of the ways in voluntary action is developing and its prospects for future growth and change has covered a good deal of ground and passed across some very different kinds of terrain. Some of the perspectives involved are fairly specific; the continuing growth in the numbers of people whose volunteering will be facilitated or supported by their employers and of those who will be involved in voluntary action in another country highlight issues of volunteer management and concerns about defining the boundaries of volunteering. The greater variety of ways in which people engage with volunteering and the diversity of activities in which they engage also raise issues for those who recruit volunteers and organise their work. We can also discuss the application of contemporary information and communication technologies to volunteering in similar terms.

The chapter has discussed the ways in which volunteering is adapting and will continue to adapt to these important incremental changes. Some of the material, however, may point to a rather different – more radical – approach to change. The implications of the new technology may be much more far-reaching and could change the relationships between volunteers, volunteer-involving organisations and beneficiaries or users dramatically and in ways which only the new generations of 'digital natives' may begin to comprehend. The huge numbers mobilised for a range of causes also points to new forms of collective voluntary action while the success of the timebanking phenomenon may be evidence that mutualism may be as useful a principle in the future as it was in the past. We will try to take account of both kinds of change in the remaining chapters.

9
Motivation and Recruitment: Why and how do volunteers come?

Introduction

This chapter discusses why people choose to give freely of their time for voluntary action. There is a compelling logic to uncovering what motivates volunteers; from a practical standpoint understanding why people are moved to volunteer is potentially useful information for recruiting more volunteers. Clary et al. (1996) note that volunteering is often not easy, people have to overcome a series of obstacles to become volunteers. What then drives them to overcome these barriers?

Perhaps, it is because the prospect of increasing volunteer numbers through understanding motivations is so beguiling to practitioners and policy-makers alike that researchers have produced such a vast number of studies that attempt to identify them. But the size of the literature, the different methods of data collection and of interpretation of results, the range of epistemological assumptions and theoretical frameworks used make the evidence on motivations hard to decipher and use practically. One handbook for volunteer recruiters simply states that there are as many motivations as there are volunteers (Ellis, 2002). If this is true, then what value is there to adding to the infinite list of reasons why people get involved? Do different groups of volunteers share broadly similar motivations? Or, can we find some underlying commonality of motivation across different groups? And, how might we use these insights to recruit and involve volunteers more successfully?

This chapter is by no means exhaustive in its review of the literature; there is simply too much. Instead, it tries to explain why research into motivation needs careful consideration. The chapter first outlines some of the methodological problems of researching why people volunteer and looks at a selection of theories relating to volunteer motivation, in particular psychological and sociological approaches. Within this, the chapter makes room to look at the Volunteer Functions Index (VFI) and the work of Omoto, Clary, Snyder and colleagues who have drawn together, and furthered, so much thinking in this field. Next, the chapter looks at survey data from the United Kingdom, disaggregating motives across different demographic groups. After reviewing a selection of studies in an attempt to see how thinking about theoretical perspectives can add meaning to research, the chapter concludes by looking at how volunteer-involving organisations make use of these ideas. We suggest that organisations view motives quite superficially and that approaches to recruitment would benefit from a more comprehensive overview of motivation.

Motivational research: trouble with method and meaning

Chapter 2 highlighted the fact that, although there is an array of explanations of why people volunteer, the 'flat-earth' view privileges altruism and the 'gift of time'. The extent to which this happens at the expense of a richer understanding of what volunteering is, may to some extent be socially conditioned. Put simply, this would suggest that when volunteers are asked what motivates them they feel compelled to say that they are involved for the benefit of others. One study demonstrated this by looking at how people defined being a volunteer. By identifying key dimensions in common definitions, they were able to analyse how people perceive what makes a volunteer by asking them to rate these dimensions. Then, developing this idea further by asking people to rate volunteer tasks by the 'net cost' to the volunteer, they found that people identified volunteers most strongly in those roles where volunteers had a 'net loss'. That is to say, volunteers should get less out of the experience than they put in (Cnaan, Handy and Wadsworth, 1996). This finding is supported to some extent by studies noted by Musick and Wilson (2008) which showed how, when talking of motives, volunteers felt compelled to give what they thought was the socially acceptable answer (it is a selfless act done to benefit others). At the same time, however, they did not want to appear 'too saintly' and so acknowledged that they themselves also benefited. This raises the question of how far we can trust answers of this kind to provide a true reflection of why people get involved?

Perhaps the notion that volunteering is driven by altruism persists because surveys have repeatedly found that this is what volunteers say (and we shall explore whether this is the case and the methodological issues of surveying volunteers below). During the 1980s, several studies tried to tease out the extent to which motivations are altruistic (primarily explained in terms of the desire to do something for others) or egotistic (volunteers looking for self-gain) by developing two-factor models. Esmond and Dunlop (2004), for example, noted the work of Horton Smith (1981) which tried to distinguish between altruistic and egotistic motives and Frisch and Gerrard (1981) and Gillespie and King (1985) who also employed this two-factor approach. They then go on to trace how researchers such as Fitch (1987) and Morrow-Howell and Mui (1989) extended the model to three factors to include motives of social obligation (Esmond and Dunlop, 2004: p. 12). Although these studies moved the field on to a better understanding, they were not without problems. The empirical evidence supporting their assertions did not seem particularly robust, sample sizes were small and limited to single groups of volunteers in particular organisations (ibid.).

These shortcomings could be addressed by making surveys more representative of volunteer demographics and organisational type. Nonetheless the problem of whether what volunteers say about motivations is what they themselves think or what they believe people asking questions want to hear remains. There are further questions. Do people really know what their motivations are? Is asking people what makes them volunteer enough to give us a clear understanding of motivations? Musick and Wilson (2008) suggest that this is a fault of many surveys. How, they ask, does it help our understanding of volunteering to know that a woman helping clean her neighbourhood explains her action by reference to her desire to see a clean neighbourhood (2008)? In particular, they argue that without asking non-volunteers (which many surveys do not) we suffer a paucity of explanation; when volunteers talk of believing in a cause, how can we know if non-volunteers also believe in the cause but just do not volunteer?

These questions mean that the obvious and simple way to find out about volunteer motivation – by asking them – may be unreliable. The large body of research which seeks to differentiate volunteers by demographics, by socio-economic status and by asking what motives are, may tell us something about the stated motivations of each group but offer little in the way of an attempt to develop an understanding of what it all means (Pearce, 1993).

Theorising motivation

To develop a deeper understanding of motivations, we may need to go beyond asking volunteers directly and then comparing their answers to see if groups of volunteers have similar motivations. Much of the data we have on motivations are still derived from surveys, and often surveys that ask volunteers to identify their reasons for volunteering against a set list. The difference perhaps is that theoretical work on motivations is available to help us interpret better what results mean – the argument 'do volunteers tell us what they think or what they think we want to hear' takes on a different significance when looked at from different theoretical perspectives. Later in this chapter, we will review data from UK surveys and studies, but first we will look at two perspectives that attempt to draw thinking together and make sense of what we know about motivations. These in turn will help us when we turn to survey data and more qualitative organisational studies. We will consider first psychological approaches to motivations and then look at sociological perspectives.

Psychological approaches

The most widely known work on volunteering from a psychological perspective is that of Clary and Snyder and colleagues (Clary and Snyder, 1991; Clary et al., 1992, 1996, 1998; Omoto and Snyder, 1995) which they operationalise through the VFI.

This work challenges directly the idea that there are an infinite number of motives through building on existing psychological theories of functional analysis. This is based on the idea that all people have the same basic psychological needs. These needs are broadly

- a need to acquire an understanding of the world through acquiring knowledge;
- a need to act on and express values; and
- a need to somehow protect the self.

People are motivated to act when they perceive that an activity will answer a particular need. Importantly, the same act can satisfy different needs, and people with the same need may choose different ways to satisfy it (Clary et al., 1996; Musick and Wilson, 2008). That is to say, for example, that volunteering can satisfy all these needs, but people do not need to use volunteering as their way of answering their own needs.

The functional approach attempts to link motive to behaviour. Therefore, some people see volunteering (behaviour) as a way of answering some need (motivation). Clary et al. (1996: p. 486) explain it as motivations that are '[i]nternal psychological forces that move people to overcome obstacles and become involved in volunteer activity'.

Applying the functional approach to volunteering, they identified six categories of motivation that can be addressed through volunteering:

1. *Values:* Volunteering affords the chance to express values around altruism or concern for others.

2. *Understanding:* People volunteer to experience new learning experiences, develop or practise skills that might otherwise be unused or to increase their knowledge. This is not, however, the same as volunteering to gain skills for employment – this comes under the *career* function.

3. *Career:* Volunteering serves to provide experience for furthering careers, this may be gaining career-related skills or experiences.

4. *Social:* Volunteering affords the opportunity to be with friends; it is about the 'social rewards of volunteering'. But 'social rewards' can also be negative, and people may volunteer to avoid social disapproval from not getting involved.

5. *Protective:* People can volunteer to escape 'negative feelings' and protect the self. For example, volunteering may help them escape feelings of guilt about being more fortunate than others.

6. *Enhancement:* Volunteering for enhancement is about personal development and growth and about self-esteem. This may sound similar to the protective function but Clary et al. (1998) suggest it is a contrast to it. They suggest that research indicates negative and positive effects are separate dimensions not just two ends of one scale and that helping others can promote positive effects rather than just lessen negative ones. Therefore, whereas the protective is focussed on eliminating negative feelings, enhancement is about how the ego grows and develops.

Although the work of Clary and Snyder and colleagues with the VFI is perhaps the best known in this field, it is not the only attempt to construct an inventory. Jacobsen-D'Arcy and McEwin developed a scale which was tested and refined by Esmond and Dunlop (2004). This inventory finished with ten categories, adding four to that produced by Clary et al. (1992). Dolnicar and Randle (2007) explore a different approach by segmenting volunteers. Their research in Australia found six groups of volunteers: 'classic volunteers' who are involved in a worthwhile cause, want to help others and gain personal satisfaction; 'dedicated volunteers' who contribute the most hours and to a multitude of organisations; 'personally involved volunteers' who are likely to limit their involvement – the research identified these typically as people who are involved in an organisation because their child is active in that organisation and will move on when the child moves on; 'volunteers for personal satisfaction' are the ones who are most likely to look for personal gains; 'altruists' volunteer specifically to help others (the research uses befrienders as an example) and 'niche volunteers' who are looking for roles to answer particular needs such as gaining experience, but acting on religious beliefs comes under this category. Although this research is specific to Australia and seems to offer less distinct groupings, the authors argue that an approach like this is useful for recruitment, about which we say more below. Meanwhile Batson et al. (2002) divide volunteers into four motivational types focussed on the ultimate goal for each action. They identify egoism, where the goal is one's own welfare; altruism, focussed on the needs of others; collectivism, which focuses on the welfare of groups; and principalism, in which the goal is to uphold moral principle or principles.

Sociological perspectives

Viewing motivations from a sociological perspective provides a different understanding of why volunteers do what they do. Sociologists are less sympathetic to the view that there are a finite number of underlying individual needs that explain volunteer involvement. Motives are not the answer to some inner need but explanations; they are the way in which people make sense of their own involvement. This, as Musick and Wilson (2008) say, puts a different perspective on how we view surveys that ask people to account for why they volunteer. Psychological explanations say that such surveys tell us little of what motivates volunteers; sociologists acknowledge this but argue that we are not asking them to pinpoint the cause of their volunteering but to express how they view their own involvement. Furthermore, this differs from the psychological approach in that it permits a social context to help explain why people volunteer. Explanations are as much about how we justify what we do to others as to ourselves and acknowledge that others too have an influence, 'Even highly motivated people are unlikely to volunteer unless they are asked, and people with little motivation might agree to do so if they are constantly badgered by friends to give some of their time' (ibid.: p. 50).

The distinction between the two approaches can be seen if we look at the view of Clary et al. (1996) quoted at the beginning of this chapter. They argue that people face all sorts of barriers to volunteering, and so we must look for motivations that answer a need, a need strong enough to overcome these barriers. Yet if we look at how people chose to explain involvement, one answer given in a 2007 national survey of volunteering by 13 per cent of people was that there was 'no one else to do it'. From a psychological perspective, this is not a motivation. The motivation for those volunteers who also believed there was no one else to do what they were doing lies hidden in this survey. Nevertheless, from the sociological perspective, these volunteers are accounting for how they got involved and locating that within a social context – they are saying, 'This is how I want you to see my involvement, I am doing this because I believe nobody else will'.

This is not to say that volunteers' needs are not taken into account in this perspective. Reasons given for volunteering may be that the volunteer wanted to meet new people and make new friends, which accords very well with the functions identified in the psychological approach. In fact, in many research reports, unless specific reference is made to researchers working within a psychological or sociological perspective, the questions asked can look quite similar.

What volunteers say: UK survey data

Having looked at some theoretical underpinnings for assessing motives, we now turn to survey data. Large-scale survey data for the United Kingdom can be found in national representative surveys for England (Low et al., 2007), Scotland (VDS, 2006; VDS Research Team, 2007) and Northern Ireland (Volunteer Development Agency, 2007). These surveys ask volunteers to identify the reasons they get involved rather looking at their underlying motives and needs. In essence, they follow a more sociological perspective believing that social groups, class position and so forth determines motive rather than individual need (Musick and Wilson, 2008: pp. 73–74). However, the questions asked can also be aligned with VFI categories, so explanations of motivations are presented in terms of the reasons people volunteer.

From a policy perspective, it makes sense to try to group volunteer motivations around how volunteers perceive their own involvement rather than trying to uncover some hidden inner need. As noted above, questions which ask volunteers to account for their involvement are not divorced from this approach. But how much more useful is it to be able to identify that people of a certain age group or socio-economic group tend to report their motivation in terms of, say, wanting to improve the community in some way, learn new skills or make new friends, than it is to be able to say that a certain percentage of volunteers get involved from a need to use volunteering as enhancement? In practice, both have their uses, and it is this we shall attempt to address in the final part of this chapter. First, let us turn to what volunteers tell us.

Data on motivations for England are available in the 2007 *Helping Out* survey referred to in Chapter 4 (Low et al., 2007). Although the questions were not explicitly set within a psychological or sociological framework, the answers can be grouped into altruistic and instrumental reasons.

Just over half of current volunteers (53 per cent) in England indicated that a reason for getting involved was that they wanted to help people. Interestingly, the second most important reason was that 'the cause was important to me' which was reported by 41 per cent of volunteers. If we want to translate this into VFI terms, we might say that both of these could be described as value led (only 1 per cent however indicated it was 'to give something back'). But with 41 per cent also indicating that they wanted to meet people and make friends, the social aspect is important too (although making new friends is part of the enhancement function too) while 29 per cent said it was connected to the needs and interests of friends or family, and 21 per cent because family and friends did it.

Volunteers could indicate more than one reason, so we do not know the prime reason why people volunteered, but these data give us an overall picture that volunteers see their involvement as rooted in expressions of humanity and belief in a cause; in VFI terms volunteering seems to be value-driven. Indeed, other questions also seem to have a values function underlying them; 23 per cent of volunteers said it was part of their philosophy of life, and 17 per cent said that it was part of their religious belief. There also appears to be a set of motivations that can be grouped as career-focussed: 19 per cent said they became involved in order to learn new skills, 7 per cent to get on in a career and 2 per cent to get a recognised qualification. Other motivations are interesting but, perhaps, do not give further clues as to whether volunteering is either altruistically or instrumentally driven; 41 per cent of volunteers gave as a reason for starting that they simply had time to spare and 29 per cent because there was a need within the community.

The same set of questions were asked in a survey in Northern Ireland (Volunteer Development Agency, 2007); this time, 49 per cent wanted to improve things and help people, 28 per cent said the cause was important, 24 per cent said that they had spare time, 22 per cent said that it was part of their religious belief or philosophy of life, 15 per cent said that their family and friends did it, 12 per cent said it connected with the needs of family and friends and the same proportion that they wanted to meet people, and 3 per cent said that it would help with their career.

Clearly, there are some similarities and differences. Wanting to improve things and help people was identified each time by approximately half of the volunteers. In addition, although the proportion of volunteers in Northern Ireland mentioning the cause, having time to spare, the needs of communities, and wanting to meet people were lower, if the proportion of people mentioning them are ranked, they follow a very similar order in each survey. A notable difference is the skills-related reasons: volunteering to learn new skills or for career purposes are much lower in Northern Ireland. Nevertheless, both surveys were able to say that there was clearly a mix of altruistic and egotistic motivations, with altruism just shading more instrumental reasons when looking at volunteers as a whole (Low et al., 2007; Volunteer Development Agency, 2007). Data from Scotland, derived from qualitative research, found very similar motivations – the desire to help, meeting new people, gain skills, giving something back, having something to do with their time and boosting confidence (Hurley et al., 2008).

Both the England and Northern Ireland surveys were able to look back to previous research to assess if there had been any changes. The Northern Ireland survey noted that there had been no change in the prevalence of altruistic reasons – formal volunteers in surveys of 1995 and 2001 also showed motivations connected with meeting needs in the community as the most common reason (Volunteer Development Agency, 2007). The *Helping Out* survey for England cautions against direct comparisons with the 1997 national survey of volunteering (Davis Smith, 1998) for methodological reasons, but it does note that the mention of 'wanting to improve things' become more common with 35 per cent of volunteers reporting it as a reason to volunteer in 1997 as compared to 53 per cent in 2007 while 'having spare time' also increased (Low et al., 2007).

Data available from national surveys mean that analysis can often be carried out beyond the 'headline' findings. It is useful to know that concern for others and the community are key drivers for volunteers and that the opportunities afforded to meet others is also a strong reason to volunteer, but do these reasons differ across different groups? Data from *Helping Out* also made it possible to compare the motivations of new and long-standing volunteers which showed that broadly speaking all volunteers wanted to improve things but that newer recruits were less motivated by religious belief and more by wanting to enhance skills and careers (Hutin, 2008). It also found variations in demographics (Low et al., 2007) which included the findings that

- the youngest (16–24 year olds) and the oldest (65 and over) were more likely to cite meeting people as their reason for volunteering;
- young people (16–24 year olds) were also most likely to say they were looking for benefits to their career prospects from volunteering;
- older people volunteered because they had spare time and because it was part of their philosophy of life;
- people from minority ethnic backgrounds, and those with long-term illnesses were more likely to cite religious belief than other groups; and
- Asian and Black volunteers were more likely to acknowledge that recognising a need in the community triggered their volunteering.

Analysis of Northern Ireland data shows

- volunteers aged between 50 and 64 were more likely to cite improving things as a reason to get involved, with the 16 to 24 year olds least likely to do so;
- the younger age group was more likely to be motivated by cause than any other age group; and
- older volunteers were more likely than other age groups to cite having spare time as a reason to get involved.

Unravelling the complexity

We have then a relative abundance of national data that tell us how volunteers choose to identify their involvement and to a certain extent we can express this in terms akin to the VFI approach. As we have seen from the survey data, volunteers, broadly speaking, mix altruism and egotism, and that understanding can be refined if we look at different demographic groups. While these seem to be broadly similar in different country contexts, they are also different enough to suggest that country-specific survey data are needed.

Looking at survey data helps, but the work of Clary and his colleagues suggests that universal needs can exist irrespective of demographics – is it possible that two people of different ages and ethnicities can share a motivation? Of course, it must, and it is equally possible that the motivational need they share makes them in that regard more similar to each other than to the rest of their age group or those who share their ethnicity and socio-economic status. Neither the psychological perspective, nor surveys like *Helping Out* alone can give us a clear picture of motivations. They help, they make the picture simpler, but we must be careful not to be simplistic when it comes to motivations. Some examples of research studies and the thinking behind them show how we may take these broad motivations and try to add a more subtle understanding. The authors of the following three studies have used different perspectives and methodologies to integrate broad motivational models with contextualising factors to draw out how volunteers get involved and what they want from their volunteering. Each offers an example of how research can delve under the surface of motivational thinking to try to construct the architecture to help us understand more about volunteers.

The sociological perspective argues that volunteering motivations must be seen in its social context. Hustinx (2001/2007) and Hustinx and Lammertyn (2003) illustrate this very well in their work about 'reflexive' volunteering. Although heavily theoretical, the work provides some very practical insights. It considers the apparent move from altruistic to egotistic motives in young people. Hustinx and Lammertyn argue however that this apparent feature shortchanges young volunteers. Their research suggests that for young people, volunteering provides an individualised 'self-project'. Taken as a whole, this does suggest a move away from 'collectivist' perspectives which are characterised by concepts of duty and collective identities such as class, gender and faith, and associated with altruism and accepting of one's place in a hierarchical organisation to which one is committed. The 'new' volunteering is 'reflexive', it is less about groups and duty and more about personal identity, and less about altruism and more about forming an exchange relationship. Organisations can expect less 'loyalty' which instead might be shown to the cause. On the face of it, this does seem to underscore perceived trends from altruistic to individual motivations. However, the authors argue that individualisation should not be equated with egotism; young people want greater choice, but it does not mean that they have less interest in solidarity. The key message for organisations perhaps is not that young people have no interest in volunteering but rather that they are more like consumers of opportunities who will think twice about buying if the product is not what they want.

Contextualising motivations is also the strength of Slight's research on older people in England (Slight, 2002). This research reviews recent UK government enthusiasm for volunteering and how it is framed in terms of discharging civic responsibility, civil society and social cohesion. Slight interviews volunteers who have grown up with the British welfare state and finds that their view of their involvement is contextualised by how they view the roles they feel they should have within the norms of a collectivist welfare state. Slight's perspective is that social life is stored and it is how we come to understand ourselves. She argues that policy pronouncements cut across the grain of the experience of these volunteers. Government expectations assume feelings of solidarity that are not experienced by all those that are expected to respond. In other words, we may know that volunteers of a certain age are likely to be motivated by altruism but that it is an altruism born of a particular view of society, and we may not be able to appeal to altruism alone if we do not understand how people expect those acts of altruism to be undertaken. We may appeal to volunteers to become involved in hospitals and appeal to altruism to get them involved, but if today's welfare state with its management and target-driven outlook does not correspond to how volunteers feel they can express their altruism, a simple appeal may not work. Listening to volunteers as much as surveying them can give insights into why people do what they do; take us beyond 'limiting' models that it is 'to do good' and illuminate what are invariably complex reasons for being involved (Brookes, 2002).

Goddard's (2005) attempt to understand how volunteers with personal experience of breast cancer viewed their involvement employed a number of different approaches. Using a version of the VFI, she found that the values function gave the highest return but her methodology also allowed her to discover that the understanding function was also common. This understanding is particularly related to the way these volunteers see themselves and the fact that they have experience of breast cancer; this means that 'giving something back' and providing support that they themselves did not have was a key way for them to express their involvement.

Recruiting volunteers

Understanding motivations can be a useful tool for recruitment. Clary et al. (1998) operationalise the VFI by showing that messages that appeal to particular motivational needs are picked up on by volunteers. So, if an organisation does want to focus on people who might have a value function as a motivation rather than a protective one, or an understanding motive rather than a career one, it should be possible. Dolnicar and Randle's (2007) segmentation approach helps organisations think about how to present opportunities to particular types of volunteer, those that are likely to be more committed, those that are looking for skills and so forth. Is this what organisations want? It may be and, if it is, the VFI indicates it is possible to do so while the segmentation idea offers a variation of it. Or, do organisations want to appeal to broader motives? Is it enough to know that messages couched in terms of helping people or making friends will be successful in drawing forward new volunteers?

National surveys, especially where analysis is disaggregated across different groups, help characterise what volunteers in each group are like and what they want, and this too could prove helpful. We have seen that a perhaps simplistic reading suggests young people want skills and experience while older people want social contact and to know they are helping people. Pearce (1993) looks at the propensity to volunteer by social group (explored in the UK context in Chapter 4) before attempting to integrate motivational thinking. She argues that these can also tell us a lot about why people volunteer as they do – her contention, for example, is that people from higher socio-economic groups are more attractive to organisations.

All these suggest that there is no simple short cut to explaining motivation. We need to understand motivations from different perspectives and theoretical positions to give us a deeper insight into volunteers. Young people will probably respond better to adverts that emphasise social networking and skill enhancement, and they will want their contribution to the cause explained rather than the help they can give to that one organisation. However, the context cannot be ignored; organisations will need to realise that these young people are consumers, likely to move on for the next experience. The key is to plan for that and not to assume that young peoples' enthusiasm is any the less for it. Older people may want to use spare time, and be altruistically motivated, but at what point does the baby-boom generational effect kick in resulting in 'older' volunteers being more demanding about what they want to get out of their volunteering?

Motivations are perhaps better understood alongside other types of 'triggers' – as one part of the explanation as to why people end up volunteering. Motivations in themselves cannot explain how people begin volunteering. There is a great deal of research on how volunteers get involved which consistently finds that the most important factor is personal contact and 'being asked'. How does this then translate into how involvement in volunteering is triggered? Clearly, there is a social element. The research tells that motivations to become involved and meet people are strong; to this extent, a propensity to volunteer is there waiting to be triggered. People already active in communities are likely to know like-minded people and therefore recruit from the same groups. The social route is important, but we must also be creative about how the 'ask' is used, how to appeal directly to other volunteers. One example is REACH, an organisation in the United Kingdom that places people with professional skills in organisations that need help. REACH uses an advert in the print media that asks volunteers to 'Donate your brain' thus appealing not only to altruistic motivations but also to the fact that volunteers have key skills that only they can contribute.

Too often, recruitment is seen in terms either of a mechanism or in terms of very broad motivational categories. This chapter has suggested that motivations are very complex; it has looked at two perspectives – the psychological and sociological – and noted that although they have different underpinnings, they are not incompatible. Indeed, the chapter suggests that understanding motivations needs different perspectives to illuminate the relationship between what drives people and how that may be used to recruit them to volunteer roles. The story does not, however, stop there; motivations can change and, if motivational needs are not satisfied and if organisations are not aware of how motivations can change, they will lose volunteers. This is the focus of our next chapter.

10
Rewards and Retention: Why do volunteers stay?

Introduction

The previous chapter addressed motivations to volunteer by considering how participation might be explained in terms of meeting personal needs and how attitudes and attributes influenced decisions to volunteer. In this chapter, we look at retention – what makes people stay (or not) in organisations once they have taken the decision to become involved.

Retention is every bit as complex as motivation with a variety of different theories and frameworks to explain why volunteers stay. Indeed, in their review of the literature, Locke et al. (2003) concluded, '[T]here is no "factor x" that explains why some people continue volunteering and why others withdraw. No single explanation has been found to be sufficient even in one study, and we have reviewed many studies that come to different, if not quite contradictory conclusions'. They go on to say, '[T]hus, not only has no factor x been found – it does not appear to be worth looking for one' (ibid.: p. 95).

This chapter does not attempt to review more literature in the hope that the 'factor x' can be found. Rather, it engages with the literature to outline a variety of factors that have been explored in studies on retention and in doing this, it explores why retention is about more than satisfying motivations. Researchers have attempted to find explanations of retention in the 'disposition' of volunteers; that is, in the characteristics of the volunteers themselves. They ask, for example, if older volunteers stay longer or if it is those that have stronger religious beliefs who are more likely to stay. There are also alternative theories which assert that it is how strongly volunteers identify with the organisation they volunteer for that predicts longevity of involvement. Other studies have looked at whether it is quality of volunteer management that is the key to keeping them. In this chapter, we review findings from some of the studies that have explored these factors and also look at attempts by researchers and academics to combine more than one factor into more comprehensive models. Ultimately, we find that each of these attempts has some explanatory power but that the research evidence is often contradictory when considered as a whole. However, as with motivations, by engaging with different models and perspectives, and recognising that we will not find 'the answer', we may at least be in a better position to interpret what factors are more likely to be successful in helping retention. This should also help us know better how to apply these different models in various contexts rather than assuming a single model will provide us with short cuts to our understanding.

Modelling retention

The literature on retention is vast, and it is varied. Some studies use complex statistical modelling to try to tease out the relative importance of factors hypothesised to predict engagement. Other studies adopt qualitative methods seeking to learn from long-standing volunteers what it is that makes them stay.

One of the more influential studies in the field (Omoto and Snyder, 1995), which looked at the longevity of service of AIDS volunteers, presented a model outlining a variety of factors which might influence how long volunteers stayed with an organisation. We will begin by looking at this useful model which sets setting out what Omoto and Snyder called the 'volunteering process'. This is divided into three stages. The first of these focuses on 'antecedents' – what it is about people, or the situation that they find themselves in, that gets them started as volunteers. In this stage of the process, three factors are considered – a helping personality, motivation and social support. The next stage is 'experiences' which is divided into volunteer satisfaction and integration into the organisation. This stage builds in the experiences volunteers have, whether it is their satisfaction within the organisation or how they relate to the organisation which encourages a longer stay as a volunteer. The final stage is the 'consequences' – how do the previous stages account for duration? The model – which is shown below in Figure 10.1 – demonstrates how the stages interlink, what is connected to what and how.

We are not suggesting that this model is a definitive explanation; like any theory, it is there to be challenged. However, it does provide

Figure 10.1   Structural model of the volunteer process
Source: Adapted from Omoto and Snyder (1995: p. 679)

a framework in which to analyse other studies and which allows us to look at their relative strengths. Omoto and Snyder themselves highlighted three key findings from their use of the model:

1. Motivation was linked to duration – the stronger the motive to volunteer, the more likely it was that a volunteer would stay for longer.
2. There was no direct path between motivation and satisfaction or integration; that is, being strongly motivated did not make a volunteer more likely to be satisfied with their volunteering or to be more integrated into the organisation.
3. A helping disposition influenced satisfaction and integration, but not duration. However, an indirect link was found because a helping personality was linked to satisfaction, which in turn was related to duration (although integration was not).

These findings show just how complex retention is. For example, there was no link between a volunteer feeling integrated in an organisation and staying as a volunteer; however, someone with a helping disposition was more likely to be satisfied in their volunteering and to feel integrated. In addition, satisfaction was related to duration but integration was not. At the same time, there was no direct link between a helping disposition and staying; helpful people only stayed longer if they were satisfied in their volunteering. Intellectually, it might be gratifying to unpick these relationships, but it may be fair to question whether such complexity can help where it matters – keeping volunteers in organisations. In fact, the picture is even more complex because other studies and models show different results. It may be that Omoto and Snyder's findings are true only of the volunteers they studied.

Let us nevertheless use this framework within which we can analyse other studies and which allows us to look at their relative strengths. We will start from the idea that disposition and/or motivation and/or support, and satisfaction and/or integration have an impact on duration and look at other studies to see what they have to add. Some of their findings link factors together and some of them look at factors in isolation. After this, we may not emerge with an answer about which model works, but we will have extracted some of the alternative theories that have been employed to try to make sense of retention.

Motives to stay

Omoto and Snyder's (1995) conclusion that 'motivation directly and significantly influenced duration of service' (p. 683) provides a useful starting point for thinking about retention. Their model appears to suggest that the hard work we put into understanding motivation in the previous chapter was time well spent and that identifying motivation can help retention. However, the model told us that duration was linked to the *strength* of volunteer motivation, not what that motivation *was*. According to this, a manager would need to assess how enthusiastic a volunteer was rather than what particular motivations were driving them. Other studies have focused on the issue of satisfying motivations by taking as a starting point what motivations were rather than their strength. Unsurprisingly, the literature presents a range of insights, and we look at these next.

One of the interesting features of the literature is that it reminds us that, even if we identify motivations, or the strength of motivations, these can change. Snyder and Omoto (1999) themselves note that the experience of volunteering itself will alter a volunteer's initial motivation. The practical implication is that an organisation might identify a volunteer's motivation and plan to use this in such a way that the volunteer satisfies their motivational needs but find that the motivation has changed. One study of young volunteers (Eley, 2003) not only set out to investigate whether volunteering led to changes in pro-social behaviour but also found motivational changes as the programme progressed. The study noted that, although the goal of the volunteers – to gain leadership skills within a sports context – remained strong, volunteers became much more community focussed which suggested that the programme needed to recognise that largely instrumental motivations had altered to include more altruistic ones as time went on. This is helpful if it allows us to predict that volunteers who start with the desire to do something for themselves will become aware of wider needs. We could look to ensure volunteers get the skills they wanted from the experience, but then help them to satisfy their new motivations to be, say, more useful to the wider community.

Although Eley highlights the increasing importance of altruism, other studies find the opposite and suggest that altruistic motivations diminish in favour of more instrumental ones. A review of commitment in environmental programmes (Ryan et al., 2001) found that, while attachment to the cause – in this case the environment and doing something to preserve it – was important to volunteers, social factors were more important to those who were highly committed. As Ryan and his colleagues point out, this is in line with an earlier study of volunteers in a hiking organisation which also found personal benefits to be the single greatest predictor of commitment (Dresbach, 1992 cited in Ryan et al., 2001). Furthermore, when looking at the studies which report a move from altruism to more self-interested motives, it seems that these become more important for continued participation (Mesch et al., 1998; see also Locke et al., 2003 and Omoto and Snyder, 1993).

This poses interesting questions: If some studies suggest motivations change from instrumental to altruistic, and some suggest it works the other way, what does this mean for retention? The questions are complex and unresolved. Reviewing studies does not help us, moreover, to identify whether the trend is more likely to be from altruism to instrumental motives or the reverse; or whether one motivation was more of an indicator of longevity as a volunteer than the other (Locke et al., 2003).

We can suggest, using Omoto and Snyder's model (1995), that stronger motives suggest that volunteers will stay longer, but we cannot say that someone with one motive is more likely to stay longer than someone with a different motive. The model included other influences at work at the same time, not least of which was the finding that volunteers stay as long as they are satisfying motivations *relevant to them* (Clary and Snyder, 1991; Clary et al., 1998). While this ongoing search for the complexities of volunteer longevity remains largely an academic exercise, for organisations trying to retain volunteers, it does seem that people who are more motivated to volunteer will stick with it but that even they need to feel satisfaction in their role in terms of meeting their motivational needs. Satisfaction, however, is not simply the result of motivations being met but may also depend on volunteers' feeling that they have been well supported and managed. It is to these concerns that we now turn.

Organisational and management factors

One way of helping to understand how volunteers might come to feel satisfied with their volunteering is by paying closer attention to the literature on organisational and management influences. We have to look a little more widely because many of the sources focus not on why volunteers stay but on why they leave. Studies examining the organisational and management features that cause volunteers to drop out seem to point the finger at volunteering being poorly organised (Locke et al., 2003). The 1997, National Survey of Volunteering in the United Kingdom is the one most frequently referred to in this context showing that 71 per cent of volunteers said that their volunteering could be better organised (Davis Smith, 1998). This finding has been a staple for those arguing for a greater understanding of what good volunteer management should look like and how it should be developed. Dissatisfaction seems to have reduced considerably since 1997 – in the *Helping Out* survey (Low et al., 2007), the comparable figure had fallen to 31 per cent – but this still means that nearly a third of volunteers questioned the adequacy of volunteer management. It is, however, questionable that the case has been convincingly made that poor organisation causes volunteer loss. Analysing further data from *Helping Out*, Machin and Ellis Paine (2008b: p. 6) note,

> Concern about poor organisation and management do not seem to be causing individuals to stop volunteering. The study suggests that it is more likely for volunteers to leave their organisations for personal reasons, in particular changing home or work circumstances.

However, there is evidence (Alexander, 2000) that some ex-volunteers who have said, in reply to a straightforward question that they left for personal reasons will, if the researcher probes further, reveal that the reasons were more complex and may well have involved managerial issues. In any case, it seems that improving how volunteers are looked after may maximise the chances of keeping those whose circumstances are not changing to the extent it causes them to withdraw. As one study observes, 'virtue might be its "own reward" but intelligent and progressive management practices would not hurt either' (Penner, 2002: p. 464).

But what constitutes good management? Chapter 11 looks further at models of management, but here we consider how studies have tried to link management practice to retention. Moreover, there is plenty of it; Locke and his colleagues' (2003) literature review seems to identify scope for organisations to correct management faults. Among the factors they identify are inadequate supervision, poor communication, lack of training, volunteers feeling under-valued and being ill-deployed, volunteering taking up too much time and volunteers feeling stigmatised or embarrassed (see, for example, Alexander, 2000; Bebbington and Gatter, 1994; Gaston and Alexander, 2001; Omoto and Snyder, 1995).

Wider policy factors have also been identified as having an impact on retention. The steady increase, for example, in the number of volunteer-involving organisations who have entered into contracts for service delivery has been held responsible for a blurring of the boundaries between paid and unpaid work and has been seen as impacting negatively on the volunteer experience through an increasing formalisation of volunteering (Gaskin, 2003; Low et al., 2007; Russell and Scott, 1997; and see also Chapters 11 and 16 of this book).

In general, studies have found that organisations can address negative experiences of volunteering by developing appropriate management practices: '[B]roadly, however, it seems that continuation is more likely if volunteers are managed in an explicit, developmental, supportive and appreciative way' (Locke et al., 2003: p. 87). From this perspective, we might want to consider research that, while not necessarily focussed explicitly on retention, does offer a view of what this developmental, supportive management might look like. The IVR has undertaken a programme of work on this theme. An early study from IVR was Gaskin's (1998) work on young people which culminated in a 'wish list' of what young people want from volunteering. Its implicit message is that, if this is what young people say they want, then addressing that list would go some way to satisfying their needs and expectations. The study produced the well-known FLEXIVOL list which suggested that young people wanted the following: Flexibility (to allow them to fit volunteering around busy lives); Legitimacy (organisations need to demonstrate just why young people should see volunteering as a normal activity for a young person), Ease of access (a recurring barrier for many people including the young); Xperience (very important – how can young people use volunteering to develop experience they can take elsewhere including to paid work?); Incentives (important as organisations compete for young people's time, but what is a legitimate incentive? Validation of experience is one, and out-of-pocket expenses is another); Variety (in commitment, task and responsibility, to name a few important factors); Organisation (efficient but informal); Laughs (speaks for itself – it has to be enjoyable). Many of these requirements can be seen as ways of realising needs, answering motivations and ensuring satisfaction. These findings about the preferences of young people are corroborated elsewhere (see, for example, Ellis, 2004).

A later study by the same author, which explored the attitudes to management among volunteers of all ages (Gaskin, 2003), produced a four-stage model of volunteer involvement – the 'doubter', the 'starter', the 'doer' and the 'stayer'. The 'stayer' is someone who persists as a long-term volunteer. Gaskin argues that each organisation can assist people to make the transition to each of the stages. In the final stage, facilitating a volunteer to be a 'stayer', the organisation needs to pay careful attention to management and support. Volunteers want a blend of formal and informal management: well organised but flexible enough to accommodate both young and older people and their preferences for shorter-term engagement. This can be achieved, for example, by organising one-off or episodic volunteering or developing a pool of volunteers to rotate duties and reduce demands.

Gaskin also found that the atmosphere of organisations is important to volunteers; it should be welcoming and show that the people in the organisation value the volunteer's contribution. Volunteers value training, including training about volunteering in the organisation and about client groups – young people, BME people, disabled people, or older people. The research suggested that volunteers wanted to feel part of the organisational culture and identify with its philosophy. In other words, organisations needed to help volunteers express values and develop role identity. Volunteers themselves also suggested that satisfaction with the support and supervision they received was a key to keeping people volunteering. Volunteers wanted to know that there was someone to whom they could go for support, both personal and professional. Supervision was accepted by volunteers but it needed to be 'light-touch' rather than make their experience resemble paid work.

These findings seem to resonate with many agencies. Studies from organisations that have surveyed their volunteers seem to agree by and large with Gaskin's findings. One study of a Black volunteers' organisation concluded that volunteers were looking for high-quality training, adequate formal and informal support, confirmation that the organisation was well run and the offer of challenging tasks that matched their skill but were also flexible (Britton, 1999). Another study – of Home Start volunteers – identified management, meeting expectations, and support as the key factors (McCudden, 2000). Similarly, studies of volunteers in the HIV/AIDS sector in British Columbia and of Canadian volunteers in general noted that successful organisations needed appropriate policies and strong communication mechanisms as well as providing access to volunteer managers; the reimbursement of expenses; limits in involvement to avoid burnout; flexibility of roles; and strong orientation, training and recognition (Barker, 2005; Phillips and Little, 2002). Completing the circle, Ellis Paine (with Ockenden) who was part of the team which reviewed the literature (Locke et al., 2003) looked at the retention of volunteer governors in higher education. While personal factors proved to be the decisive factor in drop out, support in terms of induction and continuing advice from the clerk to the governors was the crucial element in satisfaction, while feeling valued was also important (Ockenden and Ellis Paine, 2006).

Volunteer characteristics and helping personalities

Omoto and Snyder's (1995) model also looked at the idea of a helping personality as an 'antecedent' of the volunteering process. We mentioned above that the model found connections to duration of volunteering but that the pathways were complex with helping personality only linked to duration when mediated by satisfaction. The picture is further muddied when other studies find that a pro-social personality did not predict if a volunteer would stay (Penner and Finkelstein, 1998).

Other studies have searched for a link between retention and the characteristics of volunteers, whether this was, for example, a predilection to helping or age. Researchers have used survey data over time to show how particular categories of volunteers are associated with longer service. Some of these data seem to suggest that older volunteers stay with their organisations for longer, but we need to resist the temptation to draw crude generalisations from this evidence. It can, however, be useful to begin by looking at retention in this way as long as we recognise that it can lead to what Sayer would call a 'bad abstraction' or 'chaotic conception' (1992: p. 138) if it divides groups by characteristics that are by themselves unlikely to have a causal connection. Is it likely that older volunteers stay longer simply because they are older? Might there not be some other reason why older people appear to stay longer? Nevertheless, looking at how studies have grouped characteristics can be helpful in separating the cul-de-sacs from more fruitful ways forward.

Once again, however, the evidence is inconclusive, even if it does throw up questions to explore. Overviews of the evidence seem to suggest that demographics are not generally linked to continuation; there is no link between age and/or gender and length of volunteering (Hiatt et al., 2000; Locke et al., 2003; Nathanson and Eggleton, 1993; Omoto and Snyder, 1993). Other studies have, however, uncovered connections. Rohs's (1986) study of youth club volunteers, for example, found a correlation between age and length of service, while studies of special constables by Alexander (2000) and Gaston and Alexander (2001) found that those who joined younger, and women, did not stay as long. Other traits and characteristics that have been used to explain retention are duration of education and higher levels of education (Wilson and Musick, 1999) and previous experience of volunteering (Gidron, 1984).

Searching for evidence is made harder by the fact that studies that have also involved thinking about dispositions have used Omoto and Snyder's model and plugged in slightly different factors. This often makes it hard to pinpoint cause and effect. One study (Penner, 2002) analysed both dispositional variables such as personal beliefs and values, personality traits and motives and organisational variables such as an individual's feeling about how they are treated by the organisation and the organisation's reputation and personnel practices. The conclusion was that personality and attributes are important in explaining why some people are more likely to volunteer and are more susceptible to pressure to volunteer if asked. Once a person has decided to volunteer, however, the organisation's reputation and practice become important. Therefore, what seems to be a study in dispositional variables leads us back to management considerations.

Other perspectives

Through using these few examples, we hope we have shown that, although many studies exist that purport to explain retention, they give the enquiring practitioner several problems. One is the sheer complexity of the model. In social science terminology, it is easy to think that retention is 'over-determined', that it is connected to so many factors that isolating a key one is extremely hard. Furthermore, most of the studies focus on volunteering in a specific area or field and it is not clear, for example, how similar AIDS volunteers are to other volunteers. Attempting to look across the studies, as Locke et al. (2003) did, simply highlighted the difficulty of identifying the factors which explain retention from a range of studies each of which focuses on different issues and factors.

Life cycles

Omoto and Snyder's model, which we have used as a framework for our analysis so far, is a useful starting point but it is by no means the only way to look at the subject. We might be able to explain other 'antecedent' factors by reference to other theory. One such theoretical insight is that volunteering is related to family life cycles. As Knoke and Thomson (1977: p. 56) found, '[A]t different stages in the life cycle, certain types of voluntary association activity become more compatible with current roles like mother, breadwinner, retiree and so forth'. Further weight has been given to this explanation by Rotolo's (2000) use of survey data to argue that people will stay or leave organisations in rhythm with life cycles. Men and women with pre-school children, for example, will stay affiliated with youth clubs largely because most will have children there, and 'the appearance of even younger children only lengthens the duration of attachment, presumably because when these younger children reach the requisite age, they too will likely begin to participate' (Rotolo, 2000: pp. 1154–1155).

Such theorising might help explain the trends noted by Locke et al. (2003: p. 83) in their review as 'continuation factors': that 'stability or continuity in personal life – such as marriage and already having children – are correlated with continued volunteering'. Such evidence can be easily found: married volunteers stay longer (Hiatt et al., 2000) as do volunteers who have children (Wilson and Musick, 1999). Life cycle theory might also help explain the 'withdrawal factors' noted by Locke et al.: volunteers leave to find or look for paid work (Wardell, Lishman and Whalley, 2000), or to start higher education or because of other family commitments (Blake and Jefferson, 1992; Iveson, 1999).

While it is interesting to explore these findings, there must be questions about how many of these factors organisations can do much to influence. Marriage might be a reasonable predictor of retention, but what can an organisation do about that? It is possible that some organisations might favour married volunteers, but this hardly progresses diversity agendas. It may also be that some organisations will be more likely to attract volunteers that will remain longer; the example of organisations that involve the parents of children participate in its activities seems to be one that suggests that those volunteers are more likely to stay. Ultimately, of course, even those volunteers leave, a reality starkly outlined by Wilson and Pimm (1996: p. 25):

> One other factor which requires consideration is that the useful 'life' of a volunteer may be limited by the purpose of the organisation itself. Few parents remain active in a parent-teacher association when their children have left the school. Single issue campaigns obviously disband when the cause is won or lost. In either of these circumstances it is possible to place a time limit on the voluntary services sought, which itself may be an attraction to those who wish to see the way out (Equally it could be a disincentive to others who want long-term commitments).

Role identity theory

Another useful theoretical perspective that can add value to Omoto and Snyder's framework is role identity theory. The use of this theory in the context of volunteering is usually attributed to Piliavin and colleagues (Chacón et al., 2007; Finkelstein, Penner and Brannick, 2005; Penner, 2002). They argue that people have a variety of roles when they begin their volunteering but, as they participate, so they begin to identify themselves more and more as a volunteer within the organisation and they act to maintain that self-view (Grube and Piliavin, 2000; Lee, Piliavin and Call, 1999; Piliavin and Callero, 1991). This theory has been used to explore volunteer expectations and integration; within Omoto and Snyder's model, it can help explain the 'integration' part of the process. Using role identity, we can postulate that as volunteers identify more and more with their roles and the organisation they are with, they feel as though they are getting more from their volunteering and stay longer. A study pursuing this line was unable to specify whether long-tem volunteering was a result of developing role identity or whether a strong role identity was the result of staying longer as a volunteer. It does, however, suggest that organisations should cultivate role identity, for example, through appreciation events which affirms publicly the volunteers' contribution and may strengthen identity (Finkelstein, Penner and Brannick, 2005).

The idea of role identity was further pursued in another study which also tried to think through the idea of identifying motivations. This suggested that motivations and role identity are important, but at different times. When a volunteer first begins, it is most important to satisfy motivational needs. Although satisfaction is important at all stages, its importance diminishes over time: in the first flurry of enthusiasm, volunteers do not consider the cost of volunteering, but after a time the costs become clearer, and this will trigger some to drop out. However, the ones that are less likely to quit are volunteers who have developed a strong role identity within the organisation (Chacón et al., 2007).

However, the limitations of this theoretical discussion have been demonstrated by Chacón et al. (2007). They found that the best predictor, and a factor which mediated all their other findings, was obtained when they asked volunteers a simple question: 'how long do you intend to stay?' The underpinning of this is the idea that intention to volunteer as planned behaviour is known best by the volunteer. Therefore, along with their model of satisfying motivations and developing role identity, they recommend that volunteer managers should find out from volunteers how long they think they will be likely to stay.

Conclusions

This chapter has explored retention by reviewing a range of ideas. It has looked at the view that retention can be predicted from the characteristics of volunteers and that volunteers can be encouraged to stay longer if the organisations with which they are involved can meet their personal expectations. We also explored theories that volunteers stayed longer once they saw volunteering as part of their identity and were able to express personal values through the work of the organisation. The chapter also drew on research linking management to retention as well as life cycle theory and the idea that asking the volunteers themselves was the best means of predicting the duration of their commitment.

It might be argued that retention is not a subject organisations take particularly seriously. In one study, for example, it was reported that many were untroubled by retention with over half (56 per cent) of respondents saying that their organisation did not have any problems with keeping volunteers (Machin and Ellis Paine, 2008a). Keeping volunteers caused some problems for 35 per cent of respondents, while 9 per cent reported they had a lot of difficulties. Retention will affect organisations, but the impact will be felt differently. For some organisations, a turnover of volunteers is expected and may even be desirable. For some, such as an organisation that has matched a volunteer with a vulnerable client, keeping volunteers will be more important. Other organisations will be concerned about the costs of recruiting and training new volunteers. In addition, competition between organisations for volunteers means that retention should be something managers think about. Like motivation, however, it is a complex subject; this chapter has sought to set out the issues in such a way that a reflective practitioner might be able to gain a greater understanding of the subject. Clearly, management issues figure largely in this, but what is good and appropriate management? We attempt to answer this question in the next chapter.

11
Issues of Coordination and Management: How can the activities of volunteers be best organised?

Introduction

This chapter looks at the ways in which the work of volunteers can be coordinated or managed. It starts from the understanding that the debate about *whether* volunteers should be managed, which was a feature of the not-too-distant past, has been resolved and that the discussion has moved on to focus on *how* the work of volunteers should be organised. We will begin by tracing the way in which the consensus about management has developed and the increasingly common adoption and adaptation of the language and techniques of managing paid staff. It will then make the case for caution in applying these practices to volunteering and the need for a range of management approaches to reflect the diversity of volunteering opportunities. The chapter will then introduce two models of volunteer management – the modern 'workplace' model and the less formal 'home-grown' alternative – and discuss the strengths and weaknesses of each of them.

The need for management

Two of the foremost thinkers, practitioners and authors of good practice guides for volunteer management in the United States have argued that when an organisation takes on a volunteer, there is an obligation to provide good support. They say that 'with paid staff this is commonly understood. Hiring any staff requires basic planning and management related to work space, supervision, record-keeping. With volunteer workers come many of the same responsibilities' (Noyes Campbell and Ellis, 1995: p. 2). It is a view that is difficult to argue against, and one wonders why it needs to be re-stated, involving any-one, paid or unpaid, must imply some managing or organising of their efforts. After all, thinking about managing volunteers as a way of max-imising their contribution is not new and can be traced to Victorian charities (Davis Smith, 1996); while recognition of the formal need to manage volunteers in more modern times begun with the appoint-ment of a volunteer manager at Fulbourn Hospital in Cambridgeshire in 1963 (Gay, 2000). Six years after that first manager was appointed, the Aves committee suggested that a national volunteer centre needed to be created to sustain and increase the contribution of volunteers and suggested that developing management should be part of the new Centre's role (Davis Smith, 1996).

Tracing the development of volunteer management can give the impression of a teleological inevitably that volunteers will be ever more tightly managed using techniques usually associated with man-aging paid staff. However, the emergence of the 'workplace model' as a dominant model has been relatively recent. A little over a decade ago, it was noted that while there was an acceptance that volunteers needed some form of management, there was opposition to the adop-tion of more formalised forms of management based largely on the techniques of managing paid staff (Davis Smith, 1996). At that point, it was noted that, while the managerialists had not won an outright victory, the trend suggested that the organisation of volunteers' work was becoming more managerial in style and content. It is possible to see how this has happened by looking at literature almost by random and noting how the language, while not always advocating a man-agerial approach, reflects the growing influence of more structured management. One of the most thoughtful writers on the history and influence of volunteering in the United Kingdom noted in one essay (Sheard, 1996: p. 122) that organisations needed to respond to volun-teers by putting in place ways of meeting volunteers' motivations and desires to feel supported:

> Thus, a checklist of items to be addressed by any organisation wish-ing to develop an effective strategy for volunteer recruitment and retention might read as follows:
> * Selection/screening;
> * Equal opportunities;

- Job descriptions/guidelines;
- Training and information;
- Regular support and supervision;
- Someone to talk to about any problems or queries;
- Out of pocket expenses;
- Health and safety (including the provision for safe transport);
- Insurance cover

While this list did not include suggestions for how it should be delivered, its scope and the nature of the tasks listed show the hand of managerialism being brought to bear. It is an influence that can be found across sectors; for example, a review of volunteers in the heritage sector noted

> The management of volunteers in the heritage sector has increasingly become a specialised function. Volunteer co-ordinators, both paid and unpaid, have been introduced. Many organisations have produced volunteer handbooks. (Holmes, 1999: p. 29)

It also found

> Mattingly recommended that each museum should formulate a policy for volunteer involvement, defining the nature and extent of that involvement in consultation with appropriate trade unions: that museums should carefully examine their management of volunteers and where standards fall below those observed in the management of paid staff, the shortfall should be remedied. (ibid.)

More recent evidence suggests that the trend towards management has become irresistible; a recent survey of volunteer-management capacity reported that almost half of the organisations surveyed funded volunteer management through core or main budgets and that managers filled a broadly middle management role (although less than 10 per cent spent all their time managing volunteers). Furthermore, when the organisations surveyed were asked about good practice, 79 per cent reported that they carried out equal opportunities monitoring; 77 per cent had a written policy on volunteer involvement; 84 per cent always had an interview or chat with volunteers before they started; and 54 per cent always produced written task descriptions for volunteers (Machin and Ellis Paine, 2008a). While this does not in itself indicate formalisation, most of these elements can be seen as indicators of a more systematic approach to volunteer management and one that is quite formal. It is also interesting that the report states that someone with a remit to look after volunteers and more formal policies and procedures were more likely to be present in larger organisations (ibid.). The picture this gives is of management in organisations in which the tools of the manager are formal procedures.

For organisations looking to recruit volunteers, there is evidence to support the idea that volunteers are looking to be managed; they want to know that somebody within an organisation is thinking about the best and most effective way to involve them. Gaskin (2003) found that volunteers had firm ideas about how they wanted to be managed and that appropriate management was key to getting, and keeping, volunteers. Locke et al. (2003) noted the 'vast' quantity of guidance on volunteer management and closely analysed 80 articles, papers and reports. They found that, despite the complexity of withdrawal and continuation factors, 'Broadly however, it seems that continuation is more likely if volunteers are managed in an explicit, developmental, supportive and appreciative way' (Locke et al., 2003: p. 87).

One size does not fit all

The establishment of the first volunteer 'manager' in the United Kingdom in the 1960s and the call on organisations by Noyes Campbell and Ellis (1995) to shoulder responsibility for managing volunteers are both examples of the general trend towards more systematic thinking about organising volunteers. Few people now argue that volunteers should not be managed; it is accepted that to attract and keep volunteers successfully, organisations must not abuse the gift of volunteer time and this includes using that gift wisely with careful deployment and support of volunteer effort. But *how* they should be managed raises questions. What is good practice in volunteer management and can that be implemented flexibly across organisational types? Is there more than one model for thinking about volunteer management? Is volunteer management a distinct role with a distinctive set of skills? There are some, often small organisations and especially those that are volunteer-led, that eschew management, or at least do not see the relevance of thinking about management styles to their work. It is interesting, however, to speculate whether this means that there is no management, or rather that it is there, but in some form that the organisation is comfortable with. In other words, there exists an alternative form of management.

The 'workplace model'

For many organizations, the adoption of a 'workplace model' makes perfect sense. This idea of volunteering which resembles paid work but without the pay has two key drivers. In the first place, organisations are working in an environment which is signalling that unless they adopt more formal styles of volunteering, they will lose out on potential volunteers to organisations that do manage volunteers and manage them well. We noted above that research with volunteers tells us *they* expect to have their work properly organised. This is further underlined where organisations that have a service delivery role are finding that eligibility for funding requires some demonstrable way of indicating how volunteers will contribute to the work of the organisation.

The second key driver in explaining why organisations are showing a keener interest in management is the trend for organisations to have to demonstrate their effectiveness and efficiency as potential providers of public services (Rochester, 2006). To be seen to be fit to deliver services, voluntary organisations need to show prospective funders that a service is cost effective and reliable. Much of this makes sense. While voluntary organisations are providing services that are being paid for by statutory sources, it is right and proper that they are accountable for that money. Where organisations and people who have an interest in volunteering need to be vigilant is when these necessities are translated into how organisations work with volunteers. Again, much of this makes sense at face value, at least when looked at from a single organisation. Where, for example, an organisation is contracted to provide a service and needs to recruit volunteers to do some of the work the management of volunteers will almost inevitably take on a sharper focus.

Alternative approaches

Although the workplace model seems to be gaining widespread acceptance, alternatives do exist. Volunteer-involving organisations vary enormously while volunteers can be found not only in the voluntary but also in the public or even the private sector. The roles volunteers play also vary enormously and, as we have seen in Chapter 3, there are a variety of different characteristics which contribute to the definition of a very heterogeneous volunteer population. The workplace model seems to suit organisations that involve volunteers in much the same way they do paid staff – to deliver a service or product of some kind.

But what of other types or organisations that involve volunteers for other reasons?

In an attempt to distil different models of volunteer involvement, Zimmeck (2001) reviewed a number of research studies which looked at what roles volunteers performed and how organisations conceptualised volunteers. Two of these have significant implications for volunteer management. The first of these is the seminal 'worlds' theory developed by Billis (1993). In its simplest form, the theory argues that there are three unambiguous 'worlds' in which social problems are addressed, each of which has its clearly understood 'rules' by which it operates. In the personal world, problems are addressed with the help of members of one's family and friends. In the associational world, people come together to form organisations to pursue a shared agenda. These 'associations' are formally established: there are clear boundaries between members and non-members; the purposes of the organisation are defined in writing; and there are rules for the election of officers and a committee whose members undertake the operational activities of the association. The third world is the 'bureaucratic': here, there is a clear separation between those who own the organisation; those who carry out its work; and those who use its services. At the heart of the organisation are the paid managers and staff who are organised into a hierarchy in which the roles, responsibilities and degrees of autonomy and authority of each person are clearly defined. This is the dominant organisational form in the private sector corporation and the governmental department or agency. Billis argues that these unambiguous worlds overlap or intersect to create ambiguous organisational forms of which the voluntary agency is a prime example, located in the area of overlap between the associational and the bureaucratic worlds and possess some of the characteristics of both. The other intersection is between the personal and the associational worlds.

We can thus distinguish four kinds of organisational context for the involvement of volunteers and assess the degree to which the workplace model of volunteer management is appropriate to each of them. Formal methods of management clearly sit most comfortably within purely bureaucratic organisations like the National Health Service and local authority departments. They are of little or no relevance in associations and those informal organisational arrangements in the overlap between the associational and the personal worlds. Moreover, their introduction and implementation might be complex and difficult in ambiguous voluntary agencies.

The second key study identified by Zimmeck throws further light on the relationship of volunteers to the organisations within which they are involved. Drawing on her study of the welfare activities of congregations, Cameron (1999) suggest that the personal world consists of individuals, the bureaucratic word of employees and the associational world of members. In this schema, she places volunteers in an ambiguous area where they will sometimes be treated like employees and sometimes like members. Clearly, the 'workplace' model is of some relevance but it does not take account of the extent to which volunteers may be more like members than volunteers.

Two models

After reviewing the literature on organisational types and the possible models of volunteer involvement, Zimmeck – to her surprise – found that there were only two models of volunteer management. 'Although the multifarious types of volunteer-involving organisations ought logically to have generated multifarious models of managing volunteers to suit their portfolios of characteristics, they have not. Indeed, mountains have produced molehills, and there are but two models, best understood in the light of Weberian sociological theory – the "modern" and the "home-grown" – in general use to provide an overview of this complexity' (Zimmeck, 2001: p. 15).

Looked at closely, the two models illustrate very well some of the fundamental issues that run through this book. The 'modern' is characterised as being practised by bigger organisations with hierarchical structures, based on rules and divisions of labour. In contrast to this bureaucratic approach is the collectivist-democratic idea. This is, as the name suggests, less hierarchical than the bureaucratic approach and is more egalitarian with a minimum application of rules and procedures.

By locating the characteristics at these apparent poles on a continuum of management types, Zimmeck is able to contrast how volunteers may be managed in a 'modern' management setting, with management in the 'home-grown' organisation. This is shown in Table 11.1.

It is a schema that neatly describes the literature that looks at volunteering from an organisational perspective, offering as it does a contrast between organisations that involve volunteers largely as a means to an end and those that involve volunteers more from a core expression of values. What this contrast of models does is show how the difference is extended across key elements of involvement – from the construction of tasks to criteria for involvement.

Table 11.1   Two models of managing volunteers

	'Modern'	'Home grown'
Aim of organisation	Most perfectly structured and efficient bureaucracy	Fullest expression of core values
Form of authority	Formal and universal: maximum application of rules and procedures	Informal and *ad hoc*: maximum application of values
Role of volunteers/ employees	Equal (both 'human resources')	Different in principle but potentially equal in practice
Distribution of authority between volunteers and employees	Hierarchical, with volunteers subordinate to employees	Shared with volunteers and employees as partners
Control	Direct, formal	Indirect, loose
Social relations	Functional relations with managers and employees	Permeable boundaries: personal/functional relations between and among volunteers. Managers, employees, clients, members etc.
Criteria for recruitment and advancement	Process-based: equal opportunities, risk management	Intuitive: shared ideals and interests, friendships
Incentive structure	Intrinsic, with emphasis on most employee-like (expenses, training)	Intrinsic, with emphasis on fulfilment, enjoyment
Construction of tasks	Maximum division of labour (e.g., between 'intellectual' and 'mechanical')	Minimum division of labour
Construction of expertise	Specialist	Generalist

Source: Zimmeck (2001: p.19)

Other approaches to model building

Perhaps reflecting the dominance of the workplace/formal model, research tends to focus on organisations working at this end of the management spectrum. However, other studies have drawn out the way in which some forms of volunteering are less likely to flourish with the more formal approach to management. Meijs and Hoogstad (2001), for example, look at volunteers in terms of service delivery organisations and their goals, and membership goals. They put forward a distinction between management focussed on programmes and on management focussed on membership. Their conclusion, when looked at in the light of the two models, is that managing service delivery volunteers might employ the modern approach but members are more likely to be organised in a much more 'home-grown' way. Cameron's (1999) study of church groups also considered the distinctions between volunteers and members and, while noting that the distinction was often a fine one, she observed differences. In her study, volunteers were more likely to be in service delivery organizations, and members were more likely to perform different roles. She suggests that members have a greater commitment than other volunteers, expect to have a greater say in the organisation, have a greater sense of reciprocity and a better overview of the organisation and its work, and they distinguish less between their private and public roles. In other words, the context of their involvement and the tasks they undertake mean that they are more likely to respond to (and demand) involvement that is not like the workplace model.

Other studies have underscored the idea that volunteer involvement is as much about how volunteers see their role as it is about simply directing effort. Netting et al. (2005) also look at volunteer roles in faith-based organisations, trying to identify how participants, staff and volunteers negotiate roles in organisations where the mission is the prime mover. The study concurs with Cameron's findings that role salience is a useful way to explain how volunteers relate to their involvement. Members of faith communities are less likely to identify with a particular role and more likely to come to volunteering with a history of attachment to a cause or belief. This means that they will accept a variety of roles. These volunteers do not perform one task which can be managed from beginning to end. Rather, they see themselves as members who range over tasks, doing what is necessary when it is needed.

We are therefore arguing that it is not the purpose of the organisation *per se* that determines how volunteers are involved nor is it the role volunteers are given. It is a combination of these, together with the way in which volunteers themselves see their role. It is not simply that we are characterising bureaucratic/formal management as happening only in large service delivery organisations. However, it is more likely that formal bureaucratic management will take place in larger organisations and those that have a service delivery remit. We can find small organisations managing projects and adopting the 'modern' model, but we would argue that it is more likely where the purpose of the organisation is to deliver a service of some kind, and less likely where the organisation's role is to provide a space in which to collective interests can be explored or pursued.

While the modern/home-grown model sets out a broad distinction between formal and less formal styles of management, some work has been done to add a more fine-grain appreciation of the interplay between organisational purpose, the role of the volunteers, and whether volunteers are seen as 'hired hands' or part of the organisation. Rochester's (1999/2007) study of small organisations develops this idea by outlining how different types of volunteers could be managed. While acknowledging the limitations of the study's focus on small organisations with few paid staff, Rochester was able to identify four modes of volunteer involvement, each of which has characteristic motivations attached, ways of recruiting volunteers and ways of supporting volunteers. These models are service delivery, support role, member/activist and co-worker. In each case, volunteers have a different attachment to the organisations and a different view of what their role is. They come to the organisations in different ways and expect to get different rewards from being involved. Therefore, for example, when Rochester looks at service delivery, he finds that volunteers are more likely to be recruited in an open process and are managed by the workplace model. However, volunteers who perform a support role for paid staff may well have come to the organisation to help out on non-operational functions and found the task through networking. These volunteers may be managed in quite a formal way because the volunteer role might be well defined. However, as the volunteer is there to help out, the management may be more 'hands off'. Rochester's other two models – the member activist and the co-worker – are more likely to be found where the volunteer is involved because he or she associates with the organisation, its aims and values and will pitch in with a variety of tasks. Volunteers involved as activists or co-workers are involved in organisations that 'operate on a very different set of "rules", where roles are negotiated and subject to change rather than fixed and specified in advance' (Rochester, 1999/2007: p. 17). In other words, Rochester identifies sub-groups within Zimmeck's two models and finds – as the title of his article suggests – that 'one size does not fit all'.

Horses for courses: saddling the right model

It should be clear by now that the workplace/modern model with its associated bureaucratic and formal style is not the only game in town.

However, there will be times when it is the right one. We would suggest that organisations should think in terms of congruence. Trends may suggest that volunteer management should be more formalised, but this could be counter-productive for some organisations. In one study of small volunteer-led groups, the researchers found that informality was key to how the groups functioned and, despite being aware of more formal systems of volunteer management, respondents to the research argued that it was not needed: 'As one volunteer said of their informality *"don't knock it if it works"* '(Ockenden and Hutin, 2008: p. 23).

But does it work? There is very little systematic evidence that one model has advantages over others. Simply, and obviously, there is space for more than one model, and different organisational settings will need a different approach. There is very little evidence to suggest that one model should dominate. Instead, the guiding principle might be to look to employ (or not employ) managerial models rather as Rochester (1999/2007) and Meijs and Hoogstad (2001) suggest by looking at who is volunteering and the role they undertake.

There is some other guidance we can glean from research that points us towards the strengths and weaknesses of each model and also helps synthesise some key elements that ought to be present in some form for all volunteers.

Volunteers want more management

Throughout this book, we have considered evidence that volunteers themselves want more management. The often-quoted figure of 71 per cent of volunteers who say that their work could be better organised (Davis Smith, 1998) is taken as a sign that management is needed. Yet other evidence tells us that too much management and bureaucracy is off-putting to volunteers (IVR, 2004a). Mediating between these findings is Gaskin's research which makes it clear that volunteers want *A Choice Blend*. They do not want to be left to twiddle thumbs until somebody thinks of a task for them to do, but neither, it seems, do they want the workplace replicated. This suggests not only certain strength in the idea of formality but also the need for it to be tempered. It also needs to take account of the diversity of roles in just one organisation; Age Concern can have very different types of volunteers in one location. Some may be giving complicated advice about benefits and financial matters while others may be working in the shop. Experience shows that these volunteers need different management styles. A strength of the 'modern' model is that it is quite clear what management looks like. Its weakness is the seeming inability to be flexible. The strength of the 'home-grown' model is that it is flexible, but its weakness is that it has few codified practices; because it is 'home-grown', there are fewer instances of accounts of 'what works' that can be passed on to other less formal groups.

Bureaucracy isn't always bad

Zimmeck (2001) argues that the problem with the bureaucratic model is that it is a model with no boundaries; it exerts its influence over all aspects of organisations and often without any regard to whether it actually produces a better outcome. Yet Weber claimed that bureaucracy was the best model for organisational effectiveness not least because it helped to ensure stability and ensure impartiality. Echoes of this can be found in advice on good practice today. VE urges all organisations to think about having a volunteer policy and that 'while volunteering is flexible and spontaneous, organisations should...have procedures and rules in place to cope with the day-to-day situations that crop up' (Bowgett et al., 2002: p. 8). The policy should provide the overall framework for volunteer involvement defining the role of volunteers and drawing together the elements the organisation has put in place to ensure volunteers are managed well – how they are recruited, reimbursed, supported and so on. It is argued that having such a policy demonstrates the organisation's commitment to its volunteers, ensures that volunteers know where they stand, and offers consistency of decision-making across the group of potentially diverse volunteers. While recent research (Machin and Ellis Paine, 2008a) suggests it is larger organisations that are more likely to have policies, it may also be helpful to more informal organisations to have some reference point so that volunteers can be treated and seen to be treated equally.

The volunteer comes first

All organisations, if they want to keep their volunteers, need to look after them. However, what does this mean in management terms? The evidence suggests that 'bad management' contributes to volunteers leaving (Locke et al., 2003), but it does not tell us what good management is. In a study of volunteers from socially excluded groups, one report suggested that organisations can help volunteers by not just matching volunteers to roles but meeting half-way; in some instances, it is right to design a role with a volunteer in mind. That study included interviews with a group which was delighted if a volunteer joined, learnt new skills and moved into the paid labour market (IVR, 2004a). Yet many organisations will argue (and so will managers of volunteers) that the purpose of their organisation is to provide a service for a client and, in this instance, a volunteer is someone who helps the organisation do more than they could do without the volunteer's assistance. In the latter case, volunteers are more like support to paid staff. This entirely understandable focus on the needs of service users means, however, that the organisation will not be able to play the role of offering opportunities to 'less productive' volunteers and enable them to learn how to make a contribution to the work.

It need not be either/or

There are advantages in adopting some formal measures. Written policies which outline the role for volunteers and what they can expect from an organisations can be seen as safe-guards against the arbitrary nature of informal groups where decisions either do not get made because the flat, informal nature of the group means nobody is in charge or the organisation is at the whim of a *de facto* leader. While being able to distil management into two models helps to contrast approaches, it also limits us. It seems inappropriate to talk about them simply in terms of their strengths and weaknesses; they are just different. It is quite possible to think of examples of volunteer involvement where volunteers in quite similar settings are in fact managed by very different models. In the heritage field, for example, the steam enthusiast in a working railway museum might feel himself or herself to be akin to a member of a club, whereas another volunteering as a room steward in a museum might see himself or herself as an additional pair of hands helping paid staff. It should be possible to acknowledge room in the heterogeneity of volunteer-involving organisations for both ends of the managieral spectrum and all points in-between. Nevertheless, what seems to come through from research is that any organisation fares better when somebody is looking after the needs of volunteers.

There also seems to be general agreement among practitioners that certain elements should be in place if volunteers are to be successfully involved. There should be some sort of application process which allows volunteers and organisations to choose each other. There should be some statement about what is involved in terms of task, hours and so on. There should be some support available to volunteers with supervisions to help review how volunteers are involved. These practices can be found in good practice guides (see, for example, Bowgett et al., 2002) and are codified in Investing in Volunteers (IiV) – VE's quality assurance programme that will badge organisations as good at management. The good practice guides will say that it is the practice that is important and variations can be implemented whether the organisational setting is formal or informal.

A supervision could be a scheduled meeting between volunteer and volunteer managers, or it could be an informal chat over a cup of tea.

The important point is that volunteers have access to support and not how the practices are implemented. After all, volunteers tell us they want to know that they are supported, that they are having an impact with the work they do and that they have a chance to develop as people (Gaskin, 2003), but this will not come through encouraging or enforcing one model. This was brought home by one manager who took part in a research study looking at the way organisations managed without recourse to formal methods. He felt under pressure to introduce tighter systems and said,

> There are expectations, funders expect volunteers to be involved, or it is a good bell to ring. Often funders question 'what is the organisation doing to involve volunteers'. If I go to (the local volunteering infrastructure) or (local university) looking for volunteers there are boxes on their forms, 'do you have this policy or that policy' I feel I have to tick those boxes.
>
> Why have we got a handbook? I don't know...We give them this in a way because it feels like it covers us to some extent, they know what our expectations are and what our legal requirements are as well. But actually we manage them in an informal way really. We try not to make it too...not intimidating that isn't the right word...too structured.

Conclusions

This chapter has looked at models of volunteer involvement and reviewed how, broadly speaking, two models can be identified. It has discussed how a more formal managerial or 'workplace' model which treats volunteering as paid work but without pay had come to dominate thinking and presented some reasons for this. It has also looked at why an informal management model may seem appropriate to some organisations. Each model has its strengths and weaknesses, and problems are most likely to occur when one model is applied in the wrong setting. Trends suggest that the formal model is expanding to become the dominant approach to volunteer management, but it can be harmful when a formal approach is attempted in an informal setting. This theme is explored further in Chapter 16 which looks at how volunteering can be defended from formalisation.

12
Measuring the Impact of Volunteering

Introduction

The language of regulation, accountability and performance measurement has become as familiar across the third sector as it is in the public and private sectors (see, for example, Billis and Harris, 1996; Ellis, 2008; Kendall and Knapp, 1996). Monitoring, evaluation and impact measurement have become part of everyday organisational life (Ellis, 2008; Wainwright, undated). Organisations have to prove their worth and provide evidence to back up claims of their effectiveness. As Saxton and Greenwood (2006: p. 2) put it, 'We must replace trust with evidence'.

Volunteering is not immune from this trend. As we have moved into an era of evidence-based policy and practice (or at least so it is claimed), volunteering increasingly has to go beyond assertions that it is 'a good thing' to demonstrate why it is worth investing in. As Chapter 7 highlights, there have certainly been a number of promises made on behalf of volunteering over the past few years. Evidence that volunteering can deliver on these promises, that 'volunteering works', is now being called for.

This demand is being driven by a range of stakeholder – funders, regulators, individual employees, donors, service users – and by volunteers themselves (Kendall and Knapp, 2000; Wainwright, undated). Funders want to know that they are getting a good return on their investment, and organisations want to know 'what works' so they can assure their efforts are being appropriately channelled. As for volunteers, Ellis (1996) reminds us that no one wants to give their time for something that has no impact.

Within these debates, language is important. Discussions have moved from concerns about outputs (things produced through action) to outcomes (changes that happen as a result of activities) and impacts (longer-term changes, whether positive or negative, intended or unintended) (Cupitt and Ellis, 2004; Ellis, 2008; Wainwright, undated). It is worth noting, however, that different authors use different definitions of impact. Within this chapter, we take a more pragmatic approach, using 'impact' in a shorthand way to effectively encompass all these three concepts.

There is a growing amount of documentation on the importance of evaluation and impact assessment. Guidance on how to do it, or at least how to report it, is also becoming increasingly prolific. It would seem, however, that many organisations continue to struggle with reporting outcomes or measuring impacts (Ellis, 2008). Many continue to lack the support they need in understanding the meanings of these different concepts, in using the relevant language to discuss the value of their work and in getting to grips with exactly how to measure or assess their effectiveness.

This chapter discusses the ways in which the assessment of the impacts of volunteering have been conceptualised and undertaken. It considers who or what is impacted upon by volunteering and what those impacts are. It explores methodological issues faced in assessing these impacts; alongside, some of the tools created help meet the challenge. In particular, it draws on work by the IVR in the development of its VIAT (involving two of the authors of this book), which aims to assist organisations in a 'D-I-Y' assessment of the impact of volunteering across a range of stakeholders.

To whom does volunteering make a difference?

Volunteering has the potential to impact upon a wide range of stakeholders. Rochester (1998) suggests that impacts of community-based organisations, which are often reliant on volunteer efforts, are split between 'members' and 'public'. Extending this model to focus specifically on volunteering, the IVR (2004b) has identified four stakeholder groups upon whom, it argues, nearly all volunteering is likely to have an impact: volunteers, organisations, service users and communities. Below, we summarise the key impacts that research has identified on each stakeholder group; we do this in brief as the following section focuses in more detail the different impacts of volunteering.

Volunteers

Whether positive or negative, the experience of volunteering has an impact on those who do it. The 2007, *Helping Out* survey of volunteers in England found that for 97 per cent of volunteers, getting satisfaction was an important benefit of volunteering; 96 per cent said they enjoyed it; 88 per cent got a sense of personal achievement; and 86 per cent said meeting people and making friends was an important benefit (Low et al., 2007; see also Murray et al., 2008 for a discussion of the positive benefits of volunteering on individuals). A whole host of other personal benefits were also identified.

There is increasing recognition of the skills that volunteers can gain through participation, and a growing evidence base to back up this claim (see, for example, Davis Smith et al., 2002; Eley, 2003; Low et al., 2007). Volunteers have also been found to gain in terms of personal development (Eley, 2003; National Youth Agency, 2007); enhanced employability or a route into education (ibid.); and improved mental and physical health and well-being (Casiday et al., 2008). The evidence for the impact of volunteering on volunteers themselves is probably the most comprehensive out of all the stakeholder groups. It is still, however, relatively scarce and some of what does exist seems to provide contradictory results. For example, despite all the recent policy attention, there has been very little research into the links between volunteering and employability. One of the notable exceptions was a study commissioned by the Department for Education and Skills in 2000, which reported that volunteering might have an impact on employability amongst unemployed people but only when it was used as part of a direct strategy to move into employment (Hirst, 2000).

Volunteer-involving organisations and their staff

The organisations that involve volunteers are also impacted upon in a range of ways as a result of their engagement. Volunteers, for example, provide the organisation with a bigger and often more diverse workforce. They enable the organisation to deliver more services and provide value for money to the organisation which can then be passed on to service users (see, for example, Gaskin, 1999b). The evidence on the impact of volunteers across organisations is relatively thin. Most research to date has concentrated on the economic contribution that volunteers make through their unpaid labour, and even that is relatively sketchy. A growing evidence base is being developed by and within individual organisations as part of the performance measurement drive, but these are often unpublished and not comparable.

Service users

There is not always an easily identifiable service user associated with volunteering. Who, for example, would be classified as the service user of an environmental project in which volunteers were erecting dry stone walls? In many cases, however, there is either an immediately apparent user – such as a sick child in a children's hospice – or one that can be identified with some thought – ramblers, for example, might be impacted upon by the dry stone walls built by the heritage volunteers mentioned above when those walls mark the edge of the footpath.

Again, there is a range of potential impacts of volunteering on service users. Being provided with a service, often for free, is the first. Increased social contact and enhanced feelings of mental and physical well-being and health (Casiday et al., 2008) are among other reported impacts. Other impacts will depend on the nature of the service provided by volunteers. Compared to other stakeholder groups, the evidence base on the impact of volunteering interventions on service users is relatively strong. Usually, however, the evidence relates to the impact of the service in general, regardless of whether it is provided by volunteers.

Communities

Members of the public within the communities in which volunteering takes place are also impacted upon. These may be geographical communities, such as members of the village in which a local shop is run by volunteers, or interest communities, such as staff and pupils at a school within which a group of pupils have volunteered to redevelop an overgrown garden area.

The impacts on communities have, for example, been reported to include: service provision; social cohesion (see, for example, Kearney, 2003); enhanced social capital (see below); reduced crime; and enhanced well-being. As Whitely (2004) concluded at the end of an extensive study into participation in the United Kingdom, '[V]oluntary activity in the community is associated with better health, lower crime, improved educational performance and greater life satisfaction.'

More broadly, it has been argued that volunteering contributes to social cohesion, build active citizenship and strengths democracy. Volunteers, for example, have been found to be more likely to vote, more likely to join political parties, and generally more likely to engage in the broader governance of their communities (Verba, Schlozman and Brady, 1995). As Dekker and Halman (2003; p. vii) note, [V]olunteering 'generate[s] social cohesion and societal self-regulation as well as strengthening political democracy by developing individual citizenship and organizing countervailing powers'.

It is at this level, however, that the claims for volunteering are hardest to prove. The 'community' is arguably the hardest stakeholder group on which to generate evidence for the impact of volunteering. Even defining it is problematic. With the heightened policy interest in volunteering and the growing academic interest in concepts such as social capital and community cohesion, however, there is a growing evidence base.

What difference does volunteering make?

Reviewing research and practitioner literature – or indeed taking an intuitive approach and reflecting on what we 'know' about volunteering – could lead to the creation of an almost endless list of the different impacts that volunteering does or could have. Many have been mentioned briefly in the section above. This section discusses in greater detail what these impacts are and what evidence has been collected about them. It does this through the lens of two frameworks, both developed by the IVR (and the authors of this book have been involved with both of them). The first framework was designed to demonstrate to policy-makers the impact of volunteering on some of their key agendas (Ockenden, 2007). The second was designed to help practitioners in their own assessments of the impact of volunteering, for a range of external and internal purposes (IVR, 2004b).

Volunteering Works (Ockenden, 2007) categorises the evidence on impact of volunteering in five key policy areas, as follows:

1. *Development:* Volunteering has been found to contribute to economic development, through the value of volunteer efforts (see below). It has also been seen to contribute to sustainable development, both through the environmental activities and campaigning led by volunteers and through engendering a bottom-up approach to development in which the sense of ownership of the issue and its solution is enhanced.

2. *Safer and stronger communities:* Research has found that those who engage in volunteering are more likely to have positive views about their neighbourhood; they are also likely to have higher levels of trust (see below). Volunteering, it is argued, also leads to safer communities. A study of one village in Yorkshire, for example, found that the establishment of a Neighbourhood Watch scheme by a group of volunteers reduced car crime by 44 per cent and burglaries by 24 per cent, while at the same time increasing community spirit and trust (ODPM, 2005).

3. *Social inclusion:* Volunteering, it has been argued, can help to address feelings of social isolation and to enable individuals and communities to integrate (see, for example, Involve, 2006). Meeting people,

making friends and generally increasing social contact is certainly an important part of volunteering (Murray et al., 2008). Older people are particularly likely to cite it as a benefit of volunteering (Low et al., 2007) as are people with experience of mental ill health (Murray et al., 2008). A key policy focus has been on the potential of volunteering to help tackle social exclusion, particularly through providing a route to employment but also more generally through tackling social isolation, and there is evidence to support this. However, as we have seen in Chapter 4, people do not participate equally: those from groups who are at risk of social exclusion are often found to volunteer less (Teasdale, 2008c).

4. *Quality of life:* Many studies have pointed to the enjoyment gained through volunteering. Nearly all (96 per cent) of the volunteers surveyed in *Helping Out* said they enjoyed it (Low et al., 2007). It has also been linked to feelings of well-being, or, as Luks and Payne (1991) put it, it leads to a 'helpers' high'. It has also been found to improve the mental and physical health of volunteers and, when it take place within health and social care settings, of service users too (Casiday et al., 2008).

5. *Lifelong learning:* Increasing attention is being paid in policy-making and research circles to the links between volunteering, skills development, and lifelong learning. The skills that volunteers develop through their participation have been of particular interest. There is growing evidence to substantiate the claims being made on behalf of volunteering in terms of skills development (National Youth Agency, 2007). Surrounding the debates on the links between volunteering and skills development have been discussions on assessing the learning gained through volunteering and a drive towards accreditation.

There are, however, other ways to 'slice the cake'. The IVR's (2004b) *VIAT*, for example, suggests that the impacts of volunteering can be categorised into five areas or types of 'capital': economic, physical, human, social and cultural. In doing so, it draws on the thinking of Wilson and Musick (1997) who argue that, as well as producing physical capital, volunteering is: productive work that requires human capital; collective behaviour that requires social capital; and ethnically guided work that requires cultural capital. Each of these forms of capital are brought into the assessment framework within the *VIAT*, with indicators for each 'capital' against each stakeholder group (see Table 12.1).

We borrow from this framework for our discussion below. It is worth noting, however, that each of these concepts is subject to considerable academic debate. Rather than engage seriously in those debates, the

Table 12.1   A matrix for identifying the impacts of volunteering

	Physical capital	Human capital	Economic capital	Social capital	Cultural capital
Volunteers	Tangible benefits accruing to volunteers (training courses attended; social events; certificates)	Personal development (confidence; self-esteem); Vocational skills (IT; public speaking; team-work); Employability	Individual costs of volunteering (expenses; opportunity-costs); and individual value (training courses attended)	Increased trust; higher rates of participation in public affairs etc.	Attachment to cultural identity; appreciation and understanding of other cultures
Organisations	Identifiable outputs (number of meals delivered; trees planted etc); Quantity and quality measures	Impact of volunteers on staff development; diversity of workforce	Value of volunteering minus the cost of volunteering	Increased status and reputation; enhanced recruitment and retention of staff and volunteers	Services more reflective of cultural diversity within community
Service users	Enhanced quantity and quality of services provided	Personal development and skills enhancement of users	Access to services which would otherwise have to be paid for	Increased networks; enhanced trust and participation	Appreciation and understanding of other people's cultures
Community	Enhanced quantity and quality of services provided	Happier communities; better-skilled citizens	Enhanced value for money in public services (lower crime; increased health)	Increased networks; enhanced trust and participation	Appreciation and understanding of other people's cultures

Source: Volunteering Impact Assessment Toolkit, 2004

Toolkit, rightly or wrongly, uses the concepts as convenient 'badges' to tie together groups of impacts. We take a similar approach in this chapter. In addition, briefly considering the different types of impacts of volunteering encompassed within each of these 'capitals', the following section also introduces considerations for how these have been or might be assessed – themes that are picked up in the final section.

Money: economic capital

Traditionally, there has been a concentration on the economic approach when considering the impacts of voluntary organisations and charities

(Burns and Taylor, 2000; Rochester, 1998). Volunteering has not escaped this.

In many organisations, the largest expenditure is on staff wages. In volunteer-involving organisations, when volunteers devote their time for free, a method is needed to establish the monetary value of the volunteers' time. When calculating the equivalent of the volunteers' 'wage bill', organisations can assess the value of each volunteer assignment based on what it would cost them to purchase that type of work in the market place. Generally, this is done by totalling the number of hours volunteers 'donate' to an organisation, and then multiplying it by the national average wage (with considerable discussion as to whether it should be the average or the minimum wage which is used, and whether different tasks should be allocated different 'wage' equivalents).

National figures on the economic impact of volunteering make for impressive reading. According to the 2007/2008 Citizenship Survey, England's 17.7 million formal volunteers contributed an average of 98.8 hours in the 12 months before interview: a total of 1.75 billion hours of formal volunteering in 2007/2008. Using the national average wage, their contribution was worth £22.7 billion (see Chapter 4 for similarly impressive figures from Scotland and Northern Ireland).

Individual sectors and organisations have also reported figures calculated along similar lines. A study of 59 hospices in the United Kingdom, for example, found that the economic value of volunteering was £112 million – a figure equivalent to nearly a quarter of the running costs of the organisations and nearly equal to the funding received by the hospices from the NHS (Help the Hospices, 2006).

However, these figures provide only the value of the volunteering in terms of the worth to the organisation of the volunteers' time. In some calculations, a notional 15 or 20 per cent is added to account for on-costs (Gaskin, 1999a), but in our experience this is not common practice. Neither do such calculations include a consideration of the investment costs necessary for the organisations to involve volunteers.

Gaskin and Dobson (1996) have moved beyond these mostly simplistic studies to look in more detail at the value of volunteer contributions in terms of how much it would cost to an organisation to replacing volunteers with paid staff while also considering the investment costs made by the organisation in their volunteers. The investment costs of volunteering included all direct and indirect payment to and for volunteers, including items such as recruitment, training and ongoing support. The study produced a basic equation – known as the Volunteer

Investment and Value Audit (VIVA) – whereby the value of volunteers' contribution is compared to the cost of involving them.

In a comparative study between organisations in the Netherlands, Denmark and England, VIVA ratios were found to vary between 1:2 and 1:13.5 (Gaskin, 1999a,b). In other words, for every £1 that was invested in volunteers, a notional return of between £2 and £13.50 was generated. A more recent study of volunteering in five NHS Trusts in England used VIVA to report returns on £1 investments of between £3.38 and £10.46 (Teasdale, 2008a). Meanwhile, one environmental organisation reported that for every £1 invested in their volunteers, they received a return of £4 (BTCV, 2008).

Volunteering has other economic impacts beyond the value of volunteers' time and the cost of their involvement, and on other stakeholders beyond the organisations that involve them. For the volunteers, for example, a range of more indirect economic impacts may be considered, including the value of training courses undertaken by volunteers (see, for example, Mook et al., 2003). They may also benefit from enhanced earning power through new skills gained from volunteering. There are also opportunity costs for volunteering. Time spent volunteering may mean, for example, time that would otherwise have been spent earning money. Unclaimed or unpaid expenses are also a direct cost to volunteers. For communities, the health benefits that volunteering has been found to bring might have knock-on effects in terms of saving for the NHS. Murray et al. (2008), for example, found that among volunteers with experience of mental ill health, there was a small reduction in the average cost of a hospital stay among the volunteers, from £2,767 prior to their volunteering experience to £2,102 after 12 months of participation. Volunteers also had less contact with psychologists, reducing the cost of such consultations from an average of £13 across the whole sample prior to involvement to an average of £2, 12 months after getting involved. Similarly, reduced crime rates may bring savings to the police force. These wider economic impacts, however, require a more sophisticated measurement approach.

Equating volunteering so directly to money is also problematic. Volunteers have told us they feel uncomfortable seeing the impact of their efforts reduced to a '£'. It risks promoting volunteering as a way of saving money and undermining the wider value of volunteering. When they are viewed in isolation, figures such as those produced by VIVA give a partial view of reality, and a tendency to compare ratios across organisations is problematic when the wider context is unknown (Gaskin, 1999b). It has been argued that within the voluntary sector in general, the relative ease of evaluating and reporting on the economic value means that it has often been undertaken at the expense of other more complex assessments of wider impact (Burns and Taylor, 2000); the same is true for volunteering.

Things: physical capital

Alongside the economic value of volunteers, the things that they produce or services they deliver also have a value in and of themselves. 'Physical capital' refers to the quantifiable, physical products produced by voluntary activity; it consists of the inanimate objects that may either result from the direct aim of the voluntary activity or as a by-product (Kendall and Knapp, 2000).

Within some organisations, the concrete products created as a direct result of volunteering may be more tangible than for others but in most cases they can be identified; it is these tangible outputs that are considered in this framework to be physical capital. Methods to measure physical output are relatively straightforward: an organisation can simply count or calculate the number of things produced as a result of their projects. For example, it could be the acres of trees planted in an environmental project, the number of telephone calls responded to in a helpline, the number of young people mentored, the number of elderly people visited, the number of clients that received advice in a counselling service or the number of visitors guided around a historic property. The ways in which organisations count these outputs, or what exactly is counted, will depend on the nature of the project, but it is generally the 'stuff' of standard monitoring procedures used by many organisations.

There is, however, a need to consider the quality of the work undertaken by volunteers and the appropriateness of such developments for the communities in which they are delivered. Consideration needs to be given, for example, as to whether the needs of the service users and/or the wider 'community' have been taken on board before the schemes were implemented and then whether the schemes have been implemented in line with these needs. A community centre built by volunteers to a 'professional' standard and directly meeting a community's need is likely to be worth more than that of a shabbily built centre undertaken with little public consultation and out of keeping with the community context. One training course run by volunteers and evaluated as effective by participants is arguably worth more than four training courses that are evaluated as ineffective. Measures of quality are therefore important.

People: human capital

While the discussions on economic and physical capital have focused mainly on the value of volunteering to organisations and communities, the concept of human capital focuses more on the impacts on individuals – volunteers, service users, and staff within organisations. It relates to personal development and the acquisition of skills as a result of volunteering (Knapp, 1990).

The opportunity to learn new skills is a reason given for starting volunteering, particularly for young people, and a commonly cited benefit of involvement (Low et al., 2007). Four-fifths of volunteers aged 25 to 34, for example, reported gaining new skills through their volunteering in *Helping Out* (Low et al., 2007). In addition, some of the most frequently reported impacts on individuals include a sense of satisfaction, a sense of achievement, increased self-confidence, self-esteem and enjoyment (see, for example, Davis Smith et al., 2002; Low et al., 2007; Luks and Payne, 1991). Depending on the volunteering activities being delivered, these impacts may also be true for the service user.

However, volunteering may not always lead to an increase in human capital. If, for example, someone has a particularly bad volunteering experience then this may conceivably knock their self-confidence or leave them feeling 'de-skilled' and so reduce their level of human capital, or at least not increase it.

When it comes to assessing impacts in terms of human capital, 'measures' vary from quantifiable (e.g., number of training schemes attended or level of skills obtained) to qualitative (e.g., reported development of self-confidence). Evaluations often rely on self-reporting from volunteers, rating their sense of confidence, for example, at the start of their volunteering and at the end, or simply reflecting back to report on how they felt their confidence had developed over the duration of their volunteering experience. This is, however, a growth area of research.

Relationships: social capital

While physical capital is concerned with inanimate objects and human capital is concerned with individuals, social capital is about relationships between people (Kendall and Knapp, 2000). It is about the trust and norms of behaviour that develop as a result of those relationships. The Home Office (2000) has described social capital as the 'raw material' of civil society.

Much has been written about social capital, by policy-makers keen to make use of the concept and by academics keen to develop it, test it out and pull it apart (see ONS, 2001 for a review of the literature). It is not the purpose of this chapter to go into detail about either the meaning or the usefulness of the concept in general; we shall leave that to others. Here, we focus instead on the links being made between volunteering and social capital, and, more specifically, on how the links are being measured.

Putnam (1993, 2000), whose work has received most attention in policy and practice circles, defines social capital as networks, norms and trust which enable and enhance cooperation. Social capital is generated through the relationships among groups of people so as to facilitate cooperation, coordination and action: it makes things possible that would otherwise not be achievable (Putnam, 1993). It is created as a by-product of participation within voluntary organisations (Kendall and Knapp, 2000), and in turn makes that voluntary action easier. Davis Smith (1999) argues that social capital facilitates the success of volunteering in a number of ways: it facilitates the sharing of information among members of a group; it increases cooperation; and it facilitates collective decision-making.

As with human capital, social capital can also have its downsides. While some have argued that social capital can provide a resource for socially excluded groups who lack other forms of capital (Putnam, 1993), others have argued that not everyone has equal access to the social capital reserves: it is more available to certain people than others (see, for example, Johnston and Jowell, 1999), and overly strong ties can be exclusionary.

There has been much discussion on the best ways in which to measure social capital, with many attempts being based on the compilation of a range of indicators, including, for example, membership of voluntary organisations and volunteering (see, for example, the ONS Social Capital Question bank: http://www.statistics.gov.uk/about_ns/social_capital/default.asp). There is growing evidence on the impact of the volunteering on the development of social capital (Muthuri et al., 2006; Wilkinson and Bittman, 2002). To give but one example, taking the indicator of trust, research has suggested that volunteers are more trusting than non-volunteers. In one survey, 54 per cent of volunteers said that they felt many people in their neighbourhood could be trusted as compared to 45 per cent of people who did not volunteer (Kitchen et al., 2006b).

Understanding: cultural capital

Cultural capital is used here to refer to assets such as a shared sense of cultural and religious identity, including language, heritage and an underlying possession of knowledge on culturally specific social meanings. These facets of cultural capital can enhance the level and quality of volunteering. In turn, cultural capital can itself be developed by those voluntary activities.

For example, the impact on language is a key issue on some areas, where a local voluntary project can either promote or erode a language. The use of local heritage within voluntary initiatives may also be of importance. Again, by promoting specific features of local heritage, certain individuals may feel that their culture is being promoted, in ways which some may approve of while others object. Other people, however, may feel theirs is neglected (see Ray, 1998 for an interesting discussion of the development of the 'culture economy'). In other words, consideration could be given as to whether a project is representative of the whole catchment community or just a select few within it.

The impact of volunteering in terms of the development of cultural capital is arguably one of the hardest areas to measure. Perhaps for this reason, it is an under-studied area of research.

How can we tell if volunteering makes a difference?

It is all very well identifying these impacts and referring to, what is often expensive, research undertaken to understand them, getting organisations themselves to assess the impact of their volunteering programmes is a different matter. Identifying the impacts of volunteering is tricky. They are often intangible, subjective, hard to verify and a matter of degree rather than being absolute (Annabel Jackson Associates, 2000; Ockenden, 2007). Cause and effect is also an issue – does volunteering make people healthier and happier, or do happier and healthier people volunteer? There are also issues of the 'durability' of apparent impacts. Some research, for example, has suggested that while positive benefits may be reported soon after a period of volunteering, these may fade over time (see, for example, Brandeis University, 1999). How organisations grapple with negative outcomes can also be an issue. There are also issues of attribution: how to disentangle the influence of volunteering from other developments.

In short, proving the impact of volunteering is not easy. As Neuberger (2007: p. 3) notes, this makes it both attractive and frustrating for policy-makers:

> It is this very elusiveness, the power of volunteering to act upon people in mysterious ways, that makes it so powerful an intervention – for

those who volunteer, those who are helped by volunteers, and the community generally that benefits from the contribution of volunteers – and that makes it so frustrating for government.

A wide range of toolkits, guides, training sessions and other resources are now available to help organisations monitor and evaluate their work. A review of available monitoring and evaluation tools by the Charities Evaluation Service identified over 100 books, guides, toolkits, discussion papers, fact sheets and other resources; it also found 14 online tools (see Ellis, 2008 for a discussion based on this review). Just two of these resources were classed as focusing specifically on volunteering, with one focusing on the impact of volunteering through the volunteering infrastructure and the other on volunteer-involving organisations. That is not to say, of course, that many of the other tools were not or could not be used or adapted to evaluate volunteering or assess its impact, but that was not specifically what they were designed to do. We also add the VIVA to the list:

VIVA: As introduced above, VIVA provides organisations with a tool, or formula, to establish return on investment: the value of volunteers' time compared to the costs spent on involving volunteers. It provides guidance for different ways to calculate value and a check-list of different costs to consider. It also provides suggestions for how organisations might collect these data. VIVA has provided organisations with a straightforward and effective tool for establishing and reporting on value (Gaskin, 1999a). The results have been used to convince funders of the value of volunteering and convince trustees or senior management teams of the value of investing in volunteer management. The limitations of VIVA are, however, also acknowledged (Gaskin, 1999b).

VIAT: As illustrated in Table 12.1, VIAT takes the approach of identifying (a) the main parties or stakeholders who are affected by volunteering and (b) classifying the major ways in which they may be affected. It provides a set of research 'tools' – questionnaires, interview topic guides, focus group guides, diary sheets – which users are encouraged to adapt. A range of different organisations have used the toolkit, and a number of studies have been undertaken to test out the toolkit across multiple organisations (see, for example, Gaskin, 2008; Teasdale, 2008a,b). Such studies suggests that it provides a useful framework, but that organisations often require additional help in getting to grips with some of the concepts used and the analysis of any data collected.

Learning, Evaluation and Planning (LEAP): LEAP was developed by the Scottish Community Development Centre, with a specific tool tailored for volunteer centres and other volunteer-involving organisations. The focus of this tool, however, is more on the organisation in terms of evaluating how well it has achieved its desired outcomes, rather than on volunteering per se.

Outcome measures: Several other tools designed to help with measuring outcomes have been applied to volunteering, to explore either the impacts on volunteers or on service users. Among others, these include the Outcomes Star (used mainly in the homelessness sector – see http://www.homelessoutcomes.org.uk/About_the_Outcomes_Star.aspx) and Spiritlevel (an IT-based tool developed to assess 'distance travelled' in terms of changes in young people's attitudes and quality of life – see http://www.spiritlevel.org.uk/).

Conclusion

The push towards monitoring, evaluation and impact assessment looks set to continue. Until recently, attempts at evaluating the impact of volunteering have tended to focus on the economic value – what it would cost the organisation, or the country, if all volunteers were paid. While there is a growing body of research looking at the wider contributions of volunteering, many evidence gaps remain.

Several guides, tools and training programmes have been developed to help organisations assess impact, a small number of which have focused specifically on volunteering. These in themselves, however, are not enough to overcome some of the barriers that exist to organisations developing better monitoring, evaluation and/or impact-assessment processes. As the Charity Evaluation Services' review of the implementation of evaluation and monitoring within charities attests, the language of outcomes, a danger of getting bogged down in detail, a lack of skills and most significantly a lack of time act as the biggest barriers (Ellis, 2008).

Furthermore, many organisations continue to focus on the external value of evaluation – especially being able to report to funders – rather than recognising the organisational learning that can be gained through such processes. This restricts the types of impacts which are assessed, it dictates how that assessment is done, and it shapes the analysis of the results; it also limits the value of the exercise as a whole.

13
Changing the Image of Volunteering

Introduction: an enduring challenge

In 1992, the editors of a book which can be seen as a precursor to this volume (Hedley and Davis Smith, 1992) argued that 'the volunteer movement' needed to 'rediscover its identity and to develop a new "public culture"' which 'should stress that volunteering is no longer (if it ever was) about charity and dependency, but is about mutual support and reciprocity...It should stress the role of volunteering as advocacy and as campaign work, and not just as service delivery in the health and personal social services' (pp. 5–6). This process of rediscovery would be helped by widening the base of volunteering: while, they caution, the 'stereotype of a volunteer as a middle-aged, middle-class woman has never been entirely true', nonetheless some socio-economic groups were over-represented and some were under-represented in the volunteer population.

Sixteen years later, the Manifesto of the Independent Commission on the Future of Volunteering (2008) found that public understanding of volunteering had changed little in the meantime: 'sadly, there are still negative perceptions and associations with volunteering, particularly amongst those who do not volunteer...outmoded stereotypes may persist...volunteers being seen as do-gooders or as people who volunteer only in traditional volunteering environments' (p. 17). It also echoed the earlier call for a change of public perception 'based on inclusion, and on revitalising and reshaping the culture of volunteering' (p. 25).

Despite a series of initiatives by government and the 'volunteering industry' itself during the intervening years and the identification by the then Chief Executive of VE (the body formed by the merger of the key infrastructure organisations in England) of developing volunteering as a brand as one of the four key challenges for the new body (Spence, 2003) volunteering continues to face the enduring problem of overcoming a negative and unhelpful image.

In this chapter, we will explore the nature of volunteering's continuing problem with its image and look at the implications for volunteer-involving organisations; distinguish between the different perspectives represented by image, brand, culture and vision; and review a number of different ways in which they might be deployed to change the perception of volunteering.

The nature of the problem

The problem of volunteering's unhelpful image has at least two different dimensions. On the one hand, the flat-earth map of volunteering which reflects what we have called the dominant paradigm (discussed in Chapter 2) excludes very large tracts of voluntary action and tends to perpetuate the narrow view of the scope of volunteering criticised by Hedley and Davis Smith in 1992. In this view, volunteering is essentially philanthropic in purpose and involves the provision of unpaid labour for the benefit of people seen to be less fortunate or more 'needy' than the volunteers and organised by formally constituted charities. This perception excludes consideration of the tradition and practice of self-help and mutual aid which, as a root of voluntary action, is as significant as altruism as well as the large number and variety of volunteering activities which we have defined (in Chapter 2) as volunteering as activism and volunteering as serious leisure. It is also reflected in the evidence presented to the Commission on the Future of Volunteering that 'more informal types of voluntary work tend to be less recognised and valued, and the sizeable contribution of volunteers in statutory services such as health, education and the justice system can also be underestimated' (Gaskin et al., 2008: p. vii). Finally, the voluntary contribution made by the trustees or the members of the governing bodies of third sector organisations is rarely included in accounts of volunteering: tellingly, ChangeUp – the government's programme of investment in the voluntary and community sector – included different and separate 'hubs of expertise' devoted to 'volunteering' and to 'governance' (www.capacitybuilders.org.uk/).

Even within the sector of volunteering defined by the dominant paradigm, however, the gap between how volunteering is widely perceived and the reality of its practice is wide and presents serious challenges for organisations which involve volunteers in their work and those seeking to promote volunteering. In the first place, the image of volunteering has been identified as a major barrier to the involvement of young people. Research for the Russell Commission (Ellis, 2004) found that 'a narrow, stereotypical view of volunteering still prevails among young people who don't volunteer' (although evidence suggested this was shifting) and that 'many young people who are not volunteers lack knowledge on the breadth and diversity of volunteering' (p. 9). They tended to think of it as 'either travelling abroad, making cups of tea, helping old people, working with children, or helping homeless people' (ibid.). By contrast, young people who had become involved in volunteering had a less stereotypical and more 'positive and progressive' image of volunteering. Other evidence suggests that young people feel that volunteering is worthy, dull, boring, old fashioned and 'not cool' and believe that it is largely undertaken by the middle-aged (Gaskin, 1998; Niyasi, 1996).

At the other end of the age spectrum – the over 50s – we have evidence from a review of the 26 projects that constituted the Home Office Older Volunteers Initiative (HOOVI) (Rochester and Hutchison, 2002) and from a more recent study of the role of volunteering in the transition from work to retirement (Davis Smith and Gay, 2005). Like the young people of 'Generation v' (Ellis, 2004), older people encountered in the HOOVI programme who were not involved in volunteering had narrow and stereotypical views of the range of possible activities while those who had become volunteers had been pleasantly surprised about the degree of enjoyment and the variety of benefits they had derived from their involvement.

Similarly, a review of the barriers to the involvement in volunteering of people at risk of social exclusion (IVR, 2004a) found that the image of volunteering was a major factor which was common to the experience of the three different kinds of people involved in the study – individuals from BME communities; people with disabilities or long-term health conditions; and ex-offenders. The 'long-standing stereotype...that [volunteering] is a formal, organisation-based activity carried out by white, middle-class, middle-aged people...is persistent; this means that many people continue to feel that volunteering is not an activity they can identify with' (p. 24). Respondents also felt that volunteering was an activity which was not valued in the materialistic society in which they lived while many of them were unaware, on the one hand, of the full range of volunteer roles open to them and, on the other, of the variety of ways in which volunteering could enhance their lives.

The nature of the gap between the common perception of the nature of volunteering and the complex reality is thus fairly clear. There are four principal elements to this:

1. *The range and scope of activities:* The common perception of volunteering ignores or excludes a wide range of the opportunities available; these include activities based on mutual aid; informal as well as formal volunteering; campaigning and advocacy; participation in decision-making and the direction of third sector and some statutory organisations; contribution to the work of public agencies such as schools; and volunteering in a wide range of sports, recreational and cultural activities and other leisure pursuits.

2. *The nature of the rewards and the benefits of involvement:* Volunteering is generally seen as a selfless and altruistic activity rather than a kind of exchange in which the benefits to service users and the organisations that seek to meet their needs is balanced by the rewards experienced by the volunteer in terms of the acquisition of knowledge, understanding and skills; personal and social development; involvement in an enjoyable leisure pursuit; and the opportunity to meet and share the company of other people.

3. *The kinds of people who volunteer:* While, as we have seen in Chapter 4, the levels of participation in volunteering vary across different socio-economic groups, the common negative image of volunteering as the preserve of the 'blue rinse brigade' and the 'twin set and pearls' set ignores the involvement in volunteering of people of all ages, classes and ethnic origins.

4. *The status of volunteering:* A combination of these unfortunate images helps to explain the view expressed by participants in many studies that volunteering has a low status and that volunteers were not given the respect they deserve. As a result, some kept quiet about their activities and could be seen as 'closet volunteers' while others studiously avoided using the 'v' word. Interestingly, the volunteering undertaken by lawyers and other professionals, aspires to a higher status by using the term 'working on a pro bono basis' (Hankinson and Rochester, 2005).

How can we explain the persistence of these widely held but erroneous beliefs about the nature of volunteering? An important part of the answer may be found in the historiography of voluntary action. Lukka and Ellis Paine (2001/2007) summarise the argument that the service delivery model of 'doing good' which is at the heart of the image of volunteering emerged from Victorian practices of benevolence, in which those who 'had' were encouraged to help those who 'had not'. 'It was from this era that the predominantly middle-class image of volunteering arose, through the idea of "Lady Bountiful" helping the poor and needy' (2007: p. 31). The notion is both class- and gender-based. The 19th-century philanthropists were celebrated by the middle classes and became hate figures for politicians of the Left. In the process, this ensured that the extent of voluntary action in working-class communities was – and to an extent still is – overlooked. The unpaid labour force of 19th-century charity was largely recruited from the many middle-class women who were increasingly well educated and independently minded but were nor permitted to enter the labour market; for them, volunteering offered an alternative to the paid work from which they were barred.

Since the 1960s, the idea that volunteering is about helping others has been maintained and reinforced by a series of government initiatives which aimed to promote voluntary action as a panacea for a variety of social ills such as juvenile delinquency and large-scale unemployment (Sheard, 1996). The more recent of these have been described as 'Tory initiatives about helping others and service to the community. These are dated concepts about helper and helped, powerful and powerless' (quoted in Lukka and Ellis Paine, 2001/2007: p. 90). Commentators have also found that the early rhetoric of the Blair administration about 'active communities' boils down to 'an emphasis on individual responsibility, "active citizenship", and also on employment' (ibid.).

As well as tending to exclude volunteering in working-class communities, the 'Western construct of volunteering' – as Lukka and Ellis Paine (2001/2007) call it – is, they argue, at odds with the experience and aspirations of people from three specific groups – BME communities, young people and people with disabilities – each of which highlights ways in which the dominant perspective is 'a potentially exclusionary one' (p. 87). In the case of people from BME communities, the issue is the gulf between the formality of 'mainstream volunteering' in which they are under-represented and the informal arrangements that characterise voluntary action within their own communities where rates of involvement are much higher. This latter kind of informal community activity was not seen as volunteering: Lukka and Ellis Paine quote research that found less than a quarter of those involved in it considered it to be volunteering. They saw it instead as 'a natural form of mutual support' as against 'the dominant Western construct based on the service delivery model with a formal relationship between the helper and the helped' (p. 92).

In the case of young people, failure to recognise many of the activities in which they are involved as volunteering is associated with the prevailing perception that volunteers tend to incur high individual costs in engaging in an activity which is essentially altruistic. Lukka and Ellis Paine (2001/2007) draw on a study by Gaskin (1998) to show that young people wanted to participate in 'mutually beneficial activities' and they report that three of the eight criteria on which young people assessed volunteering opportunities 'were based on their need for returns: that is, Incentives, Experience and Laughs' (p. 36).

The third group which tends to be excluded from volunteering because of the nature of the dominant perception of voluntary action – disabled people or people with long-term health conditions – are often seen simply in terms of their disability and thus seen as the 'helped'. They are regarded solely as passive recipients of the activities of volunteers rather than people who can make their own active contribution. The 'Western construct' of volunteering can thus be seen as reflecting and reinforcing wider societal attitudes towards disability. In the course of research carried out for the IVR on volunteering and social exclusion, one informant highlighted the issue by suggesting that the researchers should avoid using the term 'volunteer' during their study and instead refer to 'activists'; 'as people seek to move away from the traditional, passive image of disabled people as the subject of volunteering to a far more proactive image associated with activism' (Lukka and Ellis Paine, 2001/2007: p. 98).

The persistence of narrow, outdated and stereotypical images of volunteers and volunteering and the hegemony of what Lukka and Ellis Paine (2001/2007) have termed the 'Western construct' of voluntary action raise a number of related issues and challenges for policy-makers, practitioners and researchers alike. On the one hand, they act as a powerful disincentive for people of all ages, classes and ethnic origins to become involved in volunteering. Second, they put especially high barriers in the way of participation by specific socio-economic and cultural groups and, by thus discouraging their involvement, contribute to the continuing lack of diversity in the volunteer population. These represent key challenges for volunteer-involving organisations and the specialist infrastructure organisations that promote volunteering. The gap between the popular perception of volunteering and its reality, however, raises a more fundamental issue for researchers and policy-makers as well as practitioners; how can we develop the 'round-earth' map that will capture the diversity of voluntary action and provide us with the means of exchanging an exclusive construct of volunteering for one which is truly inclusive.

Clarifying some terms

At this stage, it may be helpful to look critically at some of the terms with which the discussion is carried forward. Much of the earlier part of this chapter has concentrated on *images* of volunteering, but we have also mentioned the concept of a *brand* and the idea of a *culture* of volunteering. And another key term in common usage – employed, for example, by the Commission on the Future of Volunteering (2008) – is *vision*.

The literature of branding and brand management makes a clear distinction between images and brand identities. Hankinson and Rochester (2005) draw on the work of Kapferer (1997) to illuminate the differences:

> Images, he argues, are reflections, associations and perceptions about a product, an organisation or a service. The image 'is the way in which (people) decode all of the signals emanating from the products or services'. It is something 'received' by stakeholders. But it may also be dated and lag behind the reality. (quoted in Hankinson and Rochester, 2005: p. 94)

While images are thus essentially the messages people 'receive' about a phenomenon, brand identities are the signals transmitted by the senders:

> They involve a particular vision or aim and intend to be different, unique and permanent. They also involve a set of values that support the organisation or service and with which stakeholders may identify and engage. Unlike images, ... brands may be seen and used as a strategic resource to achieve lasting and competitive advantage, financially or, alternatively, in terms of public awareness and support. Many writers ... argue that the brand is an active agent in the communication process, one that deliberately promotes desired messages that describe what the product, service or organisation does and the values for which it stands. (pp. 95–96)

According to Hankinson and Rochester (p. 95), the literature suggests that 'volunteering is more of an image than a brand'. There is, however, some evidence that there is the beginning of 'a move from a received image of volunteering towards a more managed presentation which is consistent with a branding approach'. This has been highlighted in studies of younger volunteers which have identified the need for a 'make-over' to promote a more up-beat and modern presentation of volunteering (Gaskin, 1998) and an 'overhaul' which would give it a 'funky image' (Ellis, 2004). It has also been taken on board as a more general need; according to its first chief executive (Spence, 2003), 'The creation of Volunteering England was an opportunity to develop a single, strong, nationally recognised brand' (p. 3) as part of shaping a new future for volunteering.

Brand management can be seen as a set of techniques which can be employed to help develop a culture of volunteering of the kind called for by Hedley and Davis Smith in 1992 and the Commission on the Future of Volunteering in 2008. Culture is a very broad term which embraces 'what we think, how we act and what we own' (Macionis and Plummer, 1998 quoted in Dekker and Halman, 2003) and embodies a combination of collective values. The culture of volunteering will be shaped by wider cultural norms but will also help in turn to shape them. The Commission on the Future of Volunteering's *Manifesto for Change* (2008) defines its aim as 'a culture change in society so that helping others and benefiting from a culture of mutual dependence become a way of life, from which the whole of society benefits. We would like to see a society where not volunteering would be seen as missing out on something that was life-enhancing, enjoyable and useful' (p. 2). More succinctly, it wanted volunteering to become 'part of the DNA of our society' (ibid.). Furthermore, one of the key themes identified in the Commission's review of the evidence submitted to it (Gaskin et al., 2008; p. x) was the need for 'our cultural understanding of volunteering ... to be more inclusive, more flexible, and more expansive in its definitions. In this we can learn from other cultural traditions of volunteering but we also have our own lessons from the history of voluntary action in this country and the current under-valued involvement of so many people in their communities'.

Such cultural changes need to be driven by a radical vision or visions of what volunteering can and should be. Those who looked to the Commission on the Future of Volunteering for such a lead will have been disappointed; the 'vision' set out in its manifesto does not provide the means of replacing the current dominant view of volunteering with a new paradigm or the inspiration for a radical change in the way in which voluntary action is recognised, pursued and promoted.

Challenging and changing the current perception

The extent to which perceptions of volunteering could be reshaped by the adoption of a brand development and management programme has been explored by Hankinson and Rochester (2005). In order to take account of the range and diversity of forms of volunteering, the authors conducted focus groups with volunteers from very different arenas of voluntary action as well as interviewing senior staff from generalist and specialist volunteering infrastructure organisations. The focus groups consisted of members of the St John Ambulance (who were seen as part of the service-providing stream of voluntary action); a branch of the Muscular Dystrophy (MS) Society (embodying the self-help or mutual aid stream); a local action group formed to oppose a property development (the campaigning stream); and the governing bodies of a number of voluntary and community sector organizations.

The study explored informants' positive and negative perceptions of volunteering in general and of each of the four different areas of voluntary action, looked for commonalities and linkage between their views of the specific areas and their general perceptions and then considered which perceptions and associations might be used to promote volunteering and how volunteering could be managed as a brand.

As well as a marked degree of consensus about negative perceptions of volunteering (which have been incorporated into the discussion in the previous section of this chapter), the study found a considerable degree of agreement about the main positive features of volunteering as a generic concept. This had three dimensions:

1. Its *social purpose*: volunteering was seen to make a difference either (a) by providing help to individuals or (b) by helping to shape communities to the benefit of all;
2. Its *benefit to the volunteer*: as a means of (a) acquiring new skills (both personal and career-enhancing) and (b) meeting new people or making new friends; and
3. The *nature of the activity*; including both (a) flexibility of engagement (from episodic to regular commitment) and (b) the range of opportunities.

The research also found that there were significant differences in the way in which the various areas of volunteering were perceived. This suggests that there is a need, within the generic concept, to recognise the distinctive flavour of different types of activity by creating 'sub-brands'. Significantly, there was little, if any, linkage between the

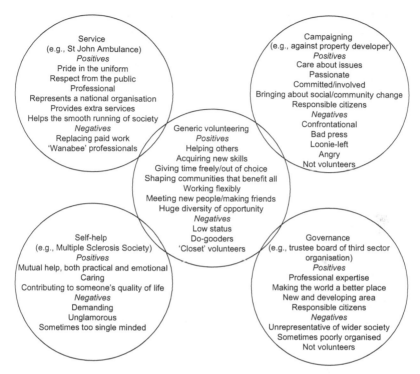

Figure 13.1 Perceptions of volunteering

Source: Hankinson and Rochester (2005)

different areas represented by the four case examples. It was the construction of the generic concept that enabled the researchers to see what they had in common rather than what distinguished them from one another.

Figure 13.1 provides a summary of the perceptions of the general concept of volunteering and the four disparate areas of voluntary action reported by participants in the study.

Finally, the study identified a substantial amount of support for the development and management of a volunteering 'brand'.

As Hankinson and Rochester remind us, this was no more than a pilot study and more substantial action research is needed, possibly with the *pro bono* help of one of the major brand agencies with experience of the non-profit sector. Nonetheless, they feel that they are able to identify some key implications for the development of a volunteering brand.

They suggest that the process of developing a volunteering brand and the subsequent management of its generic elements should be led by the leading infrastructure organisation in England, VE (presumably in concert with its counterparts in the other countries of the United Kingdom). The process should involve the development of sub-brands for each of the different areas of volunteering activity (however defined) within the general framework of a generic brand and every effort should be made to maximise the links between the sub-brands and this overall construct. It should also be an inclusive process. In the first place, the development of the sub-brands would require the active involvement of the key organisations working in each of the specific areas. Second, 'boards, members and staff of national and local bodies concerned with the promotion of volunteering should be involved in the development of the generic and sub-brands' (p. 104). Finally, 'volunteers involved at national and local level should play a full part in the brand development process' (ibid.).

Developing a brand, they suggest, would involve three kinds of activity. The development of key messages along the lines of those identified by the research (and summarised in Figure 13.1) needed to proceed hand in hand with the development of 'the visual identity including the logo, graphic, motif, colours and strap-line' (p. 102). This would need to be matched by the development of an *internal* brand focused on the understand and behaviour of the staff (and volunteers) who are responsible for its delivery; 'there needs to be a seamless coupling between the external face of the brand – its key messages and visual identity – and the internal face that represents staff understanding of what the brand does and the values it represents' (ibid.). As well as refining the account of what volunteering 'does' and what it stands for and creating a visual identity for it, the brand-development process needs to engage and educate all those involved 'to ensure a clear and consistent delivery of key brand messages' (p. 104).

Brand development and management thus offers one possible means of challenging and changing the image of volunteering. There are, of course, a number of problems or difficulties involved in implementing this approach. Foremost among them are the issues of authority and accountability in what is an institutionally fragmented field; the idea of brand management may not transfer easily from the hierarchically and bureaucratically organised companies and agencies in which it has been developed and practised. The key prescription of identifying compatible, clear and cogent messages at both generic and specific levels and equipping those responsible for involving volunteers and promoting volunteering with the means of communicating them does offer a potentially useful way of creating a new culture of volunteering. It is difficult, however, to envisage how one could build a consensus about the process through which it could be pursued; bring the many interests involved to accept leadership by VE (or anybody else); and reach agreement about the key messages and how to communicate them. The mixed experience of re-branding local volunteer centres does not suggest that volunteering is a fruitful soil for this kind of approach.

Other ways of promoting volunteering and, in the process, challenging misconceptions and building a new culture of voluntary action which have been advocated include campaigning and promotional events, the creation of 'volunteering champions', attempting to 'embed' volunteering in social institutions and finding a new name or identity for it. The Commission on the Future of Volunteering (2008) followed the Russell Commission (2005) in calling for action to promote awareness of volunteering. The former's *Manifesto* (p. 27) recommends 'a sustained high-level approach to raising the profile of volunteering', but its only concrete proposal is that existing events like Volunteers Week and Make a Difference Day should be 'hugely enhanced' through the involvement of politicians as well as volunteer-involving organisations. Similarly, 'major media companies, both traditional and new media' should be 'invited to play a part, in order to extend profile and reach'. It suggested that the cultural change it was calling for would 'need to be underpinned by public debates about the nature of volunteering – for example, how it interfaces with paid work, and when it is not desirable for volunteers to do the same work as paid colleagues' (p. 25). For its part, the Russell Commission also recommended that the profile of youth volunteering should be raised by the organisation of an annual award ceremony 'to recognise and reward young people for their contributions to UK society'.

Hankinson and Rochester (2005: p. 104) recommended as part of their strategy for brand development that 'consideration should be given to the appointment of one or more celebrity champions for volunteering and its brands'. The Commission on the Future of Volunteering also recommended the appointment of champions, but here they were thinking not of celebrities but of volunteers at local level who would be located in 'existing volunteer development agencies or other relevant agencies or within the local authority itself' and given training to undertake the role (p. 25). Essentially, this would extend v's strategy for youth volunteering to other groups of volunteers.

The Commission also follows Russell's lead in seeking to embed volunteering in educational and other institutions. Like Russell, the *Manifesto* looks to 'schools, further education and higher education institutions ... to support a culture of volunteering linked to personal development, civic engagement and active citizenship' (p. 25). But it goes further: 'we would expect business and public leaders to set an example and to demonstrate that making a voluntary contribution to the public good is an expectation of people in a senior leadership position' (ibid.).

Another approach to changing the image of volunteering is to try to find an alternative word or phrase to replace the 'v-word'. Hankinson and Rochester (2005) are merely the latest to note that some volunteers and volunteer-involving organisations avoid using the term or simply do not think of what they do as 'volunteering'. Much of the activity we include on our 'round-earth' map of volunteering has never been given the label. In addition, there have been recent conscious attempts to use a different language; TimeBank, for example, uses the terms 'Time Givers' and 'Time Partners', and v has been trying to provide a different badge for the activities it is promoting to young people. This is and has been a controversial approach. The research reported by Ellis (2004: pp. 12–13) found that 'young people want to see the volunteering "brand" given an overhaul but don't think it should be abandoned altogether'. They – like many others – were unconvinced about any alternative formulation.

Conclusion

It has proved a good deal easier to analyse the nature of the problems associated with common perceptions or images of volunteering and their implications for volunteer-involving organisations and agencies that promote voluntary action than to identify the ways in which those perceptions can be changed. The *Manifesto* of the Commission on the Future of Volunteering has failed to set out a convincing plan of action to bring about the cultural change it has called for. Its aspirations for high-level awareness raising and embedding volunteering in the institutions of UK society are couched in the most general terms and are not supported by concrete proposals. However, the attempt made by Hankinson and Rochester to employ the techniques of brand management to volunteering, while setting out a clear way of doing so, is unlikely to be implanted in the diverse and disorganised world of voluntary action. There are, it is clear, no magic bullets or quick fixes for volunteering's problem with its image. Replacing the narrow and stereotypical perceptions which are so predominant will be a long-term project and will need be based on more research to develop the 'round-earth' map of voluntary action and to disseminate its findings.

14
Making Volunteering Inclusive

Introduction

While the stereotyped image of the typical volunteer is far from true, it remains the case – as earlier chapters have noted – that participation in voluntary action is not evenly distributed across the United Kingdom's population. There are some key groups whose involvement is comparatively rare. Exploring the reasons behind these patterns of volunteering, in particular identifying barriers to participation, and identifying and taking the necessary steps to make volunteering more inclusive has become a key component of volunteering practice, policy and research across the United Kingdom. It is also the focus of this chapter.

In terms of policy, the Compact's Volunteering Code of Good Practice recognises the need to 'effectively tackle discrimination to ensure that volunteering is open to all' (Commission for the Compact, 2005: p. 2). The government has, since 2004, had a Public Service Agreement (PSA) aimed at increasing volunteering amongst those at risk of social exclusion and has launched a series of initiatives, including, for example, Volunteering for All and GoldStar, to increase the inclusiveness of volunteering (see Chapter 7). It is soon to launch a new 'Access to Volunteering' scheme, which will provide funding to enable organisations to make 'reasonable adjustments' and so increase access to volunteering for disabled people in particular.

Many volunteer-involving organisations will have given at least some thought to increasing the diversity of their volunteers, with some developing specific initiatives to target groups that have previously been under-represented in their volunteer numbers. Numerous 'good practice' guides have been produced by and for practitioners focusing on developing more inclusive volunteering programmes (Mencap, undated;

Moore and Fishlock, 2006; Wilson, 2003). Within the research community, several studies have been completed which explore the obstacles to volunteering (Ellis, 2003a; Gaskin, 1998; IVR, 2004a; Scope, 2005). This chapter will review what we know about the different kinds of barriers which prevent more people from volunteering and discuss what is being done and can be done to overcome these barriers and meet the challenge of making volunteering truly inclusive.

Who is excluded from volunteering?

As Chapter 4 discussed, participation in volunteering is not even across the population. While not wanting to repeat that earlier analysis, it is worth reiterating some of the key trends. People from several key groups are found to volunteer significantly less than the population as a whole or to experience particular barriers to volunteering in the United Kingdom; each of these groups is discussed in brief below.

Disabled people and/or those with a Long-term Limiting Illness (LLI) are less likely to volunteer than the population as a whole. For example, in England, 22 per cent of people with a disability or LLI regularly took part in formal volunteering in 2007/2008 compared to 27 per cent of all adults (CLG, 2008). In Scotland, one study found that 17 per cent of disabled people volunteered compared to 24 per cent of the population as a whole (Reilly, 2005). The same study found that disabled people used slightly different routes into volunteering, with, for example, a greater use of Volunteer Centre services. They were also found to undertake slightly different roles, being more likely to be involved on committees and less likely to be involved in fund-raising or event organising than the population as a whole (ibid.). Elsewhere, research has found that people with mental health problems also tend to volunteer less (Clark, 2003). So too do people with learning disabilities. One study, for example, reported that only 6 per cent of people with learning difficulties volunteer (Mencap, undated).

People who have *no formal qualifications* are less likely to volunteer than those who do. For example, the 2007/2008 Citizenship Survey found that 15 per cent of those who had no qualifications, compared to 30 per cent of those who had a qualification and 33 per cent of those with a degree or higher qualification, were regular formal volunteers. Another study found that people with no qualifications were particularly unlikely to get involved in committee roles as volunteers and in educational organisations: 22 per cent of volunteers with no qualifications, for example, helped out in educational organisations as compared to 31 per cent of all volunteers (Teasdale, 2008c).

Among BME groups patterns of participation are relatively complex. In general, however, people from Asian and Chinese groups in the United Kingdom volunteer less than Black, mixed race or White people. These overall figures, however, mask considerable differences in volunteering within ethnic groups and across different types of volunteering. For example, among Asian groups in England, Pakistani and Bangladeshi people tend to volunteer less than Indian people (CLG, 2008). As Chapter 4 discusses, those born outside the United Kingdom are particularly less likely to volunteering, accounting for at least some of the difference among ethnic groups. Levels of volunteering in 'mainstream' organisations are particularly low. Refugees and asylum seekers, for example, tend to volunteer within refugee community organisations but not – or at least not to the same extent – in the mainstream voluntary and community sector (Wilson and Lewis, 2006).

Young people (especially those aged 20–24) and *older people* (those aged 75+) tend to volunteer less than those from other age groups. The 2007/2008 Citizenship Survey, for example, found that 20 per cent of 20 to 24 year olds and 24 per cent of those aged 75 and over were regular formal volunteers, compared to 27 per cent of the population as a whole (CLG, 2008). Levels of participation in informal volunteering, however, tend to be higher among young people.

Those living in *economically and socially disadvantaged* communities are less likely to volunteer. The lowest levels of volunteering in England have been found to exist in areas classified as 'Council Estate Residents, High Unemployment' and 'Multi-Ethnic Low-Income Areas'.

Although subject to less scrutiny, *other groups* such as homeless people (Bowgett, undated), single parents (Ellis, 2003a) and ex-offenders (IVR, 2004a) have also been found to experience barriers to volunteering.

As indicated above, there are also differences in patterns of participation within different forms of volunteering and for different types of organisations. There is a particular lack of diversity, for example, among volunteers in a governance role (Akpeki, 1997, 2001; Brown et al., 1999; Cornforth, 2001; Ellis, 2003a; Ellis and Brewis, 2005). A number of these studies have reported that, in contrast to many other roles, women are included among the under-represented groups of volunteers in many governance positions. People from BME groups, with LLI and no qualifications (i.e., the PSA4 groups), have been found to be under-represented in sports-based organisations and in those concerned with conservation (Teasdale, 2008c). Conversely, those from BME groups were particularly likely to volunteer for religious groups, while a disproportionate number of disabled people volunteer for disability-related organisations (Scope,

2005). Similarly, there is a tendency for people with mental ill health to volunteer for mental health charities (Clark, 2003) and for refugees and asylum seekers to volunteer in refugee organisations (Wilson and Lewis, 2006).

How are they excluded from volunteering?

We now turn our attention to exploring the reasons behind these unequal patterns of participation. We focus in particular on the barriers which have been found to exist to volunteering. We focus first on what have been found to be cross-cutting barriers, before highlighting any barriers that have been found to disproportionately affect specific groups of the population.

The chapter draws heavily on the framework provided by the IVR in its publication *Volunteering for All* (2004a), co-authored by two of the contributors to this book. We have, however, made a few additions and changes within the overall framework, which considers both practical and psychological/attitudinal barriers to volunteering. As will become apparent, a number of the specific barriers could have been placed in either, or indeed both, these categories.

Psychological barriers

Time is consistently reported to be, or at least one of the, key barriers to volunteering. In the *Helping Out* study (Low et al., 2007) eight out of ten people who were not currently volunteering but who would like to do so cited a lack of time as a reason for not getting involved (see Table 14.1 below). Similarly, time-related factors – having more spare time, working less, having fewer other commitments – were the most commonly cited factors when respondents were asked what would encourage them to get involved in volunteering: three out of ten said that having more spare time would make it easier for them to get involved in volunteering (see Table 14.1 below).

Young people in particular are likely to cite time as a barrier to volunteering. For example, in *Helping Out* 93 per cent of 16 to 24 year olds gave this as a reason for not volunteering, compared to 87 per cent of 55 to 64 year olds and 42 per cent of those aged 65+ (Low et al., 2007; see also Ellis, 2004).

It may seem strange to classify time as a psychological barrier. It is, of course, also a practical barrier. It is placed here, however, for two reasons. First, it reflects peoples' perceptions of what constitutes 'spare time' and how much spare time they have. Yet, what we know about

Table 14.1   Reasons for not volunteering, among people who have not volunteered in the past year but would like to start helping out

	Applies a lot (%)	Applies a little (%)	Does not apply at all (%)	Base
Not enough spare time	60	23	18	*638*
Putt off by bureaucracy	17	32	51	*632*
Worried about risk/liability	16	31	53	*635*
Don't know how to find out about getting involved	12	27	61	*636*
Not got the right skills/experience	6	33	61	*635*
Wouldn't be able to stop got involved	7	29	64	*632*
Worried about threat to safety	8	19	73	*636*
Worried about ending up out of pocket	6	19	75	*637*
Worried about fitting in with other people involved	4	20	77	*638*
Illness or disability	13	9	78	*638*
Feel too old	8	11	80	*638*
Family/partner wouldn't want me to	5	15	80	*638*
Worried about losing benefits	3	4	93	*633*

Source: Helping Out, 2006/2007

people who volunteer tells us that it is actually those who are likely to be the busiest who volunteer most. For example, people in employment volunteer at a higher rate than those who are unemployed. This suggests that time is less of a 'real' practical barrier than it may be perceived to be. Second, when probed it is often not time *per se* that is a barrier to volunteering, more a fear of over-commitment and a lack of knowledge about the time commitments involved in volunteering. It would seem that there is a general assumption among those who do not volunteer that volunteers would automatically be expected to give up a regular amount of time each week and that that time would be substantial (IVR, 2004a).

To put this in context, the Time Use Survey conducted by the Office of National Statistics in the United Kingdom found that British adults, on average, undertake four minutes of volunteering per day and eight minutes of 'helping' (National Statistics, 2003). By way of contrast, they spend on average 150 minutes watching TV or videos and 44 minutes socialising.

Time does, of course, affect some people more than others. For some people in certain types of employment or disabled people with certain impairments, it is a lack of flexibility in their time which is the biggest barrier to volunteering. As noted above, young people arguably have multiple demands on their time, which make fitting in volunteering more difficult (Ellis, 2004).

As discussed in Chapter 13, a *stereotyped image* of who volunteers and what volunteers do pervades the public conscience, and this in itself creates a barrier to participation, effectively alienating large parts of the population. The image of volunteering, as something that only 'older people' or 'do-gooders' do, can create a particular barrier to young people (see Chapter 13). Attempts by the youth volunteering charity v to rebrand volunteering as 'favours' is but one example of an organisation trying to challenge this barrier. Research among young people has found that alternative concepts may be equally problematic, leading to the conclusion that it may be better to challenge people's understanding of what volunteering encompasses rather than to do away with the idea of volunteering altogether only to replace it with another equally problematic concept (Ellis, 2004). This is an ongoing debate, which resurfaces on a periodic basis across the volunteering movement in the United Kingdom.

The image of volunteering may also be particularly problematic for disabled people, as there has been a tendency to depict disabled people as the recipients rather than the givers of help (IVR, 2004a; Retired and Senior Volunteers Programme, 2000; Skill, 1999). While there is widespread evidence to counteract this view (see, for example, Skill, 2005), with disabled people particularly active, for example, as volunteers in the form of self-help and campaigning groups (Oliver, 1990), the stereotype is persistent and this can be off-putting.

It is also true that many people volunteer but never classify it as such. They consider their acts of volunteering to be helping out, 'acts of kindness' or just 'part of what we do'. Others consider what they do to be 'activism' – in their minds at least a more overtly political form of engagement. While the definitions of volunteering discussed in Chapter 2 would encompass all these activities, it is clear that many people reject the term or simply do not think it applies to them. While this has little consequence in many ways (why should it matter if someone calls what they do volunteering or not?), it does have clear implications for whether people get counted as volunteers (see Chapter 4).

Self-image and a lack of self-confidence also create significant barriers to volunteering. Two-fifths of those who were not currently volunteering but would like to do so in the *Helping Out* study said that a concern about not having the right skills or experiences was the reason they were not volunteering (see Table 14.1). In addition, one-quarter of respondents said that concerns about 'fitting in' were putting them off from getting involved. As one respondent in a study we undertook said, 'what organisation would take a chance on me?' (quoted in IVR, 2004a: p. 30).

A lack of self-confidence seems particularly problematic for those who have experienced or are at risk of social exclusion (ibid.). Experiences such as a loss of employment and a breakdown of social relationships soon erode confidence. In one study of volunteers with experience of mental ill health, half the respondents said that they had lacked confidence and were concerned about having the right skills before they got involved (IVR, 2003). It also seems particularly problematic when the volunteering takes place in an unfamiliar or in some way alienating environment. In one study of school governors, for example, the formal educational environment was found to be particularly off-putting to some, particularly those who either had a bad or no experience of the United Kingdom's educational system (Ellis, 2003a). This may go some way towards explaining, for example, the low levels of volunteering in educational organisations found amongst those with no qualification (Teasdale, 2008c). It may also be particularly problematic for certain volunteer roles, such as those involved in governance, where requirements for particular skills or knowledge are perceived to be higher (ibid.).

For some people, concerns about being unreliable or letting people down may create additional self-confidence issues. This has been found to be particularly true for disabled people with certain impairments that affect their daily functioning (Corden and Ellis, 2004) or their ability to commit to something on at a set regular time and especially among those who themselves have been let down by 'unreliable' volunteers in the past (Corden and Sainsbury, 2001).

Direct discrimination and prejudice is also a barrier to volunteering. People may experience discrimination by paid staff, existing volunteers or service users. At a very general level, it is apparent that some staff are opposed to working alongside volunteers altogether, and this can create an (at best) uncomfortable environment for volunteers to come in to. Prejudice is often, however, more specifically targeted, with individuals subject to the same forms of discrimination when they are volunteering as experienced in other areas of their lives. Those who have been discriminated against in the past are likely to be more hesitant about opening themselves up for further discrimination. Discrimination can stop people getting involved in volunteering, reducing their chances of getting a placement; it can also stop people staying involved in volunteering (IVR, 2004a).

Concerns about *losing welfare benefits* create another barrier to volunteering which can be considered both psychological and practical. It is probably the barrier which has received greatest policy attention; yet it remains unresolved. Regulations permit all benefits recipients to volunteer for an unlimited amount of time. It is apparent, however, that many are stopped or discouraged from doing so by ill, informed or misguided benefits staff (e.g., those in Job Centre Pluses). Numerous stories circulate around the sector about people who have had their benefits stopped because of their volunteering or who have been told that they are not allowed to volunteer while claiming benefits (IVR, 2004a contains some examples; see also Restall, 2003). Others simply do not understand the rules or how they apply to their circumstances (Corden and Sainsbury, 2001).

Despite the relatively high level of attention that this barrier to volunteering has received recently in policy and practice circles, however, only 7 per cent of respondents in *Helping Out* who were not volunteering but would like to start cited concerns about losing benefits as a reason for not volunteering (Low et al., 2007). These concerns were, however, greater among those with LLIs and those with no qualifications (arguably groups more likely to be claiming benefits) (Teasdale, 2008c).

Health and safety, risk and liability have become defining features of 21st century Britain (as discussed in Chapter 6), and concerns about them have affected volunteering. Nearly half of the people questioned in *Helping Out* said that the reason they had not got involved in volunteering, despite wanting to, was because they were worried about risk and liability; one-quarter were concerned about threats to their safety (see Table 14.1) (see also Gaskin, 2005).

Practical barriers to volunteering

A whole series of more practical barriers to volunteering have also been identified. It is these that policy-makers and practitioners have tended to focus on.

Not knowing how to get involved in volunteering, what opportunities are available or where to go to find out is a commonly identified barrier to volunteering. With a general over-reliance on word-of-mouth recruitment methods for volunteering, there is a danger that those who are not connected to relevant social networks will simply not be asked to get involved. One-third of respondents who were not currently regular formal volunteers in *Helping Out* said that they would be 'pleased to help' if asked to get involved in volunteering, while less than two-fifths said they would refuse outright (Low et al., 2007). In the same study, two-fifths of those who were not volunteering but who wanted to help out gave not knowing how to find out about getting involved in volunteering as a reason for not doing so (see Table 14.1). It is not always, however, a total lack of information that creates a barrier to volunteering. Conversely, some have argued that there is a plethora of information available but navigating through that information is what is problematic (Ellis, 2004).

Looking again at the *Helping Out* study, when those who were not currently regular formal volunteers were asked what would make it easier for them to get involved, one in ten said having more information (the third most common factor identified – see Figure 14.1). Young people in particular said that more information would help them get involved (Low et al., 2007). As well as a lack of information, misinformation can also be a problem, whether it is misinformation about benefits regulations (see above) or about whether refugees and asylum seekers are 'allowed' to volunteer (Wilson, 2003).

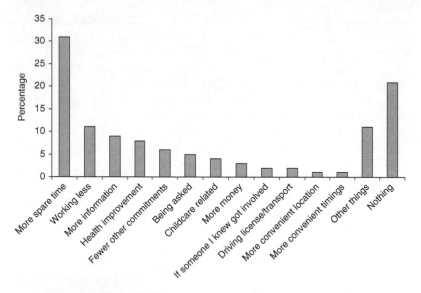

Figure 14.1 Things that would make it easier to get involved in volunteering, as identified by people who had not been regular formal volunteers in past year

Base: 1154

Source: Low et al. (2007)

A lack of appropriate or appealing opportunities for volunteers can stop people getting involved. During the consultation carried out as part of the Commission on the Future of Volunteering, one organisation reported that a survey of their members had revealed that 71 per cent would be interested in volunteering in the future. Of these, 50 per cent said that what was stopping them at the moment was 'not seeing the right sort of opportunities' (Gaskin et al., 2008: p. 9).

Poor management and excessive bureaucracy can be off-putting to potential volunteers (see Chapter 16). Overly formal recruitment procedures involving unnecessarily lengthy or formal application forms and interviews can create barriers to potential new volunteers, particularly among those who have communication difficulties, whose first language is not English or who have limited employment histories and, as such, are not familiar with these processes (IVR, 2004a).

Perhaps more concerning is the evidence of overtly bad management. Evidence suggests, for example, that a considerable number of people who make contact with an organisation to offer themselves as a volunteer have simply not heard anything back or have been kept waiting for a response for an unacceptably long period of time (see, for example, Gaskin et al., 2008).

In particular, there is growing evidence that it is organisations' management response to concerns about risk that is problematic, most notably the increasing insistence on Criminal Record Bureau (CRB) checks. Some volunteer roles, of course, require CRB checks, and it is proper that these are carried out. In other cases, however, it is apparent that organisations are blanket checking their volunteers, something which is not only bad practice but in some cases might also be illegal. It is not necessarily having to undergo a CRB check itself which creates a barrier – although this does create a particular barrier for those with criminal records or those, such as refugees and asylum seekers, who find it hard to collect together the required records and documentation (see, for example, Wilson and Lewis, 2006) – it is more the wait to get them completed that becomes an issue. Some people get fed up waiting for permission to start volunteering in one organisation and so move on to another; others put off volunteering all together.

As one volunteer said in response to the Commission on the Future of Volunteering,

> [I]f the government seriously envisages an enhanced role for volunteers it must be aware that volunteers are just that and that they will withdraw their services if the demands made on them are too great

and if over-regulation stands in the way of what they wish to achieve. Obviously there must be basic financial probity, but the ever-growing apparatus of quality assurance, compliance, etc, is driving volunteers away. (Gaskin et al., 2008: p. 10)

Whether it is through a lack of transport or poor building access, *inaccessible physical environments* can also create a barrier to involvement. It has been suggested that the voluntary sector in particular has lacked the resources necessary to make the reasonable adjustments necessary to make their spaces accessible (Scope, 2005).

Money is also an issue. A quarter of the people taking part in the *Helping Out* survey who were not volunteering but who expressed an interested in getting involved said concerns about being out of pocket was a reason for them not to do so (see Table 14.1). The *costs of volunteering*, therefore, can create a considerable barrier to participation. The costs may take the form of transport to and from the venue, childcare, covering other caring responsibilities or subsistence. It may also include the costs of 'reasonable adjustments', such as signer, specific equipment or an assistant, which are not met directly through organisations. While some organisations reimburse all expenses, others do not reimburse any, and even when they do offer expenses some volunteers might be unaware of this or they might not be willing to buck a general trend where the culture among volunteers is not to make claims (Ellis, 2003a). Only 3 per cent of current formal volunteers in *Helping Out*, for example, said they had all their expenses reimbursed; 36 per cent said they had none (Low et al., 2007). The proportion of volunteers receiving expenses had actually declined over the past 10 years (ibid.). It is worth noting, however, that when non-volunteers were asked what would help them to get involved only 4 per cent said more money (ibid.).

Moving towards more inclusive volunteering

Reasons for thinking about diversity and inclusion

As we have noted above, tackling the barriers to volunteering in order to make it more inclusive has become a key preoccupation of policymakers and practitioners. For government, it is part of a wider drive to increase participation in volunteering as part of the public service renewal and active citizenship agendas. More specifically, however, it is also related to social exclusion/inclusion agendas as volunteering is seen as useful mechanism to help tackle social exclusion, particularly by providing a stepping stone to employment (see, for example, speeches by Blunkett, 2001; Brown, 2000; Michael, 1998).

For volunteer-involving organisations, it has been argued, there are a range of reasons for them to concern themselves with increasing diversity (Clark, 2003; Mole and Harrow, 2003). These include the following:

Equity: Only through making volunteering inclusive can organisations avoid discriminating;

Effectiveness: Drawing on a wider pool of skills, experiences and perspectives enhances performance;

Representation: Reflecting the makeup and/or needs of the local community and/or service users; and

Inclusion: Contributing to the fight against social exclusion.

Developing an inclusive approach

As discussed above, a series of government initiatives, foundation-funded programmes and individual organisational initiatives have developed over recent years with a specific aim of making volunteering more inclusive. As a result, numerous good practice guides and several evaluation reports and research studies have been produced which set out the steps taken or needed to make this happen. Several common factors can be identified across these. Here we use the framework provided by the review of the 46 projects that have been funded through the GoldStar programme, which identified eight 'critical success factors' for developing good practice in managing volunteers from 'socially excluded groups' (Tribal, 2008). Into the framework we have added findings from elsewhere as appropriate.

Positive action, in terms of targeting certain 'under-represented' groups, has been found to be an important element in developing an inclusive volunteering programme (Ellis and Brewis, 2005; Tribal, 2008). This may involve, first, understanding the target population. What is the makeup of the local community? Which groups are under-represented? How do they currently engage in volunteering activities? What type of activities would they like to get involved in? What forms of recruitment are likely to work best?. The knowledge and understanding that is gained from these enquiries can be used to develop appropriate opportunities and recruitment mechanisms. This may mean changing or developing new ways of working to ensure that opportunities reflect the needs to the target population and not just of the organisation (Ellis, 2006).

In terms of *recruitment*, the need to advertise widely, to focus on the role and not simply asking for volunteers in recruitment materials and challenging any stereotypes of who volunteers have also been found to be important elements for an inclusive volunteer recruitment process (see, for example, Ellis, 2003a). Tribal (2008) lists the steps within the recruitment process that are needed to ensure that volunteering is inclusive. The key requirements are providing appropriate information to prospective volunteers, supporting volunteers at the recruitment stage, recruiting service users and ensuring that selection procedures are effective. Evidence from programme evaluations elsewhere suggests that developing partnerships with local groups representing the target population and/or local support agencies that work with such groups is an important element of developing a more inclusive volunteer programme (Ellis, 2006; Teasdale, 2008d). Working with intermediary agencies can be particularly important. Some volunteer centres in England, for example, have been found to be particularly effective at engaging volunteers with extra support needs and those from 'hard to reach' groups (Malmersjo, 2006). Offering introductory sessions, or taster days, can also be important – enabling people to dip in and try volunteering in a range of settings before they commit to anything (IVR, 2004a; Teasdale, 2008d).

Matching volunteers to roles, or rather roles to volunteers, has also been found to be important. There has been a tendency within the work-based or 'modern' model of volunteer management that has dominated in recent years (see Chapter 11) to focus on identifying a volunteer opportunity and then finding a volunteer to fit that role. Taking a more inclusive approach, it is argued, would first involve understanding the needs and motivations of volunteers and ensuring that these are met through having a range of opportunities, as recommended in most good practice guides for volunteer management. It would also, however, involve going one step further to tailor the opportunity, or come up with new opportunities, to fit the individual's abilities and interest – to start with the individual rather than the opportunity (IVR, 2004a). In general, developing a flexible approach is important (Tribal, 2008). Drawing on their experiences of running Capital Volunteering – a scheme aimed at involving people with mental health problems in volunteering – CSV (2008) argue that being flexible and responsive is one of the most important factors in being inclusive.

Particularly, for those who see volunteering as a route out of exclusion and/or into employment, there is a need for organisations to develop clear *progression pathways* and to support volunteers in identifying goals and reviewing progress (IVR, 2004a; Tribal, 2008). Developing formal structures and partnership arrangements with other organisations may help to facilitate this process (Tribal, 2008). As a result of their experience of involving homeless people as volunteers, for example, one organisation discovered the value of providing a route to progression by giving participants the opportunity to experience volunteering for the first time in the relative 'safety' of that (homelessness) organisation before then being given the opportunity and support necessary to progress on to volunteering opportunities in partner organisations (Teasdale, 2008d).

The provision of *training*, both at the point of induction and on an ongoing basis, is also recognised as an important part of developing an inclusive volunteer programme. Within this, the need to understand individual training needs and access issues and then to tailor training opportunities has also been found to be important (Tribal, 2008). This may include ensuring that training venues and materials are accessible and a variety of learning approaches are used. Indeed, for some training in itself can be an intimidating concept which some organisations have found best to avoid; integrating more informal 'training sessions' within social events, for example, have been found by some to be more inclusive (IVR, 2004a). Accreditation can be a valuable asset to some volunteers, particularly those who see their volunteering as a route out of exclusion and/or a route to employment. For some, the certificates gained through accredited training may be the first they have received, becoming a source of considerable pride and having a powerful effect on the individual (Teasdale, 2008d). Accreditation in itself, however, can create additional barriers to potential volunteers, particularly, for example, among older people who tend to be less interested in formal accreditation of learning (Rochester and Grotz, 2006).

Getting the *support and supervision* 'right' for volunteers has been found to be central to inclusive volunteering. Volunteers – particularly those from 'excluded groups' – identify the need for friendly, efficient and effective support (see, for example, Gaskin, 2003; IVR, 2004a). Peer support can be an important part of this (IVR, 2004a; Tribal, 2008). More generally, it is important to ensure that there are good communications with volunteers and that they are made to feel included within and central to the organisation.

Providing *recognition* to volunteers for their contribution has also been widely recognised as important. This refers not only to providing thanks or rewards but also to ensuring that volunteers are involved in decision-making throughout the organisation and that this involvement is reflected in organisational policies and procedures. As much as anything, it is about creating a positive and inclusive organisational ethos, which may additionally require ensuring diversity and providing volunteer-management training for existing staff and volunteers (IVR, 2004a). Ensuring that these things are addressed before seeking to recruit new and more diverse volunteers is important. An evaluation of one initiative to diversify volunteers in which ten pilot programmes operated found that the one to be most successful in terms of its recruitment was the one that set out not to recruit more volunteers initially but to ensure that the organisation was ready to do so. As a result of the process of ensuring that the organisation was ready to be more inclusive in its volunteering, many new volunteers had been attracted to the organisation (Ellis, 2006).

Underlying all of the above is a need for effective *volunteer management*. Tribal (2008) suggests that this involves clear policies and procedures, practical methods for measuring performance in terms of outcomes and impacts, appropriate management information and records of volunteers, and the establishment of effective working relationships with clients (see Chapters 11 and 16 for a wider discussion of what makes for 'effective' volunteer management).

Cutting across all of these elements, a number of reviews have highlighted the importance of developing a partnership approach to ensuring inclusivity (see, for example, CSV, 2008; Ellis, 2006; IVR, 2004a; Teasdale, 2008d). Partnership working has been found to be crucial at the point of developing appropriate opportunities, recruiting volunteers, supporting volunteers and providing opportunities for progression. These partnerships, however, take time to build and require organisations to be 'patient and persistent', 'consultative' and open so as to build trust among those with whom they are seeking to work in partnership (CSV, 2008).

Conclusion

Ensuring that volunteering is inclusive is an enduring challenge. While many organisations are seeking to involve a more diverse range of volunteers than they have done in the past, evidence suggests that there is still a considerable amount still to be done to tackle the more enduring barriers to participation. To date, much of the policy and practice focus has (perhaps inevitably) tended to focus on tackling the more practical barriers to volunteering, with little consideration to how the more entrenched psychological barriers might be addressed.

Different organisations are adopting different approaches to this challenge. On the one hand, there are some organisations that have adhered to the view of volunteering as unpaid labour, 'using' volunteers to deliver public servicing and developing a work-based model of volunteer management, with little commitment to investing the time and resources required to make their volunteering more inclusive. On the other hand, there is another set of organisations that have adhered more to the view of volunteering as activism or serious leisure (see Chapter 2); they have recognised the developmental potential of volunteering and saw volunteer involvement as fundamental to their organisational ethos. Such organisations have tended to adopt a more flexible approach to their volunteer management (although arguably often still a predominantly work-based model) and have been willing to invest more in their volunteers than they may immediately get in return in order to meet additional support needs. These organisations are interested in much wider outcomes from involving volunteers than a simple return on investment. Of course, there are also many other organisations in between these two approaches, working in different ways and to greater or lesser extents to address issues of inclusivity.

All this requires time. Perhaps, one of the biggest contradictions within the numerous initiatives that have been set up to increase access to volunteering is that they have generally set high targets for the numbers to be included and done so within time-limited periods. Many programmes, for example, have set about increasing the diversity of volunteers within a one-year period. Evidence gathered through evaluating such initiative – and more generally through attempts by organisations to be more inclusive – suggests that one year is not enough and that a target-based approach is not the most appropriate way forward.

Finally, this chapter and much of the existing literature focus on formal volunteering much of which takes place within comparatively large organisations. Relatively little is known about the extent to which more informal forms of volunteering or volunteering within small community-based organisations is inclusive, what the barriers are to volunteering in these contexts and what can be done to tackle them.

15
Maintaining the Independence of Voluntary Action

Introduction

As we noted in Chapter 5, volunteering in the countries of the former Soviet Union and its satellites in the Eastern Bloc has a toxic heritage. This can be traced back to the weekly subbotnik – a day of compulsory universal volunteering organised by the new Soviet state in an attempt to rebuild a country shattered by civil war (Davis Smith, 2001/2007). Nothing, it seems, could be further from the theory and practice of voluntary action in the United Kingdom and other Western democracies than the requirement by the state that its citizens should provide unpaid labour. However, it is equally clear that voluntary action does not take place in a separate space where the influence of the state is not felt and its writ does not run. In the United States and Canada, compulsory or 'mandated' volunteering – to use Kearney's (2001/2007) term – is commonplace, and there have been proposals that it should be introduced in the United Kingdom. But the state can have a major impact on volunteering without turning to compulsion: it may attempt to harness voluntary action to its policy objectives; it can set the agenda for volunteering by giving greater attention or priority to some forms of volunteering over other kinds and some kinds of volunteers rather than others; and its actions can – by design or inadvertence – either make volunteering easier to access and more attractive or put barriers in the way of involvement.

In this chapter, we will discuss these ways in which the state can shape voluntary action and identify some of the possible consequences of government involvement with volunteering. Having completed the agenda of key problem areas, we will then consider the role that government can best play in encouraging or promoting voluntary action and make suggestions about what the state should and, more important, what it should not do. The chapter ends with a discussion of the grounds on which the world of voluntary action can challenge or resist government influence, including the need for independent and representative institutions and the possible role of research in forming their own agendas. Before turning to the key problems as we see them, however, we need to look at the overarching debate about the relationship between the state, civil society and democracy.

The state, civil society and democracy

In the absence of a body of theory about the relationship between volunteering and the state and its implications for democracy, we can look at the debate about the role and importance of civil society. While the idea of civil society overlaps with the concept of volunteering in associations, it is not an exact match; it excludes volunteering in statutory agencies (and in the private sector) and is of limited relevance to volunteering within the non-profit paradigm we have discussed in Chapter 2 and elsewhere in this book. However, it provides, as Davis Smith (2001/2007) has pointed out, a useful starting point for a wider view of the role of volunteering in its social and political context. It might help us to address the challenge identified by Nicholas Deakin (2007: p. iv):

> Despite the important gains that have been made, it is not hard to see problems ahead in the ways in which relationships between state and citizen are being reformulated and the tensions that are bound to develop if civil society's independence is to be protected.

In Davis Smith's summary, the argument for a direct link between volunteering and democracy rests on three legs. In the first place, people are more likely to participate in the political process if they have been involved in volunteering: 'volunteering is a nursery for citizenship' (p. 22). Second, voluntary agencies which involve volunteers offer spaces and opportunities for engagement which are wider in scope and more varied than political parties; they constitute 'an alternative political world' and 'an essential counter-balance to the power of the state' (ibid.). Third, volunteering contributes to democracy by helping to build up trust and reciprocity. While this thesis has been widely accepted since the work of De Tocqueville in the mid-19th century, there are a number of significant criticisms that cast doubt on its validity. On one front, it has been attacked for ignoring the dissident nature of much voluntary action; it has 'glossed over the essential element of conflict which lies at the heart of the civil society/state relationship' (ibid.). As well as this concentration on consensus, the neo-De Tocquevillian approach also fails to take account of the differences between volunteer-involving organisations; they do not all build trust across communities and the extent to which they allow or enable volunteers to exercise initiative and responsibility. A second line of criticism is to argue that history simply does not support the theory. There is no simple relationship between democracy and a strong civil society as illustrated by the examples of Germany, where the Nazis came to power in an environment where civil society was healthy, and Spain, where democracy has flourished despite the weakness of its civil society institutions.

The state and volunteering

How can this debate help us to understand the relationship between the state and volunteering? It suggests that we should look elsewhere than the desire to create and maintain a healthy democratic society to find a rationale for the government's interest in promoting volunteering. In the first place, the critics have argued that there is no clear link between the policy and its expected outcome. Second, it might lead to unexpected and unwanted consequences as government discovers that voluntary action may provide barriers to the implementation of public policy as well as assisting the state to achieve its ends. Ministers have spoken about the importance of voluntary organisations as advocates and campaigners – 'the thorn in the side of Government and the establishment' as David Milliband (2006) described them. He also praised the role of community groups in 'strengthening the bonds between people of similar faith, ethnicities and interests, and building the bridges between them' (ibid.).

It is, however, hard to find evidence that the expressed willingness of government to tolerate, let alone support, organisations and their volunteer leaders and activists is translated into action. In fact, the perceived threat to independent action by local organisations such as advice centres has led to the formation of a National Coalition for Independent Action which describes itself as 'an alliance of organisations and individuals who have come together out of frustration and anger to object to the state of UK Voluntary and Community Sectors. We believe there is a crisis in our ability to act independently from Government and other powerful interests, and to be part of the checks we need within our democracy' (www.independentaction.net). And the members of the Coalition tend to be drawn from the mainstream of the voluntary and community sector rather than what might be seen as the wilder fringes of civil society where groups like *Plane Stupid* are to be found.

Why else might government support and encourage volunteering? One possibility is that they are motivated by its intrinsic value. The Commission on the Future of Volunteering (2008: p. 2) based its Manifesto on its 'vision of a society in which we enrich our own lives by enriching the lives of others' and wanted to 'see a society where not volunteering would be seen as missing out on something that was life enhancing, enjoyable and useful'. While many of the Commission's recommendations were accepted by government, it is by no means clear that this vision was the key that unlocked the door to increased state funding for voluntary action. Wearing another hat as the government's volunteering champion, Baroness Neuberger, the Commission's chair, had also produced a review of volunteering in the public services which suggested that there was 'much potential to expand volunteering in health and social care to create more people-centred services, and a better understanding of service users' (Neuberger, 2008).

This finding tends to suggest that the government's interest in volunteering may be largely instrumental; rather than valuing voluntary action as a means of strengthening the democratic institutions of civil society or because of its intrinsic value the state views volunteering as a means of helping it to achieve its public and social policy goals. At various times, volunteering has been hailed as a means of addressing a whole series of social needs including providing diversionary activities for disruptive young people, offering a way of occupying the enforced leisure time of the unemployed and helping them find their way back into paid work, addressing the social isolation and health needs of older people and helping under-achieving school children (these initiatives are discussed in more detail in Chapter 7). As Sheard (1995: p. 116) commented, '[O]ne might almost say that successive governments have seen in volunteering a panacea for whatever society's current ills happen to be'.

Whatever is driving the government's engagement with volunteering, it is generally assumed that its interest is benign. This would not necessarily be the case in other societies where the state and civil society may be mutually suspicious and even hostile. Part of the explanation for this general climate may lie with the nature of the legal system. English Common Law is based on the principle that citizens are free to take any action – including setting up an association or society – which has not been specifically forbidden by the laws of the country. Other legal systems, by contrast, are based on the very different principle that the law defines what may be done as well as what may not. In countries where this system applies, the right to form association is conferred by statutes which may place restrictions or conditions on the exercise of that right. The British assumption that the state's interest in voluntary action is benign is not universally held. In his address to the National Council of Voluntary Organisations, David Milliband (who was then the Minister with responsibility for the sector) accepted that there were two schools of thought about how to tackle 'the power gap' in British society: 'in one corner are those who argue that the third sector thrives as an alternative to Government action, and on the other are those who believe that the third sector thrives in partnership with Government, not at its expense.' In addition, the Government's motives have been questioned by Andy Benson, one of the founders of the National Coalition for Independent Action. Speaking at a symposium at Roehampton University in 2007, he suggested that we should 'mistrust the State' and went on to say that 'this...may be the actual real indicator that sorts out how different people approach these issues. Do you see the state as benign, ethical, responsible and competent – there to act in the interests of the people? Or do you see the State as oppressive, repressive, willing to act outside of respectable values, incompetent and acting in the interests of political and bureaucratic elites and their associates outside of government?' (Benson, 2007).

In this remark, Benson is raising the issue of the state's competence as well as its trustworthiness in its dealing with civil society. The evidence suggests that government initiatives to foster and promote volunteering have been, at best, of limited success. Davis Smith's (1999) judgement on the Major Government's ambitious *Make A Difference* programme can be applied with equal justice to the series of initiatives taken by New Labour since 1997: 'its failures were due to a combination of insufficient resourcing, lack of strategic thinking and inability to translate high strategy into workable solutions on the ground' (p. 19). However, we also need to clarify what we mean by the state. Throughout this book, we have emphasised the heterogeneity of voluntary action and, by the same token, we need to acknowledge the variety of ways in which the state manifests itself nationally and locally – and, more recently, regionally. This case has been put with his usual elegance by Nicholas Deakin in response to Frank Prochaska's claim that voluntary organisations were swimming into the mouth of Leviathan: 'striking though this phrase may be, it is in some important respects misleading: Government is no longer, if it ever was, a single marine monster but a shoal of smaller beasts' (Deakin, 2006: p. 8).

The key issues

In this section, we turn from a general consideration of the relationship between the state and voluntary action to focus on a series of concrete issues where we perceive there to be a threat of government encroachment on the autonomy of volunteering.

The threat of compulsion

The most immediate or direct challenge is the possibility of government making some forms of volunteering compulsory. What Kearney (2001/2007) has called 'mandated volunteering' is not uncommon in the United States and Canada. The main focus is on the involvement of young people in 'community service' and the creation of a link between academic learning and the involvement of students in their local community in the form of service learning. This is defined by Learn and Serve (America's Most Comprehensive Service-Learning Resource) as 'a teaching and learning strategy that integrates meaningful community service with instruction and reflection to enrich the learning experience, teach civic responsibility, and strengthen communities' (http://www.servicelearning.org/). While much service learning is voluntary – one option among a number of possible courses of study – some US states and school districts and at least one Canadian province have made it compulsory in schools and colleges and, in some cases, have made it a condition of graduation. In Ontario, for example, high school students undertake 40 hours of compulsory community service as part of the requirements for achieving their Secondary School Diploma (Kearney, 2001/2007).

Kearney (2001/2007: p. 10) points out that 'voluntary or community youth service has not, of course, been mandated in the UK' and the government has put its emphasis on programmes like *Millennium Volunteers* which 'build on young people's interests and aspire to meet what they want out of volunteering'. Strictly speaking, that may well have been accurate at the time of writing, but, as Davis Smith (2001/2007: p. 26) has pointed out, the degree of coercion involved in participation in the subbotnik is not so very much greater than 'in a present day school-based community service programme which requires students to volunteer as a core part of the curriculum'.

Successive UK governments have, it is true, fended off recurrent proposals or demands for a national scheme of community service for young people as a replacement for compulsory military service which was phased out in 1960. The most recent expression of this view formed part of the evidence collected by the Neuberger Commission (Gaskin et al., 2008: p. 50). '[Volunteering] should be compulsory for all 14 to 18 year olds before they do any other job and it should also be part of a university course'.

A more significant problem is contained in the Welfare Reform Bill which, at the time of writing (February 2009), had reached the committee stage and has been widely criticised as introducing 'workfare' into the United Kingdom's benefits system (see, for example, Bunting, 2009). The new Bill gives JobCentre staff enhanced powers to require claimants to undertake activities which are seen as paving the way back to employment and these include 'compulsory full-time community activities that will be exchanged for the pittance that is jobseekers' allowance' (Serwotka, 2009). The meaning of the term 'community service', moreover, is also becoming blurred. As well as referring to voluntary or mandatory service by young people, it is also applied to non-custodial sentences imposed by the criminal courts.

In sum, while compulsory or mandated volunteering is not a common feature in the United Kingdom, there is enough evidence of its introduction in some areas to raise issues about its potential for development and encroachment on the idea and the practice of voluntary action.

Government volunteerism

The second issue of concern is the potential for government to harness volunteering to its own policy objectives. There is, of course, nothing new or unusual about volunteering in the public sector; lay magistrates, special constables and prison visitors are a long-standing feature of the criminal justice system, and school governors claim to be the largest volunteer group in the United Kingdom (http://www.nga.org.uk). Moreover, as we have seen in a number of places in this book, it was the growing numbers of volunteers in the NHS and the social services departments of local authorities that led to the establishment of the Volunteer Centre UK (now VE) and the development of the new role of volunteer management.

Researchers belonging to the Association for Research on Nonprofit Organisations and Voluntary Action (ARNOVA) have, however, identified Government volunteers as one of the future growth points for volunteering (Rehnborg, 2005). Again, the evidence comes from North America – although the trend may be more widespread; Rehnborg quotes from a roundtable discussion which was part of the preparation for the UN IYV and concluded, *inter alia*, that volunteering must 'be recognised as a strategic resource which can be positively influenced by public policy' (Capeling-Alakija and Pennekam, 2000 quoted in Rehnborg, 2005). It is doubtful, however, that many other countries which participated in the UN year matched the history and scale of engagement with volunteers demonstrated by the United States's Federal Government.

What Rehnborg (p. 94) calls 'the ability of government to spur service initiatives' was originally demonstrated by President Kennedy's call for international service through participation in the Peace Corps which he established in 1961. Kennedy's initiative in involving volunteers in implementing his foreign policy and international development strategy was matched on the internal policy front by his successor, Lyndon Johnson, with the establishment in 1964 of VISTA – Volunteers in Service to America – as part of his War on Poverty programme. More recently, the Clinton presidency consolidated a number of different sets of work, expertise and resources into the Corporation for National and Community Service whose activities were subsequently streamed into three major programmes – *AmeriCorps* which was a network of volunteers helping to meet critical needs in education, public safety, health and the environment; *SeniorCorps* – which was designed to mobilise older people as volunteers; and *Learn and Serve America* which promotes service learning.

Significant though these programmes are, they are dwarfed by the scope and complexity of the initiative launched by George W. Bush in the wake of the terrorist attacks of 11th November 2001. The *USA Freedom Corps* is an umbrella programme which took in the earlier initiatives and added a range of new activities. The programme is very ambitious. Rehnborg (2005: p. 102) uses the words of the Department for Homeland Security to describe it as 'designed to "inspire and enable all Americans to find ways to serve their community, their country or the world"' with a mission which 'asks every American to donate 4,000 hours of service across his or her life span'.

Setting the volunteering agenda

The investment of successive American presidents in government-led programmes of community service and the lack of any comparable activity in the United Kingdom present something of a paradox. One would have expected programmes of this kind to find more fertile ground in Britain, where the state has a history of collaboration with and mutual respect for voluntary action, than in the United States where any extension of the government role – especially at Federal level – tends to be met with suspicion. Rather than establishing programmes which involve volunteers in addressing public policy goals, the British government has preferred to influence the volunteering agenda while remaining at arms length from its implementation. As we have seen in Chapter 7, the government's priorities for voluntary action have been expressed through a series of funding programmes which have targeted specific groups of potential volunteers (such as young people, older people and students in higher education) and, occasionally, certain kinds of volunteering (such as a brief but intense flirtation with mentoring in the early years of the 21st century). The majority of these funding opportunities have been directed to existing organisations although both the Experience Corps and v were new voluntary sector 'independent' bodies albeit with significant government investment.

There is a good deal of disquiet and criticism about these initiatives on the part of people who manage and staff both volunteering infrastructure bodies, especially local volunteer centres, and volunteer-involving organisations. These feelings were reflected in the evidence collected by the Neuberger Commission (Gaskin et al., 2008). Some of the criticisms have focused on the short-term nature of the funding for government initiatives and others have been prompted by what is seen as the duplication of effort created by the establishment of new mechanisms for delivering them. At the heart of the unease, however, is the feeling that priorities are being imposed on them from government bodies which are out of touch with what is happening and with what is needed at local level where most volunteering takes place. One informant told the Commission that 'government should stop inventing new volunteering schemes and support existing organisations and infrastructure. The sector already knows what it is doing and should be trusted to get on with it' (Gaskin et al., 2008: p. 119).

Creating the environment for voluntary action

Those giving evidence to the Commission were also concerned about the ways in which the activities of government could work against their expressed policy of support for volunteering by creating an unhelpful environment. There has been a long-standing issue about the implementation of Benefits legislation with local officials advising claimants that volunteering might mean that they were unavailable for work and thus not entitled to benefits despite clear statements to the contrary at national level. More recently, the issue of criminal record checks has been a bone of contention. The evidence suggest, however, that the – largely unintended – barriers in the way of people engaging in volunteering are more numerous and more widespread. One example was the impact on purely voluntary groups and especially those involved in sport and recreation of regulatory measures which seemed disproportionate: '[H]ow can a local group interested in sports facilities on an inner city estate be expected to provide accounts that would satisfy Ernst and Young?' (Gaskin et al., 2008: p. 120). More generally, informants complained that 'regulatory bodies seem incapable of taking volunteering into account and seem keen to pass yet more regulations which effectively stop or severely curtail established volunteer activities, even when such activities have not resulted in any significant problems in the past' (ibid.). Similarly, associational activities have been affected by government policies which expect local authorities to charge market rents for the use of the meeting rooms that groups need and by the selling off or privatisation of school playing fields and other community facilities.

Respondents to the Commission on the Future of Volunteering's call for evidence identified two underlying explanations for these problems. In the first place, they suggested that government officials did not have an adequate 'understanding of volunteering and the settings in which it took place' and needed to 'increase their awareness of how volunteering is distinct from paid work, and how the contribution of volunteers actually works in practice' (ibid.: p. 115). Second, they felt that government lacked a strategic approach to volunteering. One large volunteer-involving organisation wanted to see 'a coherent overarching strategy relating to volunteering. We have seen initiatives that target specific groups, but these seemed to operate in isolation' while others suggested the need for 'greater coherence and consistency across government on volunteering issues' (ibid.: p. 114).

What government should – or should not – do?

What role, then, should government play? For the veteran academic and social commentator, Ralf Dahrendorf, the issue was straightforward; a healthy democracy depends on a vigorous volunteering sector that is independent of the state and that excludes volunteering not only in the public sector but also in voluntary agencies supported by government funding (Darhendorf, 2001). The official policy of the Conservative opposition is less radical but nonetheless starts from the injunction borrowed from the doctors' Hippocratic oath – 'first, do no harm' (Conservative Party, 2008: p. 8). Government policy should not 'attempt to compel volunteering' but to 'encourage, invest and, where necessary, simply get out of the way' (ibid.: p. 20). In practice, this stance will lead to two kinds of action. In the first place, the Conservatives pledge that they will 'make it simpler and easier to volunteer by tackling the regulatory obstacles which deter new volunteers' and 'act to dispel the confusion surrounding the benefits system so that no one is wrongly advised not to engage in community work or dissuaded by their own misunderstandings' (p. 8). Second, they will radically change the way volunteering is funded by government by 'directing support to grass-roots volunteering organisations, not quangos set up by Ministers' and supporting the development of 'new volunteer-led organisations where none previously existed' (p. 20).

Other – less minimalist – views about what government should – and should not – do have been developed in connection with the 2001 UN IYV (Davis Smith, 2000; Dingle and Heath, 2001; IAVE, 2001) by Kearney (2001/2007) and by the Commission on the Future of Volunteering (2008). There is a considerable measure of agreement between these prescriptions, but there is a clear divergence between those who, like the present-day British Conservative Party, emphasis the importance of non-interference in what should be an independent sphere of activity and others who favour a more strategic role for the state. On the one hand, the executive coordinator of the UN Volunteers at the time of IYV, Sharon Capeling-Alakija, has pointed out the danger of governments' trying to control volunteering and argued that 'in many cases the most important thing that governments can do is to get out of the way' (quoted by Kearney, 2001/2007: p. 14).

On the other hand, in his important review of the thinking behind the IYV, Davis Smith (2000) puts his trust in a 'healthy partnership between volunteering and the state' and called on the state to, inter alia, develop a strategic approach, raise public awareness, promote youth volunteering and promote private sector support. The Parliamentary Hearings organised in the United Kingdom as part of the IYV also produced a call for 'a strategic policy framework' (as well as the need to 'proof' legislation and policy against an unhelpful impact on volunteering), while the Neuberger Commission (2008: p. 32) felt that Government's contributions could include 'setting the strategic direction' and called for responsibility for volunteering to be vested in a minister of cabinet rank and a parliamentary select committee.

IAVE's Universal Declaration on Volunteering (2001 quoted by Kearney, 2001/2007: p. 13) sidesteps the issue by calling on governments

> to ensure the rights of all people to volunteer, to remove an legal barriers to participation, to engage volunteers in its work, and to provide

resources for NGOs to promote and support the effective mobilization and management of volunteers.

Having reviewed the various perspectives, Kearney (2001/2007: p. 15) concludes that 'the role of government should be to enable and encourage but not to regulate or control' volunteering and lists four key functions:

1. To uphold the values and principles of volunteering by 'proofing' legislative and policy developments and respecting the independence of voluntary action; any action to be taken by government should be subject to prior scrutiny to ensure that it will not have a negative impact on volunteering.
2. To create a policy, legislative and fiscal environment that promotes volunteering and recognises its economic, social, cultural and economic impact; this would also involve identifying and taking action to remove barriers to engagement in voluntary action.
3. To provide funding to support and sustain the volunteering infrastructure at local, regional and national level, to develop new approaches to volunteering and to commission research (the clear implication here is that the agendas will be driven by volunteer-involving organisations and the agencies that support them); and
4. To foster partnerships with the other sectors and the media through which to promote volunteering; these should be based on two principles: first, there are a wide range of interested parties with a role to play and, second, these partnerships should be designed to incorporate in their work the values and principles of volunteering.

Holding government to account

Whether we remain suspicious of the state and seek to restrict its role vis-à-vis volunteering to a minimum or embrace the idea of working in partnership with government, we can see the need for institutions which can hold the government to account and represent the views of volunteer-involving organisations. Curiously, this issue does not merit a mention in the Manifesto of the Commission on the Future of Volunteering even though the Commission had been brought into being by an organisation – the England Volunteering Development Council (EVDC) – which had been set up in 2004 to provide 'a high-level representative and advocacy mechanism for volunteering'. It is noteworthy that the Manifesto looks at the local bodies that might represent the interests of volunteers and volunteering as 'infrastructure' bodies, emphasizing their role in providing support and services to volunteer-involving organisations rather than representing their interests. In the process, it ignores the evidence it collected which includes mixed messages about how respondents viewed the representation of volunteering to government and suggestions about why it was limited in scope and impact (Gaskin et al., 2008).

The evidence suggests that, at local level, volunteer centres rarely act as representatives of volunteering largely because they focus on their primary function of promoting and brokering opportunities for volunteering and also because their resources are limited. Respondents' views of representation at national level were more mixed. A minority felt that bodies such as VE were out of touch with local concerns and too close to government. Others – and especially those from national volunteer-involving agencies – felt that the performance of national infrastructure bodies had improved. Respondents generally welcomed the establishment of the EVDC but felt that its role was, as yet, under-developed. More generally, those who gave evidence highlighted the problems of representation at both local and national level. In the first place, the second-tier bodies lacked the capacity to engage with the full gamut of volunteer-involving bodies and, second, the sheer diversity of voluntary action made it almost impossible to represent its interests and its views. One respondent underlined this point: 'it would be a mistake for government to seek some overarching body that could claim [to represent the sector] ... such a creature would be anathema to the spirit of voluntary action' (Gaskin et al., 2008: p. 113).

Conclusion

In this chapter, we have discussed the extent to which government might offer a threat to the independence of volunteering. We have identified four ways in which the action of the state might encroach on this independence. The first of these – the introduction of compulsion for some 'volunteers' – is established in the United States and Canada and is beginning to take its place in the United Kingdom. The second – government-sponsored volunteering – is, paradoxically, a major feature of the volunteering landscape in the United States but not – at least yet – in Britain. The British Government has preferred to set the volunteering agenda by prioritising specific groups and launching a series of special initiatives – our third example of encroachment on the autonomy of voluntary action. Finally, we highlight the – often unintended – impact of a variety of government actions which otherwise appear unrelated to volunteering.

Discussion of these four concrete 'threats' to volunteering's independence has been set in the context of some wider theories about the relationship between the state, civil society and democracy and some different perspectives on the nature of state power. In addition, it has led in turn to a review of the optimal role of the state vis-à-vis volunteering and the divide between those who embrace a relationship based on partnership on the one hand and those who would prefer a government approach founded on benign neglect. In either case, the ability of the world of volunteering to form an appropriate relationship with government is seriously weakened by the absence of strong representative institutions. In the circumstances, the threat to the autonomy of voluntary action is very real and offers a major challenge to all those who value volunteering's independence.

16
Defending the Spirit of Volunteering from Formalisation

Introduction

We began this book by discussing the diversity of volunteering, the variety of forms that it takes, the range of people that get involved, and the multitude of motivations that they have for doing so. Subsequent chapters have noted that volunteering has gone through something of a transformation in recent years. One of the most profound set of changes to affect volunteering has been those caused by the process of formalisation. Despite the diversity of volunteering and those who engage in it, the process of formalisation and its impacts appear, at least on the surface, to be widespread.

Chapter 11's discussion of volunteer management highlighted the increasing implementation of 'modern' (Zimmeck, 2001) or 'top-down' (Holmes, 2003) techniques for organising the work of volunteers. This approach to volunteer management is one of the key symptoms of the process of formalisation, which this chapter will critically examine. The chapter will provide a brief definition of formalisation; explore the forces, or 'drivers' for formalising volunteering; highlight the symptoms and manifestations of a more formal view of voluntary action; and assess its impact on the ways in which volunteering is understood, organised and experienced.

Defining formalisation and its key drivers

Formalisation can be characterised as the process by which voluntary sector agencies have adopted the organisational norms and ways of working more traditionally associated with their private and public sector counterparts. These include an instrumental and rational approach to their 'business', which is driven primarily by market values; clear lines of authority and accountability; and a heavy focus on 'business practices' such as performance monitoring. Indeed, it has been argued that this has happened to such a degree that it is now hard to tell which sector some organisations come from (see, for example, Harris and Rochester, 2001b). As Harris et al. (2001: p. 4) put it,

> [C]ommercial business practices became the preferred model for managing all organizations, irrespective of sector, and voluntary organizations were expected to demonstrate that they were 'business-like' if they wanted to participate in the social policy market-place. (Harris et al., 2001: p. 4)

The factors driving formalisation are well rehearsed. Welfare pluralism, in which government has repositioned itself as 'facilitator' and/or 'regulator' of services and in which voluntary organisations have been recast as providers and contractors alongside public and private sector organisation, has been a major driver. More specifically, within this hegemonic repositioning of the sector, the rise of competitive funding, tightly defined contracts and the subsequent introduction of performance measurement and regulation have led to formalisation (Harris, 2001). These developments have affected the ways in which third sector organisation structure themselves and organise their volunteers.

With particular implications for volunteering and volunteers, contract funding has brought with it new concerns for both the quality and quantity of services provided, many of which have traditionally been provided by volunteers. While this has implications for all sector workers, it has particular implications for volunteers and the ways in which their work is organised as it is apparent that there is often an underlying concern that volunteers may somehow not be up to the job or at least a more risky proposition for the delivery of tightly defined, output-driven and monitored contracts (Holmes, 2003). At best, this has led to the introduction of some fairly heavy-handed, formalised, management techniques implemented in an effort to 'control' volunteers, define their roles, and meet expected standards (Guirguis-Younger et al., 2005; Holmes, 2003). At worst, it has led to the replacement of volunteers by paid staff within voluntary organisations (Billis and Harris, 1992; Cloke et al., 2007; Elstub, 2006).

Associated with these developments are increasing levels of regulation and demands for accountability; both of which tend to lead to more formal processes, required at least in terms of monitoring activities in order to be able to report on them. More broadly, the growing concern for risk aversion and the associated rise of risk management witnessed across society has also been a key driver of formalisation in volunteering (Gaskin, 2005). Beyond the rise of service delivery and commissioning associated with welfare pluralism, funding for volunteering itself has also led to changes. Since the 1980s, the rise of government initiatives centred on funding organisations to recruit and involve volunteers, as discussed in Chapter 7, has brought stringent reporting criteria. This in turn has reinforced the pressure for formalisation already affecting volunteering.

Volunteers, and their managers, have also been instrumental in the process. Many volunteer managers, for example, have been keen to adopt a more professional and formal approach to their work. One study found that 84 per cent of volunteer managers thought that professionalising their role would give their work status, 73 per cent thought that it would give confidence to funders and 61 per cent thought it would inspire public confidence (Gay, 2000). In turn, volunteers in the 1980s and 1990s were beginning to demand that their 'work' was better 'organised' and more 'professional' in order to tackle issues that they had experienced such as boredom, poor use of their time and skill, overload and lack of appreciation (Davis Smith, 1998; Gaskin, 2003; Gay, 2000; Social and Community Planning Research, 1990).

The development of the 'volunteering industry'

The mid-90s onwards has seen growing institutional support for volunteering. This has come from government and from an increasingly prominent volunteering 'infrastructure'.

Co-opting volunteering

As Chapters 7 and 15 have discussed, the UK government has paid increasing attention to volunteering. Much of its attention has focused on the supply side of volunteering – getting more people and, in particular, a more diverse range of people to volunteer. This has two particular implications: organisations and governments, need to be able to count volunteers. How else would they know if they have recruited more or made their volunteer base more diverse? They also need to be able to monitor and review their activities, outputs and outcomes in order to be able to answer the strict monitoring criteria placed on grants. Both lead to the instigation of more formal systems, procedures and ways of working.

Recent years have also seen some attention paid to the demand side of volunteering – the need for and appropriate involvement of volunteers. The Office of the Third Sector's GoldStar programme, for example, has been concerned with the development and implementation of good practice in volunteer management. In particular, it has sought to disseminate information on the implementation of 'good' management in the involvement of 'hard to reach' groups of volunteers. While this shift is something that has been encouraged (by all of the authors of this book, as well as by many others) as part of the growing mantra of ensuring that organisations invest in their volunteers and manage them 'properly' (Neuberger, 2008), the thought put into establishing what this might mean in practice appears somewhat limited. This has given rise to a tendency of such programmes and policies to adopt a 'one size fits all' approach when it comes to volunteer management, with a seemingly unquestioned proliferation of the top-down, workplace or 'modern' model of volunteer management.

Indeed, across government volunteering policies in general, there has been a tendency to favour more formalised and 'sanitised' forms of volunteering – what Williams (2003a) has called a concentration on the third sector approach to volunteering at the expense of alternative 'fourth sector' models. All government funded volunteering initiatives bring with them requirements for reporting that inevitably reinforce, if not drive, the process of formalisation.

The rise of the infrastructure

Mirroring, or perhaps contributing to the growing involvement of government in volunteering, has been the emergence of an increasingly strong volunteering 'infrastructure'. At the national level in England, the Volunteer Centre was set up in 1973 partly in response to calls for better management and training of volunteers from the 1969 Aves Committee's report into the role of volunteers in social services. Its position was reinforced and its role broadened in light of the report of the 1978 Wolfenden Committee which called for a strengthening of national- and local-level 'intermediary' bodies and development agencies which would support and foster voluntary and community action while also providing an interface between the voluntary sector and government. Following a period of 'reconfiguration', change and merger, and now operating under the title of VE, the organisation has changed somewhat since its beginnings. It still, however, has the promulgation of 'good practice' and provision of information on volunteer management as two of its core aims. What is newer is the use of the term 'infrastructure' to describe its role.

The 'volunteering infrastructure' is a relatively new concept which seems to reflect the more industrial and bureaucratic notion of volunteering at the start of the 21st century. As a concept, it has largely replaced the notion of intermediaries or development agencies (a la Wolfenden). Although VE still describes itself as a national volunteer development agency, it is more often referred to as part of the volunteering, and/or voluntary sector, infrastructure. What is perhaps most notable about the national 'volunteering infrastructure' is that, along with government agendas, it has tended to be dominated by larger and more formal volunteer-involving organisations. The support it offers, the policies it instigates, the 'good practice' it promotes and, indeed, the research it commissions, all tend to favour a formalised approach to volunteering more akin to the service delivery and philanthropic models of volunteering than to alternative conceptualisations. It has only a residual resource for more informal and local forms of voluntary action. Indeed, it has been criticised as being remote from a significant part of its membership – local volunteer development agencies, most commonly referred to as volunteer centres.

The local 'volunteering infrastructure' has gone through a period of change in recent years, driven in part by national agendas. In 2004, for example, *Building on Success* was launched by VE as a ten-year strategy for the volunteering infrastructure (Penberthy and Forster, 2004). Integral to *Building on Success* was a call for 'reconfiguration', the introduction of a common set of six core functions, the introduction of common branding across the Volunteer Centre network, the development of a quality assurance scheme – the Volunteer Centre Quality Accreditation framework (see http://www.volunteering.org.uk/WhatWeDo/Local+and+Regional/Volunteer+Centre+Quality+Accreditation.htm). The strategy referred to all levels of the volunteering infrastructure (national, regional and local), yet its messages were largely focused on, and its impact felt at, the local level. The government's ChangeUp programme (see Chapter 7) has further reinforced calls for 'reconfiguration' and 'modernisation' of the volunteering infrastructure. Together, these agendas have attempted to standardise and formalise the local volunteering infrastructure and in turn have had a similar effect on volunteering itself.

Perhaps one of the most significant developments at the local level has been a move to refocus efforts from a concentration on the brokerage of volunteering opportunities which has been the volunteer centres' core role, to a broader range of functions (see Penberthy and Forster, 2004). The volunteering infrastructure is seeking to position itself as the voice of volunteering at national and local level. It is also increasingly concerned with supporting volunteer-involving organisations in the development of new volunteering opportunities and the implementation of good practice volunteer management. Again, however, there is often a tendency to focus on a narrow concept of volunteering within this. Through such functions then, at national and local level (some of which are discussed below), the volunteer infrastructure has arguably been one of the key drivers of formalisation and standardisation in volunteering.

The volunteer-management profession

In 1963, the first paid volunteer manager was employed in an NHS hospital in Cambridge (Gay, 2000). By 1980, the role had been explored in at least two key committees (the Taylor Committee and Aves Working Party, both of 1976 – see Gay, 2000), and there were reported to be 1,027 paid volunteer coordinator positions in local authority Social Service Departments and the NHS alone (The Volunteer Centre, 1980 quoted in Gay, 2000), with coordinating volunteers increasingly coming to be seen as an occupation in its own right (Gay and Pitkeathley, 1982). They have since become commonplace across both the NHS and the third sector. By 2007, it was reported that over two-fifths (43 per cent) of employers in the third sector had at least one member of paid staff undertaking a volunteer-management function (Clark, 2007).

Along with the growth in numbers of volunteer managers, there has been the move towards professionalising the role, although there is no agreement on how far this should go (Gay, 2000). An increasing range of training is available for volunteer managers, some of which is formally accredited. A 2006 National Training Strategy for Volunteer Managers, for example, led to the establishment a year later of the Excellence in Volunteer Management programme by VE (www.volunteering.org.uk/Resources/EVM/). National Occupation Standards have also been developed for volunteer managers, first in 2003 and revised in 2008. Then, with its origins in a loose network of volunteer managers set up in the 1990s by the National Centre for Volunteering (now VE), 2007 saw the launch of the Association of Volunteer Managers (AVM). AVM now has over 100 members. (At the same time, however, it is worth noting that the Scottish Association for Volunteer Management closed in 2008.)

Despite these developments, volunteer management often remains a relatively low status, poorly paid role within the third sector. Indeed, responsibility for managing volunteers is often something that is tagged onto someone's job, rather than a position or specified responsibility in its own right (Stuart and Ellis Paine, 2008). Only half of volunteer managers have been trained in managing volunteers (ibid.). Further, whether the available training and guidance (see below) is enough to equip volunteer managers with the fine balance of formal management skills with experience, networking, peer support, flexibility and inclusivity which is recognised as essential for the position (Gay, 2000) is questionable.

The road to quality standards in volunteer management

The origins of set guidelines on the management of volunteers has been traced by Gay (2000) back to two handbooks, both launched in 1971, which outlined the key tasks required of those managing volunteers in hospital. Such guidance documents, or good practice handbooks, have since proliferated (see, for example, Ellis, 2002; Fryer et al., 2007; Graff, 2005; McCurley and Lynch, 1998). Many of these documents have been imported wholesale from the United States. An indication of the current demand for guidance for volunteer management is the 30,000 visitors that VE's online Good Practice Bank received in 2007/2008. It is one of several online volunteer-management resource repositories. The number of guidance documents available, online and otherwise, makes the standardisation and subsequent formalisation of volunteering promulgated through them particularly powerful. As Chapter 11 discusses, these practices are now commonplace across volunteer-involving organisations.

In line with the 'quality movement', which has swept through all sectors and has seen increasing use of quality systems, or kite marks, such as Investors in People and Practical Quality Assurance System for Small Organisations (PQASSO) (see, for example, Centre for Voluntary Action Research, 2004), the volunteering sector has developed its own quality standard which can be seen as part of the trend towards embedding modern management practices. IiV was piloted in the 1990s by the local volunteering infrastructure in England and later developed by the national infrastructure, with a UK-wide launch in 2004. By mid-2008, it had been awarded to over 200 organisations (Stuart and Ellis Paine, 2008; and see Centre for Voluntary Action Research, 2006 for a review of IiV and its impacts).

What difference does it make?

Little has been done to systematically test how effective this more formalised approach to volunteering is and what its relative benefits or costs are. Indeed, the relative advantages and disadvantages of formalisation may depend upon the perspective from which we view them. The development of role descriptions for volunteers, for example, typifies a more formal approach to volunteering. According to volunteer managers, they delineate volunteer activities, give clarity and transparency, and make the role more manageable for individual volunteers:

> In the volunteer management profession, there is universal agreement that volunteers deserve written job descriptions. Such descriptions clarify roles and differentiate what volunteers do from what employees do. (Ellis, 1996: p. 88 quoted in Brudney, 2000)

Volunteers, however, are less convinced. In one study, a majority of volunteers (65 per cent) thought that having a written role description was *not* a good thing: they felt it would make their volunteering too rigid and formal and, frankly, too much like paid work (Low et al., 2007).

In the remainder of this section, we review some of the available evidence that has pointed to the positive benefits that formalisation has brought about for volunteers. We then go on to explore some of the more critical findings.

The good

Formalisation has brought many positive developments. In terms of the introduction of new management practices, for example, many of the formal, modern management mechanisms have been found to lead to better outcomes. Brudney (2000), for example, identifies 17 volunteer-management mechanisms, all but three of which were reported by volunteer coordinators to be associated with positive programme outcomes. Volunteer managers have argued that volunteers are comfortable with a more formalised approach (Gay, 2000) and, indeed, feedback from volunteers themselves confirms that there is a general consensus that things have improved. In 1997, 70 per cent of volunteers in England report that their volunteering could be better organised (Davis Smith, 1998). By 2006, this had fallen to 31 per cent (Low et al., 2007). Data from the same sources also found that fewer volunteers thought that volunteering took up too much of their time (down from 31 per cent to 13 per cent). By providing clarity in terms of rights and responsibilities, the boundaries of a role and expectations, for example, the formalisation associated with the introduction of volunteer-management practices can increase confidence among volunteers and reduce the risk of burn out or exploitation (see, for example, Musick and Wilson, 2008; Russell and Scott, 1997).

It could also be argued that a more formalised approach has opened up access to certain volunteer roles. Keeping better records on volunteers has made it possible to undertake a more careful analysis of who does and who does not volunteer within organisations. This, coupled with a more general growing recognition of the need to diversify participation, led to an attempt by a number of organisations to tackle barriers to involvement (see Chapter 14 and also below for counter arguments).

The bad

Despite these positive developments associated with formalisation, other studies have failed to find a positive link between more formal volunteer-management practices and positive outcomes. One review concluded,

> The research on organisational effectiveness in [sports] clubs could not conclude that formalising volunteer management reduced problems associated with volunteers. It found no significant relationship between having a volunteer coordinator and experiencing fewer problems with volunteer recruitment, management and overload. And it found examples of informal clubs which had successfully avoided these problems. (Taylor et al., 2007)

Others have gone further, suggesting that such processes are actually having a negative impact on volunteering. The growing bureaucracy associated with formalisation and the introduction of 'modern' top-down management techniques has received some of the loudest shouts of protest from volunteers (Gaskin, 2003, 2008). In one study, one-quarter of volunteers said there was too much bureaucracy associated with their roles (Low et al., 2007). Participants have complained that volunteering was becoming too much like paid work (Low et al., 2007; Zimmeck, 2001). Defining roles, formalising processes and standardising practices have, in many organisations, led to a loss of informality, flexibility, innovation, creativity, spontaneity, autonomy, and social interaction among volunteers (Hutchison and Ockenden, 2008; Guirguis-Younger et al., 2005). All too often, there has been a move away from volunteers and paid staff working collaboratively and sharing power and decision-making; autonomy among volunteers has given way to the implementation of objectives by volunteers through carefully defined and delineated tasks specified and controlled by paid staff.

For some, these changes are alienating (Leonard et al., 2004). They have led some volunteers to question their ongoing involvement.

Some have simply voiced concerns while others have voted with their feet and left. They are also inhibiting potential new volunteers from getting involved. Indeed, it seems that concerns about formalisation, bureaucracy and the like are even more off-putting to potential volunteers than they are to existing ones (Machin and Ellis Paine, 2008b). One study found that half of those people who were not volunteering but who would be interested in doing so had been put off by too much bureaucracy (Low et al., 2007). Other studies have suggested that these changes are likely to be particularly off-putting to the very groups that many organisations and government initiatives are currently seeking to involve through their diversity drives (Gaskin, 2003; IVR, 2004a; Rochester and Grotz, 2006; Scott and Russell, 2001; Weeks et al., 1996).

The ugly

We have argued above that formalisation has been both good and bad for volunteering. The evidence we have to drawn on, however, as with many other chapters in the book, is disproportionately weighted to volunteers within service delivery roles and more specifically to volunteers undertaking such roles within paid staff-led organisations. The implementation of formal 'modern' volunteer-management practices is more extensive in larger organisations (Machin and Ellis Paine, 2008a). While studies have identified examples of organisations that have resisted these trends (Ockenden and Hutin, 2008), formalisation processes are nevertheless affecting volunteering across the board. It is when we consider the implications for volunteering in its more diverse forms, within smaller, volunteer-led organisations, for example, or within mutual aid and campaigning groups, that we see the potential for an even more corrosive effect.

Some have argued that the promotion of some forms of volunteering, particularly that which is dominant in service delivery organisations, by government (and others) has been done at the expense of other more informal types of volunteering (see, for example, Williams, 2003a,b). In Canada, it has been suggested that government promotion of volunteering has reinforced the concept of volunteering as benevolence and social control and undermined its ability to lead to social change and democracy (Arai, 2004). These broader developments are being reinforced by developments within volunteering that are serving to formalise activities.

To date, there has been little thought given to exploring and developing different models of supporting and organising volunteering. While it is frequently acknowledged within both practitioner and academic literature that one size does not fit all, there is little attention paid to what does work and when (see Chapter 11). The danger is that the formal approach to volunteer involvement associated with 'modern management' gets applied to volunteering in more settings than it is suitable for with the potential to change fundamentally the very nature of volunteering itself. In short, we are in danger of losing the spirit of volunteering and the creativity, sociability, and autonomy which underpin it. Adopting a far more formal approach to volunteering sees volunteering increasingly cast as an instrument of delivery, and volunteers as a resource to be used, rather than as stakeholders or co-owners.

There are additional implications. A growing number of studies have raised concerns about the change in the relationship between volunteers and services users brought on by processes of formalisation. As the emphasis has moved from a central concern for the relationship between volunteers and service users to a need to meet targets, from a concern to involve volunteers with personal experience to a need for qualifications, the types of volunteers getting involved has changed, and the ways in which they can work with clients have been curtailed. Some have gone as far as to argue that the greater the degree of formalisation, the less likely the volunteers is to offer the service user the type of support they most want or need (Guirguis-Younger et al., 2005).

A delicate balance, tipping the wrong way

Formalisation is changing the ways in which volunteering is organised and conceptualised. Ultimately, there is a real danger that too much formalisation will damage the spirit and characteristics of volunteering. We are already, for example, moving away from the notion that volunteers are involved in the identification of the 'problem' and its solution through creating their own roles and activities within and through organisations – instead, we are increasingly recruiting volunteers into pre-determined posts that often leave little scope for creativity or autonomy and within which the balance of power lies almost entirely with the organisation and its paid staff. By developing recruitment criteria for volunteer selection against those posts, we are moving away from the tradition of allowing everyone who wants to join in the opportunity to do so, towards a situation in which we screen for suitability, and it is seen as perfectly legitimate and even desirable to turn volunteers away. As a result, volunteer recruitment becomes far more selective (Scott and Russell, 2001; Weeks et al., 1996). We are also changing the relationship between volunteers and users; moving towards a quasi-professional service where volunteers are increasingly remote from those they 'serve' (Bondi, 2004; Guirguis-Younger et al., 2005; Weeks et al., 1996). These are real dangers which threaten the future of volunteering.

Even if these dangers do not reach full fruition, formalisation is already contributing to the development of a dominant paradigm in which volunteering is viewed as little more than a tool of service delivery. It favours some kinds of organisations and some forms of volunteering more than others; it suits some volunteers while excluding other potential participants. It is changing the nature of the volunteering experience, making it more work-like, more regulated, less fun, creative and sociable, reducing autonomy and curtailing power, while also making the time spent volunteering more containable, manageable, better organised and, arguably, fruitful.

Most of the evidence to date, however, seems to suggest that there is a need for a balance. Formalisation is not altogether a good or a bad thing. Too much can be problematic, but so too can too little (Musick and Wilson, 2008). As Gaskin (2003) put it, what is needed is a 'choice blend': 'The task for volunteer management is to find the right blend: for the organisation, combining choice, flexibility and organisation, to be experienced by the volunteer as a blend of informality and efficiency, personal and professional support' (p. 27). Volunteers want their volunteering to be well organised, but that does not mean being managed in a formal, bureaucratic or top-down way.

Two things, at the very least, however, need to happen before it is conceivable that we might achieve this choice blend. First, there is a need for better support for volunteer managers. When asked how they saw their roles, volunteer managers in one study were clear to say that it was less about managing in terms of regulating and being in charge but more about organising and ensuring that volunteers had a positive and enjoyable experience (Gay, 2000). This seems to fit well with what volunteers themselves see as the right approach. Volunteers talk about the importance of volunteer managers having the right attitudes, about personalities, expectations, outlooks, and interactions. It is about people, relationships and doing, not about theory, structure and formal mechanisms as promulgated through much volunteer-management literature. To date, much of the emphasis has been on the 'science' of volunteer management, rather than on the 'art' of volunteer involvement (Stuart and Ellis Paine, 2008). It is hard to see how this balance will be addressed, however, within the current climate in which volunteer managers are poorly paid, poorly trained, have a low status within organisations and generally lack the institutional support they need to undertake what is often a pivotal role and one which demands a choice blend of skills and aptitudes in order to deliver the choice blend of support required by volunteers and by the organisations that involve them (ibid.).

Second, there is an acute need to explore, develop and test out alternative models for organising, supporting and managing volunteers. Much more exploration is needed of 'what works' in different settings. We need to recognise the diversity not only in volunteering roles and participants but also in the ways in which volunteering is or should be organised. At present, it seems, there has been far too little consideration of alternative approaches. There has been little debate on how volunteers and paid staff should be managed differently (Zimmeck, 2001), and there has been even less on how different types of volunteers or volunteer roles should be 'managed' differently. Perhaps, the diversity of volunteering in itself makes it too difficult to consider the many different ways in which it might need to be organised and supported, but this seems a rather poor excuse when the potential consequences of not even trying are so dire.

17
Voluntary Action in the 21st Century

Introduction: the 'round-earth' map

We began this book by arguing that the way in which volunteering is commonly understood and discussed by practitioners, policy-makers and researchers – what we call the 'dominant paradigm' – is so narrow and inadequate as to resemble a 'flat-earth map' on which much of the terrain is 'dark matter'. From this perspective, volunteering is seen essentially as an activity which is motivated by altruism – the desire to help others less fortunate than oneself; which takes place in the broad area of social welfare – for the benefit of people 'in need'; which is organised by large, professionally staffed and formally structured organisations for which volunteers represent an additional resource; and which involves selection, induction and, possibly, training for specific and pre-determined roles or functions.

In order to highlight the limitations of this understanding of volunteering as service, we put forward two other perspectives – those of volunteering as activism and volunteering as serious leisure. In the first of these, the motivation to volunteer is rooted in self-help or mutual aid rather than in philanthropy; activities include mutual support, advocacy and campaigning; the organisational context is provided by 'grass-roots' associations with few, if any, paid staff; and volunteers (who undertake all or most of the activities of the organisation) shape their individual contributions over time and in the light of experience, personal growth and reflection.

In the second additional perspective, the rewards are intrinsic; volunteers are motivated by their enthusiasm for a specific kind of activity and the desire to acquire the expertise needed to practise it; the areas of interest are arts and culture and sports and recreation rather than social welfare; the organisational context is provided by a combination of small-scale community level associations and the much wider and more formal structures to which many of them are linked; there are a wide range of volunteering roles, including performers and practitioners, coaches and teachers, directors and conductors, match officials and judges, and those who undertake administrative and support functions.

Another way of exploring the limitations of the dominant paradigm is to look at the values which, it is argued, underpin volunteering. The general principles which Kearney (2001/2007) has drawn from a discussion of volunteering's value base add up to an emphatic statement that voluntary action is a great deal more heterogeneous and generally much less tidy than the picture provided by the dominant paradigm. At the centre of Kearney's credo is the argument that volunteering is essentially an act of free will or choice. While this principle is widely accepted, the extent to which there will be agreement on the implications that Kearney draws from it is less certain. Many will agree that the right to volunteer includes not only the right to choose the nature and kind of one's involvement but also the right not to participate at all. More controversial is his argument that volunteers are 'not biddable' and can legitimately act as 'mavericks' and his support for Stowe's (2001) view that volunteering can be 'untidy, uncoordinated, awkward and irresponsible'. Other principles which sit uncomfortably with the dominant paradigm are the inclusive nature of volunteering which implies, inter alia, that people can volunteer regardless of the kind and level of skills they have to offer and that it is not a gift but an exchange in which the volunteer not only contributes to the welfare of others but also derives benefits from his or her involvement.

Finally, we deployed a number of typologies of volunteering and volunteers to throw some light on the areas of 'dark matter' in the flat-earth map. We highlighted the global perspective of the typology developed for the UN IYV (Davis Smith, 2001) in which philanthropy and service to others takes its place alongside three other 'types of volunteer activity' which are self-help and mutual aid, participation in the political process – broadly defined – and advocacy and campaigning. We also listed the 18 different kinds of activity that might be undertaken by volunteers which was also complied for the IYV as a check-list for measuring the extent of volunteering (Dingle, 2001). In addition to distinguishing between the myriad forms of volunteer activity, we also reviewed some of the ways in which scholars and practitioners have identified differences in the characteristics and attitudes of volunteers and the kind of involvement or relationship they have with the organisations through which they engage in voluntary action.

The continuing power of the dominant paradigm

Our opening chapters, then, made the case that volunteering is a much more complex and multi-faceted phenomenon than is commonly appreciated. The 'dominant paradigm' nonetheless continues to exert a powerful attraction as a kind of 'default setting' for the discussion of voluntary action. This can be seen clearly in the work of the Neuberger Commission (2008) which defines volunteering in broad terms but reverts to the narrower view of the volunteering industry when it comes down to the nitty-gritty of making concrete recommendations for the future health of volunteering. A similar fault-line runs through this book where, in certain chapters, we seem to abandon our round-earth map to concentrate on much narrower terrain.

This is especially the case with our discussion of motivation and retention (Chapters 9 and 10), the emergence of new forms of volunteering and the implications for voluntary action of changes in our society (Chapters 6 and 8) and – to some extent – the ways in which the image of volunteering can be changed and the need to ensure that voluntary action is inclusive (Chapters 13 and 14). This narrowing of the focus is not, however, the result of carelessness or lack of awareness: it reflects the scope and nature of the evidence available to us from a body of research literature which is heavily weighted towards the dominant paradigm (a point we return to later) and of the limitations within which public policy towards volunteering is conceived and implemented. For the next section of this chapter, however, we will look at the ways in which we have been able to extend our analysis beyond the 'flat-earth' view of volunteering and bring a more nuanced approach to the discussion of key issues and topics.

Taking account of the complexity of volunteering

The complex and multi-faceted nature of volunteering underpins our discussion of the difficulties of measuring its scale and the extent to which it is a normal part of every day life. As Chapter 4 makes clear, this is a difficult and complicated business even where the research is focused on one country and all the more complex if one is trying to develop an account which holds good across the four countries that make up the United Kingdom. 'Headline' figures for rates of volunteering vary according to the ways in which questions are put, and these variations may be traced to the ways in which researchers have conceptualised volunteering. There are similar concerns about the quality of the data when it comes to the key questions about patterns of participation – who volunteers and what do they do? Uncritical use of the headline figures, moreover, may tend to gloss over findings which do not support the dominant paradigm view of volunteering. These include the significant proportion of people (especially men) whose volunteering takes place in the area of sports organisations and the findings that the most common forms of volunteering are raising or handling money, helping to organise an event or acting as a committee member.

The limitations of surveys of this kind and the complexity involved in interpreting and explaining the data collected by them are underlined by our attempt to benchmark the scale and shape of volunteering in the United Kingdom against the position in other countries. Comparisons are bedevilled not only by differences in methodologies but, perhaps more importantly – as Lyons et al. (1998: p. 52) point out – by 'unconscious differences in defining the object of study'. In any case, there is little value in constructing international volunteering 'league tables'; what we need to do is to seek explanations for the differences. Chapter 5 identified social origins theory, based on the idea that the scale of volunteering in any country can be explained by a combination of historical circumstances, as the most useful approach to explanations of this kind. However, it has serious limitations which result from its focus on the voluntary sector rather than volunteering and its concentration on the economic impact of the sector. It is thus rooted in the 'non-profit' paradigm and sheds little, if any, light on the wider areas of volunteering included in our round-earth map.

Discussion of the implications for volunteering of a changing society and of new forms of volunteering is also weighted towards the concerns of the dominant model of voluntary action. In Chapters 6 and 8, we have identified two possible choices that could have a major impact on the future development of volunteering. The first of these is between 'going with the flow' or an alternative approach based on some rather unpopular or unfashionable values. The second is between a gradualist approach to change and a radical new view of the possibilities for voluntary action.

The option of 'going with the flow' is based on the belief that volunteer-involving organisations need to change in ways that acknowledge and accommodate themselves to the changes that have taken place and are continuing to happen in the society in which they operate. In a world of demographic change, weakening family ties, the loss of a sense of community based on place and a culture of consumerism and choice, organisations need to adopt sophisticated marketing techniques to define volunteering opportunities as a series of products for which they can adopt sales approaches tailored to different segments of the community – such as the young, the old and the 'baby-boomers'. This may well provide a way forward for those who think within the dominant paradigm, but it is less well suited to those engaged in the wider, less disciplined and untidier areas of voluntary action. For them, as well as asserting the importance of the diversity and sheer quirkiness of volunteers, the choice might instead involve challenging contemporary mores by promoting solidarity and cooperation against individualism, placing well-being ahead of the pursuit of material wealth and reminding people that they are citizens and not just consumers.

The second set of choices – between gradualism and more radical change – again reflects the difference between working within the dominant paradigm and working towards a more inclusive concept of voluntary action. There are at least three challenges or opportunities involved in the gradualist approach. The first of these involves engaging with the different kinds of commitment to volunteering exhibited by short-term or episodic volunteers and creating a range of opportunities that meet their aspirations. The second involves looking increasingly to employer-supported volunteering as a source of new recruits. The third is to apply ICT to the whole process of volunteering from the potential recruit identifying the kind of activity and the organisation under whose auspices he or she will pursue it through the recruitment and induction procedure to actually carrying out the work on line.

Virtual volunteering may also have the potential for much more far-reaching changes in the volunteering landscape. It could transform the relationships between volunteers, volunteer-involving organisations and service users in ways which only the new generation of what have been called 'digital natives' can begin to imagine. At the same time, the unprecedented numbers of people mobilised in support of a variety of different causes suggest that volunteering as participation and campaigning may have a new and different future while the rediscovery of the principle of mutualism by timebanking offers another way forward – especially perhaps in the aftermath of the credit crunch and recession experienced in the winter of 2008–2009.

The group of chapters which followed (Chapters 9, 10, 11 and 12) focused on various aspects of volunteer management and employed the research literature to provide a context for the discussion of the limitations and shortcomings of current practice and the growing body of 'how to' handbooks and manuals. Chapter 9 was concerned with the factors that explain why people freely choose to give time to voluntary action and overcome the obstacles in the way of their involvement. A very high proportion of the volunteering literature has been devoted to exploring the motivation to volunteer driven by a search for more effective methods of recruiting more volunteers. There remains, however, a sizeable gap between the complex reality of what a combination of psychological and sociological insights can tell us about motivation and the understanding and practices of those responsible for recruiting volunteers. Similarly, there is no single authoritative explanation of retention – why volunteers choose to stay in their volunteering role and for how long. Even within the intellectual boundaries of the dominant paradigm (which is where we can locate most of the literature on motivation and retention) the reasons for becoming and continuing as a volunteer are complex and difficult to pin down, and the most adequate accounts tend to be specific to a single organisational context rather than of general application.

One factor which may affect retention is the way in which the work of volunteers is managed. There is a good deal of evidence that people will stop volunteering if they think their work is badly organised and a growing recognition that volunteers need to be provided with the support and other resources they need to make an effective contribution to the activities of the organisation with which they are involved. There is widespread agreement that volunteers need management and the debate now focuses on how that should be done. Chapter 11 highlighted the dominance of the 'workplace model' of volunteer management which is based on the formal practices used for the management of paid staff in large, bureaucratically structured organisations.

This approach to volunteer management slots easily into our dominant paradigm of volunteer involvement in which volunteers who are recruited to act as an additional resource and to undertake predetermined tasks can be seen as playing the role of unpaid staff. In many of the other volunteer-involving organisations that can be found on our round-earth map of volunteering, the 'workplace model' is inappropriate and unhelpful. Self-help or mutual aid groups, grass-roots associations and other informal kinds of organisation operate on the basis of a completely different set of 'rules' and their characteristics have been distilled by Zimmeck (2001) into an alternative 'home-grown' model of volunteer management which she contrast with the 'modern' approach imported from elsewhere (and which is a version of the workplace model). The two models can be seen as the opposite ends of a spectrum of management practices in which where the balance between the two approaches is struck depends on the nature of the volunteer's activities and relationship with the organisation and represents the kind of 'choice blend' advocated by Gaskin (2003). These kinds of arrangement are, however, increasingly under threat from the creeping tide of formalisation which has brought with it the hegemony of the workplace model and which we have returned to in the next section.

One way in which the onward march of the dominant paradigm or default model of volunteering might be delayed is provided by Chapter 12's discussion of impact measurement. While the demand for the kind of evidence that measuring impact can provide is part of the general climate in which formalisation is flourishing, the systematic approach developed by the IVR and discussed in this chapter has two important countervailing features. The first of these is its multi-constituency approach; it goes beyond the narrow focus of service delivery and looks at the impact of the volunteer on a range of interested parties or 'stakeholders' – the volunteer-involving organisation and its staff, the volunteers themselves and the community as well as direct beneficiaries. And the second is the breadth of its conception of impact – to include unintended as well as planned consequences and 'soft' as well as 'hard' measures. A framework of this kind can be used across the complete spectrum of voluntary action.

The influence of the dominant paradigm

In the previous section, we looked at ways in which our search for a 'round-earth' map of voluntary action modified or challenged the ways in which volunteering is commonly understood and promoted. We will now move on to a discussion of what we see as the enduring challenges facing volunteering in the 21st century and the contribution of the 'dominant paradigm' to creating and sustaining them. The challenges are

- overcoming the negative and unhelpful image of volunteering;
- ensuring that voluntary action is inclusive – that it is open to all regardless of race, gender, religion, disability, age, sexual orientation and of the kinds of skills they bring to it;
- defending the independence of volunteering from interference and colonisation by the state; and
- protecting the sprit and ethos of volunteering from formalisation.

The gap between the public perception of volunteering and its more complex – and exciting – reality is not entirely due to the power of the dominant paradigm. The narrow and stereotypical views of volunteering which are commonplace do not do justice to the range of activities and roles which volunteers undertake within the non-profit paradigm of voluntary action. However, the existence of the flat-earth map does make a major contribution to the widespread lack of appreciation of the full scope of volunteering. We have distinguished four principal areas where the popular understanding of volunteering falls short of the full extent of the phenomenon.

Two of these are clearly linked to the dominant paradigm. In the first place, concentration on the provision of services to those in need leads to a failure to acknowledge activities based on mutual aid; campaigning and advocacy; participation in decision-making and the governance of a variety of agencies; a contribution to the work of schools and other statutory sector bodies; and volunteering in a wide range of sports, recreational and cultural activities. Second, a focus on the unselfish and altruistic aspects of volunteering means that the benefits and rewards it brings to volunteers in the form of the acquisition of knowledge and skills, personal development and the enjoyment of a satisfying leisure pursuit in the company of others are overlooked. The other two problem areas, which are less clearly linked to the dominant view of volunteering, are the perception that volunteering is largely a middle-aged and middle-class activity and the low status that volunteering is accorded by our society.

These perceptions are deep-rooted, with their origins in 19th-century models of beneficence which have been reinforced by a series of government initiatives from the 1960s onwards aimed at addressing social ills through mobilising volunteers to help others. They can be seen as the foundations of the 'dominant paradigm' which have been strengthened more recently as part of the harnessing of voluntary action in the service of the delivery of public welfare services. Suggestions for ways of challenging the image of volunteering and the perspectives on which it is based appear to be unequal to the task. The Commission on the Future of Volunteering, for example, puts its faith in 'beefing up' existing attempts to celebrate the full range of volunteering activities (such as Volunteers Week and Make A Difference Day), enlisting the help of media companies and appointing 'volunteering champions' at local level. Another suggestion has been to apply the techniques of brand management to the promotion of a more adequate account of volunteering (Hankinson and Rochester, 2005) but it is difficult to see how this could be translated into action in the absence of a clearly identifiable and generally accepted brand 'owner'. Finally, there have been a number of suggestions that the problem lies with the word 'volunteering' which is irredeemably associated with unhelpful perceptions, but these have yet to lead to a new formulation which would be acceptable as a way forward.

Inaccurate and unhelpful images of volunteering contribute to the persistence of another enduring challenge – the need to ensure that it is genuinely inclusive – that Kearney's (2001/2007) 'right to volunteer' can be exercised regardless of race, gender, religion, disability, age, sexual orientation and the kinds of skills people bring to it. Volunteering can be seen as an activity for people of a different class, a different age group or a specific ethnic identity which excludes those who do not match this specification. In addition, we can identify two other barriers to inclusion that can be associated with the dominant paradigm's emphasis on recruiting volunteers to carry out specific roles. The first of these is the self-image and lack of self-confidence of many non-volunteers; they feel they do not have the right skills or experience to enable them to make a contribution. Second, many do not feel that the opportunities open to them are appropriate or appealing. Other obstacles to involvement may stem from the unduly bureaucratic and risk-averse practices of volunteer-involving organisations which are associated with increasingly formal organisational methods – which are related to the dominant paradigm – and shortage of time and lack of information about how to get involved – which are not.

Our third continuing concern about the future of voluntary action is the need to safeguard its independence from government. Here, we would argue that the way in which volunteering is perceived is a key issue. The shaggy, untidy and anarchic world of voluntary action found on our round-earth map does not present an attractive proposition for government. It is unpredictable and unreliable and there are no obvious levers or mechanisms with which ministers and civil servants can engage. The narrower terrain of the dominant paradigm, by contrast, is much simpler and potentially more useful as a resource that can be drawn on in the pursuit of government's policy aims and objectives. In this arena, government can deal with a comparatively small number of organisations – compared with the myriads of mutual aid, campaigning and grass-roots groups beyond its boundaries – which are organised along lines which are recognisable to public servants and which are in the straightforward business of providing services to third parties. These are the conditions for 'partnership' between government and volunteer-involving oganisations or, perhaps more realistically, the enlistment of the latter by the former as agents for the delivery of public services.

The enlistment of volunteer-involving organisations in the delivery of welfare services has been a major factor in the increasing formalisation of the sector which puts at risk the ethos and character of volunteering. There are two major influences. The first of these is the change in funding mechanisms from grant-aid to full-blown commissioning via purchase of service contracts. This has led to radical changes in the demands made by statutory funders for accountability in the shape of clear targets and the need to meet stringent requirements for the quality as well as the quantity of the services provided. To meet these requirements, organisations have developed more formal ways of managing volunteers and monitoring and reporting activities. The second major influence has been the investment by central government in volunteering and attempts to strengthen its infrastructure. This has led to the creation of what is increasingly seen as a 'volunteering industry' which in turn has spawned more formal approaches including quality standards for volunteer involvement and the growing acceptance of volunteer management as a profession. Formalisation and standardisation, as we argued in Chapter 16, bring some clear benefits not only in achieving programme outcomes but also in improving the volunteer experience. However, they are not unmixed blessings. Volunteers have complained that volunteering is becoming associated with excessive bureaucracy and is too much like paid work. The reduction in informality has also led in some organisations to a loss of the flexibility, spontaneity, creativity and social interaction which had been a feature of the volunteering experience. Perhaps, most significantly, it has been associated with a marked change in the relationship between volunteers and service users on the one hand and volunteers and paid staff on the other.

A different vision

The previous two sections of this chapter have presented an extended critique of the adequacy of the common ways in which volunteering is understood and discussed and the contribution of this, the 'dominant paradigm', to the creation and maintenance of what we see as the key challenges for volunteering in the 21st century. It is now time for us to set out an alternative vision and an agenda for further research.

What is – and is not – volunteering?

It will be abundantly clear that our conception of the phenomenon of volunteering is broader than the perspective that informs and shapes much of the contemporary discourse and that it embraces a very varied collection of activities and organisational forms. In its broadest terms, we have added the ideas of volunteering as activism and volunteering as serious leisure to the prevailing perspective of volunteering as service.

As well as contributing – directly or indirectly – to the welfare and well-being of others less fortunate than themselves, volunteers are equally likely to be involved in mutual aid and self-help, advocacy and campaigning, participating in the decision-making systems of our society and engaging in and helping others to enjoy the full range of activities offered by the fields of art and culture and sports and recreation.

As well as working under the supervision of paid staff, volunteers may act as co-workers of equal status with them, may have more or less complete autonomy in shaping their contribution and may have responsibility for the work of other volunteers and paid staff.

They have become involved and remain committed for one or more of a variety of reasons including the desire to help others and make their contribution to their community, more 'selfish' motivations such as securing services for themselves and their families or developing their knowledge and skills and the intrinsic satisfaction of accomplishing the task itself.

In addition, their volunteering may take place within large formal structures – such as household name charities and pubic sector bodies – or grass-roots associations and informal groups and the whole gamut of organisational forms between these two extremes.

As well as the breadth of its boundaries and the heterogeneity of the activities that take place within them (or perhaps because of them), volunteering we believe, is essentially untidy and anarchic. As well as the freedom to volunteer or not, people have the right to decide on the form and purpose that their voluntary action will take. Moreover, anyone can choose to get involved – regardless of their level of knowledge, skills or understanding. Volunteering is not restricted to the qualified and the worthy, and there are no gatekeepers.

While we have characterised the arena of voluntary action as wide, sprawling and untidy, it does nonetheless have boundaries. As we discussed in Chapter 2, drawing boundaries is not a simple matter. However, we believe it is important to highlight some key areas where the integrity of the idea of volunteering may be threatened.

The first of these is the principle that volunteering is an activity that is freely chosen. This continues to be at risk from government's enthusiasm for employing 'volunteering' as a means of addressing social ills: its most recent manifestation is the proposal that unemployed people failing to get jobs will be *required* to get involved in voluntary action. In addition, the principle is also threatened by the market: increasingly access to sought-after careers depends on the ability to secure an unpaid 'internship' through which to gain the necessary work experience. There are also doubts about the practice of employer-supported volunteering where some company schemes are based on clear expectations that employees will 'volunteer'.

The second area of concern is the question of payment over and above the reimbursement of out-of-pocket expenses. This has been an issue since 1994 at least when a study by Blacksell and Phillips found that it was common to pay stipends or honoraria to 'volunteers' who were, in reality, underpaid staff. More recently, the idea that volunteering by students should be rewarded by the remission of tuition fees has gained ground. England's key national volunteering infrastructure agency has recently failed to take up a clear-cut position on the issue of material rewards for 'volunteers', with its chief executive taking refuge in an engaging, but not particularly helpful, claim by a major figure of the early Labour movement, Jimmy Maxton, that 'if you can't ride two horses at once, you shouldn't be in the circus' (Davis Smith, 2008).

Why is it an important and valuable part of our society?

Our concerns about these two defining principles are rooted in a view about why volunteering is valuable and important. The impact-assessment framework developed by the IVR identifies four constituencies which may benefit from the activities of volunteers. These are the volunteers themselves, the beneficiaries or service users, the volunteer-involving organisations and the community as a whole. We believe that the key potential or actual benefits to each of these depend to a large extent on the fundamental features that the volunteer's contribution is freely given and unpaid.

In the first place, we would argue that the benefit to the volunteer extends beyond rewards in the form of personal development, social contact with others and the intrinsic pleasure of the activity itself. Volunteering can be seen as expressive rather than instrumental behaviour which is as important for 'what its stands for' and 'how it is done' as it is for what is actually undertaken by the volunteer. This is the elusive added value of volunteering which is in danger of being lost in the commodification of voluntary action associated with the growing cultural hegemony of the market.

This expressive dimension underpins the specific contribution made by the volunteer to the well-being of the beneficiaries of his or her activities. There is widespread acceptance of the view that volunteers are more than just additional or less-expensive human resources but people who bring something which is qualitatively different to the contribution made by paid staff. It follows that the major benefit to volunteer-involving organisations from voluntary action is an additional dimension to their work. For many agencies, moreover, the presence of volunteers may be an important influence on their ability to maintain their original mission and live up to their founding values.

The argument about the value of volunteering to the community or to society at large is rather different. It has two dimensions. In the first place, as we noted in Chapter 8, volunteering offers a means of addressing the increasingly atomised society in which we live and can help to rebuild or substitute for the weakening of family and community ties. Second, it provides a means not only of challenging the received wisdom of those in power but also of ensuring that communities have access to the facilities and services they need.

Securing the future of volunteering

The Manifesto of the Neuberger Commission on the Future of Volunteering (2008) sees the way forward very much in terms of further improvements to the dominant model of volunteering and looks to employers and government, as well as the 'volunteering industry' itself, to secure the future. Employer-supported volunteering is seen as a means of 'making volunteering open to all'; government's role involves 'setting the strategic direction, acting as facilitator and enabler and by removing obstacles to volunteering' (but 'not setting up new initiatives and projects'); and both volunteer-involving organisations and the volunteering infrastructure need to be 'modernised' (p. 32) which seems to mean more and better management and a major investment in the training of volunteer managers and the volunteers themselves.

From our point of view, this is an inadequate programme. In the first place, it reinforces the role of the 'volunteering industry' – the largest of the volunteer-involving organisation and the infrastructure bodies – and perhaps, more importantly, it endorses a narrow and exclusive model of volunteering. Second, it fails to address the pitfalls and difficulties involved in employer-supported volunteering. And, most disturbingly of all, in giving government the responsibility for setting a strategic direction for volunteering, it suggests both that the messy and anarchic world of voluntary action which is shaped by the free choices of very large numbers of people can be driven by a strategy and that it would be appropriate for government to provide one.

We are sceptical about the role of government in promoting volunteering beyond removing the bureaucratic obstacles to getting involved (another recommendation from the Commission). As the Conservative Party's Green Policy Paper (2008) argues, the series of volunteering initiatives launched by central government appear to have achieved relatively little while its investment in the capacity building and the infrastructure of the voluntary sector (including volunteering) has been largely misdirected. In addition, both revenue streams have contributed to the further entrenchment of the 'volunteering industry'. The Conservatives, for now at least, propose to dismantle much of this apparatus and channel money directly to organisations working at grass-roots level where they will give priority to areas where volunteering is comparatively underdeveloped.

A recent monograph published by the School for Social Entrepreneurs (Young and Young, 2008) provides evidence of the potential for voluntary action at the community level to make an impact on the issues and problems faced by their communities. Its authors argue for a 'bottom-up' approach to addressing the needs of 'disadvantaged' areas in place of current 'top-down' models which stultify local initiative. Their recommendations include putting greater trust in the ability of local 'community activists', providing them with small pots of money as their expertise develops and giving them access to appropriate intermediaries and facilitators.

None of this is, of course, new, and community development – as this might be characterised – has had a chequered history. The analysis and recommendations of this study do, however, chime with some of our major concerns, and we would like to see a major shift in funding for voluntary action away from national schemes and 'top-down' initiatives in management and training which tend to bolster the dominant paradigm at the expense of the much wider field of volunteering and towards support for locally 'owned' action at community level. We would also like to see more systematic investment in the local infrastructure of volunteering, although the bodies we would like to see at local level would be more like the intermediaries and facilitators suggested by the Youngs and less like many of the existing bodies.

While we are clear about the need for such a shift in attention and the reallocation of funding that would accompany it, we are not in a position to spell out a detailed proposal in the absence of an improved evidence base. In the first place, we need to know a great deal more about who volunteers, where and what they do. Rather than large-scale surveys, this would be accomplished by a large number of small-scale and in-depth local studies carried out systematically in communities selected to provide a cross section of experiences. Second, we need to understand better the organisational grammar of non-bureaucratic and informal organisations and, especially their mechanisms for decision-making and the demands on their leaders. In addition, we need to explore how the organs of voluntary action at a community level can best be supported in their work.

Conclusion

In this concluding chapter, we have reviewed what we see as the limitations of the ways in which volunteering is commonly discussed and the ways in which the dominant paradigm has contributed to the perpetuation of some key challenges that voluntary action continues to face. We have then attempted to set out an alternative vision of what volunteering is and is not and why it is important. This then provides the basis for a discussion of a possible new future direction for volunteering and the need for an evidence base not available to us when we set out to provide this guide to volunteering and society in the 21st century.

References

Akpeki, T. (1997) *A Force for Change: Enhancing the quality of women's involvement on boards*, NCVO: London.

Akpeki, T. (2001) *Recruiting and Supporting Black and Minority Ethnic Trustees*, NCVO: London.

Alexander, J. (2000) *An Investigation into the Premature Wastage of Police Special Constables*, HMSO: London.

Anheier, H. (2005) *Nonprofit Organizations: Theory, management, policy*, Routledge: London.

Anheier, H. and L. Salamon (1999) 'Volunteering in Cross-National Perspective' *Law and Contemporary Problems* 62(4) pp. 43–65.

Annabel Jackson Associates (2000) *Social Impact Study of Millennium Awards: To the Millennium Commission, July 2000*, Annabel Jackson Associates: Bath.

Arai, S. (2004) 'Volunteering in the Canadian Context: Identity, civic participation and the politics of participation in serious leisure' in Stebbins, R. and M. Graham (Eds) *Volunteering as Leisure, Leisure as Volunteering: An international assessment*, Chapter 8, pp. 151–176, CABI Publishing: Wallingford.

Ashby, J. and L. Ferman (2003) *To Pay or Not to Pay? The principles and practicalities of board member payment*, National Housing Federation: London.

Attwood, C., G. Singh, D. Prime and R. Creasey (2003) *2001 Home Office Citizenship Survey: People, families and communities*, Research Study 270, Home Office: London.

Aves, G. M. (1969) *The Voluntary Worker in the Social Services: Report of a Committee jointly set up by the National Council of Social Service and the National Institute for Social Work Training under the Chairmanship of Geraldine M. Aves CBE.*, Bedford Square Press of the NCSS and George Allen and Unwin: London.

Barker, A. (2005) *Volunteers in Action – Engaging volunteers in the HIV/AIDS sector. Findings from the 2005 British Columbia Assessment*, AIDS Vancouver: Vancouver.

Batson, C., N. Ahmad and J. Tsang (2002) 'Four Motives for Community Involvement' *Journal of Social Issues* 58(3) pp. 429–445.

BBC News (2003) *'Million' March against Iraq War*. Last accessed on 15 July 2009, at http://news.bbc.co.uk/1/hi/uk/2765041.stm

Bebbington, A. and P. Gatter (1994) 'Volunteers in an HIV Social Care Organization', *Aids Care: Psychological and Socio-Medical Aspects of AIDS/HIV* 6(5) pp. 571-585.

Bennett, S., K. Maton and L. Kervin (2008) 'The "Digital Natives" Debate: A critical review of the evidence' *British Journal of Educational Technology* 39(5) pp. 775–786.

Benson, A. (2007) Contribution to seminar on the *Independence of Voluntary Action* at Roehampton University, 21 November.

Billis, D. (1993) *Organising Public and Voluntary Agencies*, Routledge: London.

Billis, D. and M. Harris (1992) 'Taking the Strain of Change: UK local voluntary agencies enter the post-Thatcher period' *Nonprofit and Voluntary Sector Quarterly* 21(3) pp. 211–225.

Billis, D. and M. Harris (1996) *Voluntary Agencies: Challenges of organisation and management*, Macmillan: Basingstoke.

Blacksell, S. and D. Phillips (1994) *Paid to Volunteer: The extent of paying volunteers in the 1990s*, Volunteer Centre UK: London.

Blair, T. (2006) Letter to Hilary Armstrong on her appointment as Minister for the Cabinet Office and Social Exclusion, 20 May.

Blake, R. and S. Jefferson (1992) *Defection . . . Why? An Insight into the reasons for volunteers leaving*. Kestrecourt: York.

Blunkett, D. (2001) *From Strength to Strength: Rebuilding the community through voluntary action*, A speech to the annual conference of the National Council for Voluntary Organisations, 7 February, London.

Bondi, L (2004) ' "A Double Edged Sword?" The professionalisation of counselling in the United Kingdom' *Health and Place* 10 pp. 319–328.

Bonoli, G., V. George and P. Taylor-Gooby (2004) *European Welfare Futures. Towards a Theory of Retrenchment*, Polity: Cambridge.

Borkman, T. (1999) *Understanding Self-Help/Mutual Aid: Experiential learning in the commons*, Rutgers University Press: New Jersey.

Bowgett, K. (undated) *Gaining Experience, Giving Time: Homeless people and volunteering*, Off the Streets and Into Work: London.

Bowgett, K., K. Dickie and M. Restall (2002) *The Good Practice Guide*, 2nd edition, National Centre for Volunteering: London.

Brandeis University (1999) *Summary Report: National evaluation of Learn and Serve America*, Brandeis University: Waltham.

Branigan, T. (2002) *400,000 Bring Rural Protest to London*. Last accessed on 15 July 2009, at www.guardian.co.uk/uk/2002/sep/23/hunting.ruralaffairs2

Brenton, M. (1985) *The Voluntary Sector in British Social Services*, Longman: London.

Brewis, G. (2006) 'Beyond Banking: Lessons from an impact evaluation of employee volunteering for Barclays Bank' *Voluntary Action* 6(3) pp. 13–26.

Brewis, G. (2008) 'Youth in Action? British young people and voluntary service 1948–70', Paper presented to the symposium on William Beveridge's *Voluntary Action* 60 years on convened by the Voluntary Acton History Society (with the Menzies Centre at King's College, London and the University of Western Sidney) at the Australian High Commission, 27–28 November.

Britton, N. (1999) 'Recruiting and Retaining Black Volunteers: A case study of a black voluntary organisation' *Voluntary Action* 1(3) pp. 9–23.

Brookes, K. (2002) 'Talking about Volunteering: A discourse analysis approach to volunteer motivations' *Voluntary Action* 4(3) pp. 13–30.

Brown, G. (2000) Speech by the Chancellor of the Exchequer to the Annual Conference of the National Council for Voluntary Organisations, 9 February, London.

Brown, A., A. Jones and F. Mackay (1999) *The 'Representativeness' of Councillors*, Joseph Rowntree Foundation: York.

Brudney, J. (2000) 'Effective Use of Volunteers: Best practices for the public sector' *Law and Contemporary Problems* 62(4) pp. 119–255.

British Trust for Conservation Volunteers (2008) *Inspiring people, Improving Places: The positive impact and behavioural change achieved through environmental volunteering with BTCV*, BTCV: Doncaster.

Bunting, M. (2009) *Workfare Has Arrived in Britain, Smuggled in with Slippery Rhetoric*, The Guardian, 23 February, p. 29.

Burns, D. and M. Taylor (2000) 'Auditing the Capacity of Institutions and Communities to Deliver Democratic Participation' *Voluntary Action* 2(3) pp. 43–60.

Cabinet Office (2008) *Briefing Note for Local Strategic Partnerships NI 6: 'Participation in Regular Volunteering'*, Office of the Third Sector, Cabinet Office: London.

Cabinet Office (2009) *Real Help for Communities: Volunteers, charities and social enterprises*, Office of the Third Sector, Cabinet Office: London.

Cameron, H. (1998) *The Social Action of the Local Church: Five congregations in an English city*, PhD thesis, London School of Economics: London.

Cameron, H. (1999/2007) 'Are Members Volunteers? An exploration of the concept of membership based on the study of local churches' *Voluntary Action* 1(2) pp. 53–66, reprinted in Smith, J. D. and M. Locke (Eds) *Volunteering and the Test of Time: Essays for policy, organisation and research*, Institute for Volunteering Research: London.

Capacitybuilders (2007) *National Support Services: Background information*, Capacitybuilders: Birmingham.

Carnegie UK Trust (2007) *The Shape of Civil Society to Come*, Carnegie UK Trust: London.

Casals, M. (2005) *Voluntary Action in Spain. Facts and figures*, European Volunteer Centre: Brussels. Last accessed on 15 December 2008, at http://www.cev.be/data/File/Facts_and_Figures_Spain_Final.pdf

Casiday, R., E. Kinsman, C. Fisher and C. Bambra (2008) *Volunteering and Health: What impact does it really have?* Volunteering England: London.

Centre for Voluntary Action Research (2004) *The Adoption and Use of Quality Systems in the Voluntary Sector*, QSTG/NCVO: London.

Centre for Voluntary Action Research (2006) *The Impact of Investing in Volunteers: Final report*, CVAR: Birmingham.

Chacón, F., M. L. Vecina and M. C. Dávila (2007) 'The Three-Stage Model of Volunteers' Duration of Service' *Social Behavior and Personality* 35(5) pp. 627–642.

Charity Commission (2003) *Looking Forward to Better Governance: Report of a seminar held in October 2003*, Charity Commission: London.

Chronicle of Philanthropy (2006) *Wikipedia*. Last accessed on 29 June 2006, at http://en.wikipedia.org/wiki/The_Chronicle_of_Philanthropy

Clark, J. (2007) *Voluntary Sector Skills Survey 2007: England*, The UK Workforce Hub: London.

Clark, S. (2003) *You Cannot be Serious! A guide to involving volunteers with mental health problems*, National Centre for Volunteering: London.

Clary, E. and M. Snyder (1991) 'A Functional Analysis of Altruism and Prosocial Behaviour: The case of volunteerism' in Clark, M. (Ed) *Review of Personality and Social Psychology*, Vol. 12, pp. 119–148, Sage: Newbury Park.

Clary, E., M. Snyder and R. Ridge (1992) 'Volunteers' Motivations: A functional strategy for the recruitment, placement and retention of volunteers' *Nonprofit Management and Leadership* 2 pp. 333–350.

Clary, E., M. Snyder, R. Ridge, J. Copeland, A. Stukas, J. Haugen and P. Miene (1998) 'Understanding and Assessing the Motivation of Volunteers: A functionalist approach' *Journal of Personality and Social Psychology*, 74 pp. 1516–1530.

Clary, E., M. Snyder and A. Stukas (1996) 'Volunteers' Motivations: Findings from a national survey' *Nonprofit and Voluntary Sector Quarterly* 25 pp. 485–505.

Cloke, P., S. Johnsen and J. May (2007) 'Ethical Citizenship? Volunteers and the ethics of providing services for homeless people' *Geoforum* 38 pp. 1089–1101.

Cnaan, R. and L. Amrofell (1994) 'Mapping Volunteer Activity' *Nonprofit and Voluntary Sector Quarterly* 23 pp. 335–351.

Cnaan, R., F. Handy and M. Wadsworth (1996) 'Defining Who is a Volunteer: Conceptual and empirical considerations' *Nonprofit and Voluntary Sector Quarterly* 25 pp. 364–383.

Commission for the Compact (2005) *Volunteering Compact Code of Good Practice*, Commission for the Compact: Birmingham.

Commission on the Future of Volunteering (2007) *Free the Power: Increasing 'volunteering literacy' through training*, Commission on the Future of Volunteering: London.

Commission on the Future of Volunteering (2008) *Manifesto for Change*, Commission on the Future of Volunteering: London.

Committee on Local Authority and Allied Personal Social Services (1968) *Report of The Committee on Local Authority and Allied Personal Social Services Presented to Parliament by the Secretary of State for the Home Department, the Secretary of State for Education and Science, the Minister of Housing and Local Government and the Minister of Health, S.O.* (Cmnd 3703), Seebohm Committee: London.

Communities and Local Government (2008) *Citizenship Survey: 2007–08 (April 2007–March 2008), England & Wales: Cohesion research statistical release 4*, CLG: London.

Community Service Volunteers (2008) *CSV Reports On: Mental health, volunteering and social inclusion*, CSV Reports On, 19 April.

Conservative Party (2008) *A Stronger Society: Voluntary action in the 21st century*, Responsibility Agenda Green Paper No. 5. Last accessed on 18 September 2008, at www.conservatives.com

Cook, L. and J. Martin (2005) 'Overview: 35 years of social change' in Summerfield, C. and B. Gill (Eds) *Social Trends 35*, Palgrave/Macmillan: Basingstoke.

Corden, A. and A. Ellis (2004) 'Volunteering and Employability: Exploring the link for incapacity benefits recipients' *Benefits* 12(2) pp. 112–119.

Corden, A. and R. Sainsbury (2001) *Incapacity Benefits and Work Incentives*, Department of Social Security Research Report No. 141, Department of Social Security: Leeds.

Cornforth, C. (2001) *Recent Trends in Charity Governance and Trusteeship: The results of a survey of governing bodies of charities*, NCVO: London.

Cravens, J. (2006) 'Involving International Online Volunteers: Factors for success, organizational benefits, and new views of community' *The International Journal of Volunteer Administration* XXIV (1) pp. 15–23.

Cupitt, S. and J. Ellis (2004) *Your Project and Its Outcomes*, 2nd edition, Big Lottery Fund: London.

Dahrendorf, R. (2001) *Challenges to the Voluntary Sector*, Speech at the 18th Arnold Goodman Lecture, Charities Aid Foundation 17 July.

Danson, M. (2003) *Review of Research and Evidence on Volunteering*, Volunteer Development Scotland: Stirling.

Davis Smith, J. (1996) 'Should Volunteers be Managed?' in Billis, D. and M. Harris (Eds) *Voluntary Agencies: Challenges of organisation and management*, Macmillan: Basingstoke.

Davis Smith, J. (1998) *The 1997 National Survey of Volunteering*, National Centre for Volunteering: London.

Davis Smith, J. (1999) *Volunteering and Social Development: A background paper for discussion at an Expert Group Meeting, New York, November 29–30, 1999*, Institute for Volunteering Research: London.

Davis Smith, J. (2000) 'Volunteering and social development' *Voluntary Action* 3(1) pp. 9–23.

Davis Smith, J. (2001) 'Volunteers: Making a Difference?' in Harris, M. and C. Rochester (Eds) *Voluntary Organisations and Social Policy in Britain*, Palgrave: London.

Davis Smith, J. (2001/2007) 'The "Inflatable Log": Volunteering, the state and democracy' *Voluntary Action* 3(12) pp. 13–26, reprinted in Smith, J. D. and M. Locke (Eds) *Volunteering and the Test of Time: Essays for policy, organisation and research*, Institute for Volunteering Research: London.

Davis Smith, J. (2006) *The Age of the Volunteer?* Speech at the Launch of the Commission on the Future of Volunteering, London, 29 March.

Davis Smith, J. (2008) *Volunteers: To pay or not to pay*, Third Sector Online, 17 December.

Davis Smith, J., A. Ellis and S. Howlett (2002) *UK Wide Evaluation of the Millennium Volunteers Programme*, Research Report RR357, DfES: Nottingham.

Davis Smith, J., A. Ellis and G. Brewis (2005) 'Cross-National Volunteering: A developing movement?' in Brudney, J. (Ed) *Emerging Areas of Volunteering*, ARNOVA Occasional Paper Series 1(2), ARNOVA: Indianapolis.

Davis Smith, J. and P. Gay (2005) *Active Ageing in Active Communities: Volunteering and the transition to retirement*, Joseph Rowntree Foundation: York.

Deakin, N. (2001) 'Public Policy, Social Policy and Voluntary Organisations' in Harris M. and C. Rochester (Eds) *Voluntary Organisations and Social Policy in Britain: Perspectives on change and choice*, Palgrave: Basingstoke.

Deakin, N. (2006) *Gains and Strains: The voluntary sector in the UK 1996–2006*, Talk delivered to the Barings Foundation, 12 December. Last accessed on 19 June 2009, at http://www.baringfoundation.org.uk/gainsandstrains.pdf

Deakin, N. (2007) 'Foreword' in J. Davis Smith and Locke (Eds) *Volunteering and the Test of Time: Essays for policy, organisation and research*, Institute for Volunteering Research: London.

Dekker, P. and L. Halman (2003) 'Volunteering and Values: An introduction' in Dekker, P. and L. Halman (Eds) *The Values of Volunteering: Cross-cultural perspectives*, Kluwer Academic/Plenum: New York, Boston, Dordrecht, London, Moscow.

Department of Health and Social Security (1984) *Opportunities for Volunteering: The future: A consultation paper*, typescript: London.

Department of Labor (2008) *Volunteering in the United States, 2007*, Bureau of Labor Statistics, United States Department of Labor: Washington, DC.

Dingle, A. (2001) *Measuring Volunteering*, Independent Sector and United Nations Volunteers: Washington, DC.

Dingle, A. and Heath, J. (2001) 'Volunteering Matters or Does it?' *Voluntary Action* 3(2) pp. 11–25.

Dolnicar, S. and M. Randle (2007) 'What Motivates which Volunteers? Psycholographic heterogeneity among volunteers in Australia' *Voluntas* 18 pp. 135–155.

Donahue, K. (2007) *Volunteering in Tower Hamlets: Local perspectives on volunteering trends and issues*, Volunteer Centre Tower Hamlets: Tower Hamlets.

Dresbach, S. L. (1992) *Commitment and Volunteer Organizations: Variables influencing participation in environmental organizations*. PhD dissertation, Ohio State University, Columbus.

Durning, J. (2006) *Review of ChangeUp National Hubs: Final Report*, unpublished, Capacitybuilders: Birmingham.

Eley, D. (2003) 'Perceptions and Reflections on Volunteering: The impact of community service on citizenship in students' *Voluntary Action* 5(3) pp. 27–45.

Elliott, S., G. Lomas and A. Riddell (1984) *Community Projects Review: A review of voluntary projects receiving Urban Programme funding*, Department of the Environment: London.

Ellis, A. (2003a) *Barriers to Participation for Under-represented Groups in School Governance*, DfES Research Report 500, Department for Education and Skills: London.

Ellis, A. (2003b) *Student Volunteering: A literature review*, Centre for Nonprofit and Voluntary Sector Management, University of Surrey Roehampton: London.

Ellis, A. (2004) *Generation V: Young people speak out on volunteering*, Institute for Volunteering Research: London.

Ellis, A. and G. Brewis (2005) *Issues of Diversity and Recruitment among Further Education College Governors*, Association of Colleges: London.

Ellis, A. (2006) *Unlocking the Potential: Reviewing the Wildlife Trusts' project to strengthen volunteering*, unpublished report (a Research Bulletin, summarising the findings is, however, available under the same title at Institute for Volunteering Research website: last accessed on 19 June 2009, at www.ivr.org.uk/researchbulletins)

Ellis, J. (2008) *Accountability and Learning: Developing monitoring and evaluation in the third sector, Research briefing*, Charities Evaluation Services: London.

Ellis, S. (1996) *From the Top Down: The executive role in volunteer program success*, Energize: Philadelphia.

Ellis, S. (2002) *The Volunteer Recruitment Book*, 3rd edition, Energize: Philadelphia.

Elstub, S. (2006) 'Towards an Inclusive Social Policy for the UK: The need for democratic deliberation in voluntary and community associations' *Voluntas* 17(1) pp. 17–39.

Esmond, J. and P. Dunlop (2004) *Developing the Volunteer Motivation Inventory to Assess the Underlying Motivational Drives of Volunteers in Western Australia*, CLAN WA. Last accessed on 19 June 2009, at http://www.morevolunteers.com/resources/MotivationFinalReport.pdf

Esping-Andersen, G. (1990) *Three Worlds of Welfare Capitalism*, Policy Press: Cambridge

European Volunteer Centre (2006) *Manifesto for Volunteering in Europe*, European Volunteer Centre: Brussels.

Evans, E. and J. Saxton (2005) *The 21st Century Volunteer: A report on the changing face of volunteering in the 21st Century*, nfpSynergy: London.

Field, J. and B. Hedges (1984) *A national Survey of Volunteering*, Social and Community Planning Research: London.

Finkelstein, M. A., L. A. Penner and M. T. Brannick (2005) 'Motive, Role Identity, and Prosocial Personality as Predictors of Volunteer Activity' *Social Behavior and Personality* 33(4) pp. 403–418.

Fitch, R. (1987) 'Characteristics and Motivations of College Students Volunteering for Community Service' *Journal of College Student Personnel* 28 pp. 424–431.

Forster, A. (2004) 'Not Always for Love but Certainly not for Money: In reply to Williams' *Voluntary Action* 6(3) pp. 37–40.

Frisch, M. and M. Gerrard (1981) 'Natural Helping Systems: Red Cross volunteers' *American Journal of Community Psychology* 9 pp. 567–579.

Fryer, A., R. Jackson and F. Dyer (2007) *Turn Your Organisation into a Volunteer Magnet*, Linda Graff and Associates: Ontario.

Gaskin, K. (1998) 'Vanishing Volunteers: Are young people losing interest in volunteering?' *Voluntary Action* 1(1) pp. 33–43.

Gaskin, K. (1999a) *VIVA in Europe: A comparative study of the Volunteer Investment and Value Audit*, Institute for Volunteering Research: London.

Gaskin, K. (1999b) 'Valuing Volunteers in Europe: A comparative study of the Volunteer Investment and Value Audit' *Voluntary Action* 2(1) pp. 35–49.

Gaskin, K. (2003) *A Choice Blend: What volunteers want from organisation and management*, Institute for Volunteering Research: London.

Gaskin, K. (2005) *Reasonable Care? Risk, risk management and volunteering in England*, Volunteering England and the Institute for Volunteering Research: London.

Gaskin, K. (2008) *A Winning Team? The impacts of volunteers in sports*, Institute for Volunteering Research and Volunteering England: London.

Gaskin, K. and J. Davis Smith (1995) *A New Civic Europe? A Study of the Extent and Role of Volunteering*, National Centre for Volunteering: London.

Gaskin, K. and B. Dobson (1996) *The Economic Equation of Volunteering: A pilot study – Final report*, Centre for Research in Social Policy, University of Loughborough: Loughborough.

Gaskin, K., R. Hutchison, M. Hutin and M. Zimmeck (2008) *The Commission on the Future of Volunteering: Results of the public consultation*, Commission on the Future of Volunteering: London.

Gaston, K. and J. Alexander (2001) 'Effective Organisation and Management of Public Sector Volunteer Workers: Police special constables' *International Journal of Public Sector Management* 14(1) pp. 59–74.

Gay, P. (2000) *Delivering the Goods: A report of the work of volunteer managers*, Institute for Volunteering Research: London.

Gay, P. and S. Hatch (1983) *Voluntary Work and Unemployment*, Research and Development Series, No. 15, Manpower Services Commission: London.

Gay, P. and J. Pitkeathley (1982) *Mobilising Voluntary Resources*, King's Fund: London.

Gidron, B. (1984) 'Predictors of retention and turnover among service volunteer workers' *Journal of Social Services Research* 8(1) pp. 1–16.

Gillespie, D. and A. King (1985) 'Demographic Understanding of Volunteerism' *Journal of Sociology and Social Welfare* 12 pp. 798–816.

Glasby, J. (2005) 'The Future of Adult Social Care: Lessons from previous reforms' *Research Policy and Planning* 23(2) pp. 61–70.

Goddard, K. (2005) 'A Different Experience? Personal experience volunteers at a cancer charity' *Voluntary Action* 7(1) pp. 9–25.

Graff, L. (2005) *Best of All: The quick reference guide to effective volunteer involvement*, Linda Graff and Associates: Ontario.

Granholm, P. (2007) *Volunteering in Sweden. Facts and figures report*, European Volunteer Centre: Brussels. Last accessed on 19 June 2009, at http://www.cev.be/data/File/FactsandFiguresSweden.pdf

Grube, J. and J. A. Piliavin (2000) 'Role Identity, Organizational Experiences, and Volunteering Experiences' *Personality and Social Psychology Bulletin* 26 pp. 1108–1120.

Guirguis-Younger, M., M. Kelley and M. Mckee (2005) 'Professionalization of Hospice Volunteer Practices: What are the implications?' *Palliative and Supportive Care* 3 pp. 143–144.

H. M. Treasury and Cabinet Office (2007) *The future role of the third sector in social and economic regeneration: Final report* (Cm 7189), H. M. Treasury and Cabinet Office: London.

Haddad, M. (2006) 'Civic Responsibility and Patterns of Voluntary Participation Around the World' *Comparative Political Studies* 39(10) pp. 1220–1242.

Hall, M. (2001) 'Measurement Issues in Surveys of Giving and Volunteering and Strategies Applied in the Design of Canada's National Survey of Giving, Volunteering and Participating' *Non-Profit and Voluntary Sector Quarterly* 30(3) pp. 515–526.

Hall, M., C. Barr, M. Easwaramoorthy, S. Sokolowski and L. Salamon (2005) *The Canadian Nonprofit and Voluntary Sector in Comparative Perspective*, Imagine Canada: Toronto.

Halman, L. and R. de Moor (1994) 'Compararive Research on Values' in Ester, P., L. Halman and R. de Moor (Eds) *The Individualized Society*, pp. 21–36, Tilburg University Press: Tilburgh.

Handy, F., R. Cnaan, J. Brudney, U. Ascoli, L. Meijs and S. Ranade (2000) 'Public Perception of "Who is a Volunteer": An examination of the net-cost approach from a cross-cultural perspective' *Voluntas* 11(1) pp. 45–65.

Handy, F., N. Brodeur and R. Cnaan (2006) 'Summer on the Island: Episodic volunteering' *Voluntary Action* 7(3) pp. 31–46.

Hankinson, P. and C. Rochester (2005) 'The Face and Voice of Volunteering: A suitable case for branding?' *International Journal of Nonprofit and Voluntary Sector Marketing* 10 pp. 93–105.

Harries, R. (2005) *Government and Volunteering: From research to policy* Presentation to the Institute for Volunteering Research Conference on Volunteering Research: Frontiers and Horizons in Birmingham, November.

Harris, M. (1996) '"An Inner Group of Willing People": Volunteering in a religious context' *Social Policy and Administration* 30(1) pp. 54–68.

Harris, M. (1998) *Organising God's Work: Challenges for churches and synagogues*, Macmillan: London.

Harris, M. (2001) 'Voluntary Organisations in a Changing Social Policy Environment' in Harris, M. and C. Rochester (Eds) *Voluntary Organisations and Social Policy in Britain*, Chapter 15, pp. 213–228, Palgrave: Basingstoke.

Harris, M. and C. Rochester (2001a) *Governance in the Jewish Voluntary Sector*, Institute for Jewish Policy Research: London.

Harris, M. and C. Rochester (Eds) (2001b) *Voluntary Organisations and Social Policy in Britain*, Palgrave: Basingstoke.

Harris, M., C. Rochester and P. Halfpenny (2001) 'Voluntary Organisations and Social Policy: Twenty years of change' in Harris, M. and C. Rochester (Eds) *Voluntary Organisations and Social Policy in Britain*, Palgrave: Basingstoke.

Hedley, R. and J. Davis Smith (Eds) (1992) *Volunteering and Society*, NCVO Publications: London.

Help the Hospices, in conjunction with the Association of Voluntary Service Managers (2006) *Volunteer Value: A pilot survey in UK hospices*, Help the Hospices: London.

Hiatt, S., P. Michalek, P. Younge, T. Miyoshi and E. Fryer (2000) 'Characteristics of Volunteers and Families in a Neonatal Home Visitation Project: The Kempe Community Caring Program' *Child Abuse and Neglect* 25(10) pp. 85-97.

Hirst, A. (2000) *Links between Volunteering and Employability*, Research Report RR309, Department for Education and Skills. Last accessed on 28 January 2009, at http://www.dcsf.gov.uk/research/data/uploadfiles/RR309.PDF

Hodgkinson, V. (2003) 'Volunteering in Global Perspective' in Dekker, P. and L. Halman (Eds) *The Values of Volunteering: Cross-cultural perspectives*, Kluwer Academic/Plenum: New York, Boston, Dordrecht, London, Moscow.

Holmes, K. (1999) 'Changing Times: Volunteering in the heritage sector 1984–1998' *Voluntary Action* 1(2) pp. 21–35.

Holmes, K. (2003) 'Volunteers in the Heritage Sector: A neglected audience?' *International Journal of Heritage Studies* 9(4) pp. 341–355.

Home Office (1967) *The Place of Voluntary Service After-Care: Second report of the working party*, H.M.S.O.: London [Reading Committee].

Home Office (1978) *The Government and the Voluntary Sector: A consultative document*, Voluntary Services Unit, Home Office: London.

Home Office (1988) *The New Adult Training Programme (Adult Training): Report of a seminar organised by the Voluntary Services Unit of the Home Office on 4 March 1988*, typescript: London.

Home Office (1990) *Efficiency Scrutiny of Government Funding of the Voluntary Sector: Profiting from partnership*, H.M.S.O.: London.

Home Office (1995) *Make a Difference: The government's action plans*, Communication Directorate on behalf of the Volunteering Unit, Home Office: London.

Home Office (2000) *Volunteering and Community Activity Today: Material assembled for the active community cross-cutting review 1999–2000*, unpublished.

Home Office (2002) *Home Office Citizenship Survey: Social capital scoping paper*, Home Office: London.

Home Office (2003) *Building Civil Renewal: Government support for community capacity building and proposals for change: Review findings from the Civil Renewal Unit*, Home Office: London.

Home Office (2004) *2003 Home Office Citizenship Survey: People, families and communities*, Research Study 289, Home Office: London.

Home Office (2005) *Volunteering Code of Good Practice*, Home Office: London.

Hughes, M. (Eds) (2009) *Social Trends 35*, Palgrave/Macmillan: Basingstoke. Last accessed on 9 March 2009, at www.statistics.gov.uk/downloads/theme_social/Social_Trends39

Hurley, N., L. Wilson and I. Christie (2008) *Scottish Household Survey Analytical Report: Volunteering*, Scottish Government Social Research: Edinburgh. Last accessed 19 June 2009, at www.scotland.gov.uk/socialresearch

Hustinx, L. (2001/2007) 'Individualisation and New Styles of Youth Volunteering: An empirical investigation' *Voluntary Action* 3(2) pp. 47–55, reprinted in Smith, J. D. and M. Locke (Eds) *Volunteering and the Test of Time: Essays for policy, organisation and research*, Institute for Volunteering Research: London.

Hustinx, L. and F. Lammertyn (2003) 'Collective and Reflexive Styles of Volunteering: A sociological modernization perspective' *Voluntas* 14(2) pp. 167–187.

Hutchison, R. and N. Ockenden (2008) *The Impact of Public Policy on Volunteering in Community-Based Organisations*, Institute for Volunteering Research: London.

Hutin, M. (2008) *Regular and Occasional Volunteers: How and why they help out*, Research Bulletin Institute for Volunteering Research: London. Last accessed on 19 June 2009, at http://www.ivr.org.uk/NR/rdonlyres/568EEABF-B25E-4E3C-870D-755FB2FA7955/0/reg_and_occ_volunteers.pdf

Inglehart, R. (2003) 'Modernization and Volunteering' in Dekker, P. and L. Halman (Eds) *The Values of Volunteering: Cross-cultural perspectives*, Kluwer Academic/Plenum: New York, Boston, Dordrecht, London, Moscow.

Institute for Volunteering Research (2002) *IYV Global Evaluation*, Report Prepared by the Institute for Volunteering Research. Last accessed on January 18 2009, at http://www.worldvolunteerweb.org/fileadmin/docs/old/pdf/2002/02_09_01GBRiyv_final_evaluation.pdf

Institute for Volunteering Research (2003) *Volunteering for Mental Health: Research bulletin*, IVR: London.

Institute for Volunteering Research (2004a) *Volunteering for All? Exploring the link between volunteering and social exclusion*, Institute for Volunteering Research: London.

Institute for Volunteering Research (2004b) *Volunteering Impact Assessment Toolkit*, Institute for Volunteering Research: London.

International Association for Volunteer Effort (2001) 'The Global Agenda for Action to Strengthen Volunteering', Paper presented to the 16th World Volunteer Conference, Amsterdam, January.

Involve (2005) *People and Participation: How to put citizens at the heart of decision-making*, Involve: London.

Involve (2006) *Involvement of Third Country Nationals in Volunteering as a Means of Better Integration: Final project report*, European Volunteer Centre: Brussels.

Iveson, C. (1999) *Recruitment and retention of volunteers*, MA dissertation, University of Manchester.

Johnston, M. and R. Jowell (1999) 'Social Capital and the Social Fabric' in Jowell, J., J. Curtice, A. Park and K. Thomson (Eds) *British Social Attitudes: The 16th report, who shares New Labour values?* National Centre for Social Research, Ashgate: Aldershot.

Jones, A. (2004) *Review of Gap Year Provision*, Research Report 555, Department for Education and Skills: London.

Jukenevicius, S. and A. Savicka (2003) 'From Restitution to Innovation: Volunteering in postcommunist countries' in Dekker, P. and L. Halman (Eds) *The Values of Volunteering: Cross-cultural perspectives*, Kluwer Academic/Plenum: New York, Boston, Dordrecht, London, Moscow.

Kapferer, J-N. (1997) *Strategic Brand Management*, Kogan Page: London.

Kearney, J. (2001/2007) 'The Values and Basic Principles of Volunteering: Complacency or caution?' *Voluntary Action* 3(3) pp. 63–86, reprinted in Smith, J. D. and M. Locke (Eds) *Volunteering and the Test of Time: Essays for policy, organisation and research*, pp. 1–18, Institute for Volunteering Research: London.

Kearney, J. (2003) 'Volunteering: Social glue for community cohesion?' *Voluntary Action* 6(1) pp. 45–58.

Kendall, J. (2005) *The third sector and the policy process in the UK: Ingredients in a hyper-active horizontal policy environment*, Third Sector European Policy Working Papers No. 5, Centre for Civil Society and Personal Social Services Research Unit, London School of Economics and Political Science: London.

Kendall, J. and M. Knapp (1996) *The Voluntary Sector in the UK*, Manchester University Press: Manchester.

Kendall, J. and M. Knapp (2000) 'Measuring the Performance of Voluntary Organisations' *Public Management* 2(1) pp. 105–132.

Kitchen, S., J. Michaelson, N. Wood and P. John (2006a) *2005 Citizenship Survey: Active communities topic report*, CLG: London.

Kitchen, S., J. Michaelson, N. Wood and P. John (2006b) *2005 Citizenship Survey: Crosscutting themes*, CLG: London.

Knapp, M. (1990) *Time is Money: The cost of volunteering in Britain today – Voluntary Action Research Paper No. 3*, Volunteer Centre UK: Berkhamsted.

Knoke, D. and R. Thomson (1977) 'Voluntary Association Membership and the Family Life Cycle' *Social Forces* 56(1) pp. 48–65.

Krishnamurthy, A., D. Prime and M. Zimmeck (2001) *Voluntary and Community Activities: Findings from the 2000 British Crime Survey*, Home Office: London.

Kutner, G. and J. Love (2003) *Time and Money: An in-depth look at 45+ volunteers and donors. Findings from a multicultural survey of Americans 45 and older*, AARP: Washington, DC.

Lee, L., J. A. Piliavin and V. R. A. Call (1999) 'Giving Time, Money and Blood: Similarities and differences' *Social Psychology Quarterly* 62 pp. 276–290.

Leonard, R., J. Onyx and H. Hayward-Brown (2004) 'Volunteer and Coordinator Perspectives on Managing Women Volunteers' *Non-Profit Management and Leadership* 15(2) pp. 205–219.

Locke, M., A. Ellis and J. Davis Smith (2003) 'Hold on to What You've Got: The volunteer retention literature' *Voluntary Action* 5(3) pp. 81–100.

Lohmann, R. (1992) *The Commons: New perspectives on nonprofit organizations and voluntary action*, Jossey Bass: San Francisco.

Low, N., S. Butt, A. Ellis Paine and J. Davis Smith (2007) *Helping Out: A national survey of volunteering and charitable giving*, Cabinet Office: London.

Lukka, P. and A. Ellis Paine (2001/2007) 'An Exclusive Construct? Exploring different cultural concepts of volunteering' *Voluntary Action* 3(3) pp. 87–109, reprinted in Smith, J. D. and M. Locke (Eds) *Volunteering and the Test of Time: Essays for policy, organisation and research* Institute for Volunteering Research: London.

Luks, A. and P. Payne (1991) *The Healing Power of Doing Good: The health and spiritual benefits of helping others*, Fawcett Columbine: New York.

Lynn, P. (1997) 'Measuring Voluntary Activity' *Non-Profit Studies* 1(2) pp. 1–11.

Lynn, P. and J. Davis Smith (1991) *The 1991 National Survey of Voluntary Activity in the UK*, Volunteer Centre UK: Berkhamsted.

Lyons, M., P. Wijkstrom and G. Clary (1998) 'Comparative Studies of Volunteering: What is being studied' *Voluntary Action* 1(1) pp. 45–54.

Matheson, J. and P. Babb (2002) *Social Trends* 32, The Stationery Office: London. Last accessed on 7 February 2009, at www.statistics.gov.uk/downloads/theme_social/social_trends32

McCudden, J. (2000) 'What Makes a Committed Volunteer? Research into the factors affecting the retention of volunteers in Home-Start' *Voluntary Action* 2(2) pp. 50–76.

McCurley, S. and R. Lynch (1998) *Essential Volunteer Management*, Directory of Social Change: London.

Macduff, N. (2005) 'Societal Changes and the Rise of the Episodic Volunteer' in Brudney, J. (Ed) *Emerging Areas of Volunteering*, ARNOVA Occasional Paper Series 1(2), ARNOVA: Indianapolis.

Machin, J. and A. Ellis Paine (2008a) *Management Matters: A national survey of volunteer management capacity*, Institute for Volunteering Research: London.

Machin, J. and A. Ellis Paine (2008b) *Managing for Success: Volunteers' views on their involvement and support*, Institute for Volunteering Research: London.

Macionis, J. and K. Plummer (1998) *Sociology*, Prentice Hall: Upper Saddle River.

Make a Difference Team (1995) *Make a Difference: An Outline Volunteering Strategy for the UK*, Make a Difference Team: London.

Malmersjo, G. (2006) *Volunteering England Annual Membership Return 2005/6: Summary findings*, IVR: London.

Meijs, L. and E. Hoogstad (2001) 'New Ways of Managing Volunteers: Combining membership management and programme management' *Voluntary Action* 3(3) pp. 41–61.

Meijs, L., F. Handy, R. Cnaan, J. Brudney, U. Ascoli, S. Ranade, L. Hustinx, S. Weber and I. Weiss (2003) 'All in the Eyes of the Beholder? Perceptions of volunteering across eight countries' in Dekker, P. and L. Halman (Eds) *The Values of Volunteering: Cross-cultural perspectives*, Kluwer Academic/Plenum: New York, Boston, Dordrecht, London, Moscow.

Mencap (undated) *Volunteering for Everyone: A guide for organisations who want to include and recruit volunteers who have a learning disability*, Volunteering England: London.

Mesch, D., M. Tschirhart, J. Perry and G. Lee (1998) 'Altruists or Egoists? Retention in stipended service' *Non-Profit Management and Leadership* 9(1) pp. 3–21.

Michael, A. (1998) 'Volunteering and Community Action: Building the future together' *RSA Journal* 5485 pp. 61–67.

Milliband, D. (2006) *Putting People in Control*, Keynote Speech to the NCVO Annual Conference. Last accessed on 19 June 2009, at http://www.ncvo-vol.org.uk/press/speeches

Mocroft, I. (1984) *Opportunities for Volunteering: The first round of the scheme: A report to the DHSS by Ian Mocroft*, Volunteer Centre UK: Berkhamsted.

Mole, V. and J. Harrow (2003) *Managing Diversity in the Workplace: An introduction for voluntary and community organisations*, NCVO: London.

Mook, L., B. Richmond and J. Quarter (2003) 'How Including Volunteers Changes a Financial Statement: The expanded value added statement' *Voluntary Action* 6(1) pp. 75–88.

Moore, D. and S. Fishlock (2006) *Can Do Volunteering: A guide to involving young disabled people as volunteers*, Leonard Cheshire and Scope: London.

Morrow-Howell, N. and A. Mui (1989) 'Elderly Volunteers: Reasons for initiating and terminating service' *Journal of Gerontological Social Work* 13 pp. 21–33.

Mraková, M. and J. Vlaicová (undated) 'Slovakia' in Spes – Centro di Servizio il Volontario del Lazio (Ed) *Volunteering Across Europe, Belgium, Lithuania, Slovakia: Organisations, promotion, oarticipation*, Spes – Centro di Servizio il Volontario del Lazio: Rome.

Murphy, F. (2005) 'Trends Affecting the Development of Volunteering Worldwide: An overview' *Voluntary Action* 6(3) pp. 45–52.

Murray, J., S. Bellinger and A. Easter (2008) *Evaluation of Capital Volunteering: Fourth interim report, at 12 months*, Institute of Psychiatry: London.

Murray, V. and Y. Harrison (2005) 'Virtual Volunteering' in Brudney, J. (Ed) *Emerging Areas of Volunteering*, ARNOVA Occasional Paper Series 1(2), ARNOVA: Indianapolis.

Musick, M. and J. Wilson (2008) *Volunteers: A social profile*, Indiana University Press: Bloomington.

Muthuri, J., J. Moon and D. Matten (2006) *Employee Volunteering and the Creation of Social Capital*, ICCSR Research Paper Series No. 34-2006, International Centre for Corporate Social Responsibility, Nottingham University, Nottingham.

Nathanson, I. and E. Eggleton (1993) 'Motivation Versus Program Effect on Length of Service: A study of four cohorts of ombudservice volunteers' *Journal of Gerontological Social Work* 19(3–4) pp. 95–114.

National Statistics (2003) *Volunteers, Helpers and Socialisers*, News Release, 6 February. Last accessed 27 January, 2009, at http://www.statistics.gov.uk/pdfdir/vhc0203.pdf

National Youth Agency (2007) *Young People's Volunteering and Skills Development*, Research report RW103, Department for Education and Skills: London.

Netting, F., M. O'Connor, M. Thomas and G. Yancey (2005) 'Mixing and Phasing of Roles Among Volunteers, Staff, and Participants in Faith-Based Programs' *Nonprofit and Voluntary Sector Quarterly* 34(2) pp. 179–205.

Neuberger, J. (2007) 'Foreword' in Ockenden, N. (Ed) *Volunteering Works: Volunteering and social policy*, The Commission on the Future of Volunteering: London.

Neuberger, J. (2008) *Volunteering in the Public Services: Health and social care*, Baroness Neuberger's review as the Governments volunteering champion, March, Office of the Third Sector: London.

Nichols, G. (2006) 'Research into Sports Volunteers: Reviewing the Questions' *Voluntary Action* 8(1) pp. 55–65.

Noyes Campbell, K. and S. Elli (1995) *The (Help) I-Don't-Have-Enough-Time Guide to Volunteer Management*, Energize: Philadelphia.

Nyasi, F. (1996) *Volunteering by Young People: A route to opportunity*, National Centre for Volunteering: London.

Ockenden, N. (Ed) (2007) *Volunteering Works: Volunteering and social policy*, Commission on the Future of Volunteering: London.

Ockenden, N. and A. Ellis Paine (2006) *Retention and Succession Planning Within Further Education Governance*, Institute for Volunteering Research, Research Bulletin. Last accessed on January 20 2009, at http://www.ivr.org.uk/NR/

rdonlyres/1225ECF3-9C69-482E-A93F-0F5D3EE8054A/0/December_2006_
Retention_and_Succession_planning_within_FE_governance.pdf

Ockenden, N. and M. Hutin (2008) *Volunteering to Lead: A study of leadership in small, volunteer-led groups*, Institute for Volunteering Research: London.

Office of the Deputy Prime Minister (2005) *Citizen Engagement and Public Service: Why neighbourhoods matter*, Office for the Deputy Prime Minister: London.

Office of the Deputy Prime Minister (2006) *Local Area Agreements: Guidance for Round 3 and refresh of Rounds 1 and 2*, Office of the Deputy Prime Minister: London.

Office of National Statistics (2001) *Social Capital: A review of the literature*, Office for National Statistics: London. Last accessed on 20 June 2009, at http://www.statistics.gov.uk/socialcapital/downloads/soccaplitreview.pdf

Office of National Statistics (2008) *Internet Access 2008; Households and Individuals* last accessed on January 30, 2009, at http://www.statistics.gov.uk/pdfdir/iahi0808

Oliver, M. (1990) *The Politics of Disablement*, MacMillan: London.

Omoto, A. M. and M. Snyder (1993) 'AIDS Volunteers and Their Motivations: Theoretical issues and practical concerns' *Non-Profit Management and Leadership* 4(2) pp. 157–176.

Omoto, A. and M. Snyder (1995) 'Sustained Helping without Obligation: Motivation, longevity of service and perceived attitude change among AIDS volunteers' *Journal of Personality and Social Psychology* 68 pp. 671–686.

Paxton, W. and V. Nash (2002) *Any Volunteers for the Good Society*, IPPR: London.

Pearce, J. (1993) *Volunteers: The organizational behaviour of unpaid workers*, Routledge: London.

Penberthy, C. and A. Forster (2004) *Building on Success: Strategy for volunteering infrastructure in England 2004–2014*, Volunteering England: London.

Penner, L. A. (2002) 'Dispositional and Organizational Influences on Sustained Volunteerism: An interactionist perspective' *Journal of Social Issues* 58(3) pp. 447–467.

Penner, L. and M. Finkelstein (1998) 'Dispositional and Structural Determinants of Volunteerism' *Journal of Personality and Social Psychology* 74(2) pp. 525–537.

Phillips, S. and B. R. Little (2002) *Recruiting, Retaining and Rewarding Volunteers: What volunteers have to say*, Canadian Centre for Philanthropy: Toronto.

Piliavin, J. A. and P. L. Callero (1991) *Giving Blood: The development of an altruistic identity*, Johns Hopkins University Press: Baltimore.

The Power Inquiry (2006) *Power to the People: The report of an independent inquiry into Britain's democracy*, York Publishing Services: York.

Prensky, M. (2001) 'Digital Natives, Digital Immigrants' *On the Horizon* 9(6). Last accessed on 20 June 2009, at http://www.twitchspeed.com/site/Prensky%20-%20Digital%20Natives,%20Digital%20Immigrants%20-%20Part1.htm

Putnam, R. (1993) *Making Democracy Work: Civic traditions in modern Italy*, Princeton University Press: Princeton.

Putnam, R. (2000) 'Bowling Alone: America's declining social capital – An interview with Robert Putnam' *Journal of Democracy* 6(1) pp. 65–78.

Ray, C. (1998) 'Culture, Intellectual Property and Territorial Rural Development' *Sociologica Ruralis* 38(1) pp. 3–20.

Rehnborg, S. (2005) 'Government Volunteerism in the New Millennium' in Brudney, J. (Ed) *Emerging Areas of Volunteering*, ARNOVA Occasional Paper Series 1(2), ARNOVA: Indianapolis.

Reilly, C. (2005) *Volunteering and Disability: Experiences and perceptions of volunteering from disabled people and organizations*, Volunteer Development Scotland: Stirling.

Restall, M. (2003) 'Breaking the Benefits Barrier' *Volunteering Magazine* 90(August) pp. 12–13.

Retired and Senior Volunteers Programme (2000) *Disability Need Be No Handicap: Creating opportunities in volunteering*, RSVP, Community Service Volunteers: London.

Rochester, C. (1997) 'The Neglected Dimension of the Voluntary Sector: Measuring the value of community organisations' in Pharoah, C. (Ed) *Dimensions of the Voluntary Sector*, Charities Aid Foundation: West Malling.

Rochester, C. (1998) *Social Benefits: Exploring the value of community sector organisations*, Charities Aid Foundation: West Malling.

Rochester, C. (1999/2007) 'One Size Does Not Fit All: Four models of involving volunteers in small voluntary organisations' *Voluntary Action* 1(2) pp. 7–20, reprinted in Smith, J. D. and M. Locke (Eds) *Volunteering and the Test of Time: Essays for policy, organisation and research*, Institute for Volunteering Research: London.

Rochester, C. (2001) 'Regulation: The Impact on local voluntary action' in Harris, M. and C. Rochester (Eds) *Voluntary Organisations and Social Policy: Perspectives on change and choice*, Palgrave: Basingstoke.

Rochester, C. (2006) *Making Sense of Volunteering: A literature review*. The Commission on the Future of Volunteering, Volunteering England. Last accessed on 18 February 2009, at http://www.volcomm.org.uk/NR/rdonlyres/6EF238B5-0425-4F99-930E-E7665CAAEEC6/0/Making_sense_of_volunteering.pdf

Rochester, C. and J. Grotz (2006) *Volunteers and Training: A report for the Commission on the Future of Volunteering*, unpublished report prepared for the Commission on the Future of Volunteering, London.

Rochester, C. and R. Hutchison (2002) *A Review of the Home Office Older Volunteers Initiative*, Research Study 248, Home Office: London.

Rochester, C. and B. Thomas (2006) *Measuring the Impact of Employer Supported Volunteering: An exploratory study*, report prepared for the Institute for Volunteering Research, London.

Rohs, F. R. (1986). 'Social Background, Personality, and Attitudinal Factors Influencing the Decision to Volunteer and Level of Involvement among Adult 4-H Leaders' *Journal of Voluntary Action Resources* 15(1) pp. 87–99.

Rooney, P., K. Steinberg, K. and P. Schervish (2004) 'Methodology is Destiny: The effects of survey prompts on reported levels of giving and volunteering' *Non-Profit and Voluntary Sector Quarterly* 33(4) pp. 628–654.

Rotolo, T. (2000) 'A Time to Join, A Time to Quit: The influence of life cycle transitions on voluntary association membership' *Social Forces* 78(3) pp. 1133–1161.

Russell, I. (2005) *A National Framework for Youth Action and Engagement: Report of the Russell Commission*, The Russell Commission: London.

Russell, L. and D. Scott (1997) *Very Active Citizens? The impact of contracts on volunteers*, University of Manchester: Manchester.

Ryan, R. L., R. Kaplan and R. E. Grese (2001) 'Predicting Volunteer Commitment in Environmental Stewardship Programmes' *Journal of Environmental Planning and Management* 44(5) pp. 629–648.

Ryan-Collins, J., L. Stephens and A. Coote (2008) *The new wealth of time: How timebanking helps people build better public services*, New Economic Foundation and TimeBanks UK: London.

Salamon, L. and H. Anheier (1998) 'Social Origins of Civil Society: Explaining the non-profit sector cross-nationally' *Voluntas* 9(3) pp. 213–247.

Salamon, L. and S. Sokolowski (2001) *Volunteering in Cross-National Perspective: Evidence from 24 countries*, Working Papers of the Johns Hopkins Comparative Nonprofit Sector Project, no. 40, The Johns Hopkins Center for Civil Society: Baltimore.

Salamon, L., A. Sokolowski and R. List (2003) *Global Civil Society: An overview*, Center for Civil Society Studies, Johns Hopkins University: Baltimore.

Samolyk, E. (2005) *Voluntary Action in Poland Facts and Figures*, European Volunteer Centre: Brussels. Last accessed on 20 June 2009, at http://www.cev.be/data/File/FactsFiguresPoland.pdf

Saxton, J. and C. Greenwood (2006) *Getting the Message Across: Practical strategies to help charities to change the ways stakeholders see them*, nfpSynergy and ImpACT Coalition: London.

Sayer, A. (1992) *Method in Social Science: A realist approach*, 2nd edition, Routledge: London.

Scope (2005) *Time to Get Equal: Tackling disablism in volunteering*, Scope: London.

Scott, D. and L. Russell (2001) 'Contracting: The experience of service delivery agencies' in Harris, M. and C. Rochester (Eds) *Voluntary Organisations and Social Policy in Britain*, Palgrave: Basingstoke.

Serwotka, M. (2009) *Labour: Ditch the banker's welfare reforms*, The Guardian, 21 February. Last accessed on 24 April 2009, at www.guardian.co.uk/commentisfree/2009/feb/21/

Seyfang, G. (2001) 'Spending Time, Building Communities: Evaluating time banks and mutual volunteering as a tool for tackling social exclusion' *Voluntary Action* 4(1) pp. 29–48.

Sharon, L. (2004/2007) 'Averting a Disaster within a Disaster: The management of spontaneous volunteers' *Voluntary Action* 6(2) pp. 11–29, reprinted in Smith, J. D. and M. Locke (Eds) *Volunteering and the Test of Time: Essays for policy, organisation and research*, Institute for Volunteering Research: London.

Sheard, J. (1992) 'Volunteering and Society, 1960 to 1990' in Hedley, R. and J. D. Smith (Eds) *Volunteering and Society: Principles and practice*, Bedford Square Press for NCVO: London.

Sheard, J. (1995) 'From Lady Bountiful to Active Citizen' in Smith, J. D., C. Rochester and R. Hedley (Eds) *An Introduction to the Voluntary Sector*, Routledge: London.

Skill (1999) 'Disability and Equality in Volunteering' *Volunteering Magazine* 45 p. 21.

Skill (2005) *Shaping the Debate*, Skill: London.

Slight, A. (2002) 'The Age of the Volunteer: Narrating generation as a motivational factor on volunteering' *Voluntary Action* 4(2) pp. 49–62.

Smith, D. H. (1981) 'Altruism, Volunteers and Volunteerism' *Journal of Voluntary Action Research* 10 pp. 21–36.

Smith, D. H. (2000) *Grassroots Associations*, Sage: Thousand Oaks.

Snyder, M. and A. M. Omoto (1999) 'Basic Research and Practical Problems' in Wosinka, W., R. B. Cialdini, J. Reykowski and D. W. Barrett (Eds) *The practice of social influence in multiple cultures*, pp. 287–307, Erlbaum: New Jersey.

Social and Community Planning Research (1990) *On Volunteering: A qualitative research study of images, motivations and experiences*, Volunteer Centre UK: Berkhamsted.

Spence, C. (2003) 'Vision, Aims and Values for Volunteering England', Background paper for the *National Centre for Volunteering Members' Consultation*, Volunteering England: London.

Stebbins, R. (1996) 'Volunteering: A serious leisure perspective' *Nonprofit and Voluntary Sector Quarterly* 25(2) pp. 211–224.

Stebbins, R. (2004) 'Introduction' in Stebbins, R. and M. Graham (Eds) *Volunteering as Leisure/Leisure as Volunteering: An international assessment*, CABI Publishing: Wallington.

Stebbins, R. and M. Graham (2004) *Volunteering as Leisure/Leisure as Volunteering: An international assessment*, CABI Publishing: Wallington.

Stowe, K. (2001) *Evidence to the Parliamentary Hearings on Volunteering in the 21st Century*, UK Volunteering Forum: London.

Stuart, J. and A. Ellis Paine (2008) *Trying to Turn Art into Science? Exploring the development of volunteer management practices and profession*, Paper presented at the 2008 NCVO/VSSN Researching the Voluntary Sector Conference, Warwick.

Taylor, P., M. James, G. Nichols, K. Holmes, L. King and R. Garrett (2007) 'Facilitating Organisational Effectiveness among Volunteers in Sport' *Voluntary Action* 8(3) pp. 61–78.

Teasdale, S. (2008a) *In Good Health: Assessing the impact of volunteering in the NHS*, Volunteering England: London.

Teasdale, S. (2008b) *Health Check: A practical guide to assessing the impact of volunteering in the NHS*, Volunteering England: London.

Teasdale, S. (2008c) *Volunteering among Groups Deemed at Risk of Social Exclusion: Research bulletin*, Institute for Volunteering Research: London.

Teasdale, S. (2008d) *Engaging Young Homeless People: Crisis' experience of being involved in the v programme*, Crisis: London.

Thomas, G. (2001) *Human Traffic: Skills, employers and international volunteering*, Demos: London.

Tihanyi, P. (1991) *Volunteers, Why They Come and Why They Stay: A study of the motives and rewards of volunteers working in Jewish voluntary organisations' day centres*, Centre for Voluntary Organisation, London School of Economics and Political Science: London.

Torry, M. (2005) *Managing God's Business; Religious and faith-based organizations and their management*, Ashgate: Aldershot.

Trades Union Congress (2009) *Work–Life Balance Campaign*. Last accessed on 15 March 2009, at www.tuc.org.uk/work_life/index.cfm?mins=469

Tribal (2008) *The Good Practice Handbook: Promoting good practice in managing volunteers from socially excluded groups*, GoldStar: London.

Tschirhart, M. (2005) 'Employee Volunteer Programs' in Brudney, J. L. (Ed) *Emerging Issues in Volunteering*, Association for Research on Nonprofit Organizations and Voluntary Action: Indianapolis.

UN General Assembly (2005) *Report of the Secretary-General: Follow-up to the implementation of the International Year of Volunteers,* last accessed on 19 July 2009, at http://www.worldvolunteerweb.org/resources/policy-documents/united-nations/doc/un-secretary-generals-report-on.html

Verba, S., K. Schlozman and H. Brady (1995) *Voice and Equality: Civic volunteerism in American politics,* Harvard University Press: Cambridge.

Volunteer Development Agency (2007) *It's All About Time: Volunteering in Northern Ireland 2007,* Volunteer Development Agency: Belfast.

Volunteer Development Scotland (2006) *Annual Digest of Statistics on Volunteering in Scotland 2006,* Volunteer Development Scotland: Stirling.

Volunteer Development Scotland Research Team (2007) *Annual Statistics on Volunteering 2007 (Survey November 2006),* Volunteer Development Scotland: Stirling.

Volunteering Hub (2006) *Report on Volunteering Hub activity for the Infrastructure National Partnership,* Volunteering Hub: London.

Wade, I., A. Mathieu and R. Perrin (2004) *Voluntary Action in Belgium Facts and Figures,* European Volunteer Centre: Brussels. Last accessed on 20 June 2009, at http://www.cev.be/data/File/BELGIUM_April_2004.pdf

Wainwright, S. (undated) *Measuring Impact: A guide to resources,* NCVO: London.

Wardell, F., J. Lishman and L. J. Whalley (1997) 'Volunteers: Making a difference?' *Practice: Journal of the British Association of Social Workers* 9(2) pp. 21–34.

Wardell, F., J. Lishman and L. J. Whalley (2000) 'Who Volunteers?', *British Journal of Social Work* 30 pp. 227–248.

Weber, M. (2003) 'What Can Be Learned about Episodic Volunteers from a National Survey of Giving and Volunteering', Paper presented to the annual Meeting of ARNOVA, Montreal, 14–16 November.

Weeks, J., P. Aggleton, C. McKevitt, K. Parkinsonand and A. Taylor-Laybourn (1996) 'Community and Contracts: Tensions and dilemmas in the voluntary sector response to HIV and AIDS' *Policy Studies* 17(2) pp. 107–123.

Whitely, P. (2004) Quoted in 'The Art of Happiness...Is volunteering the blueprint for bliss?' *Scienceblog.* Last accessed 20 June 2009, at http://www.scienceblog.com/cms/node/4096

Wiedermann, A. (2004) *Voluntary Action in Germany. Facts and figures,* European Volunteer Centre: Brussels. Last accessed 20 June 2009, at http://www.cev.be/data/File/FactsFigures%20Germany%20final.pdf

Wieloch, A. (2007) *Volunteering in the Netherlands Facts and Figures Report,* European Volunteer Centre: Brussels. Last accessed 20 June 2009, at http://www.cev.be/data/File/Facts_Figures_NL_FINAL.pdf

Wilkinson, J. and M. Bittman (2002) *Volunteering: The human face of democracy,* Social Policy Research Centre Discussion Paper No. 114. Last accessed 27 January 2009, at http://www.sprc.unsw.edu.au/dp/DP114.pdf

Williams, C. (2003a) 'Cultivating Voluntary Action in Deprived Neighbourhoods: A fourth sector approach' *Voluntary Action* 5(3) pp. 11–25.

Williams, C. (2003b) 'Developing Community Involvement: Contrasting local and regional participatory cultures in Britain and their implications for policy' *Regional Studies* 37(5) pp. 531–541.

Williams, C. (2004a) 'Giving Credit to Active Citizens' *Voluntary Action* 6(3) pp. 27–36.

Williams, C. (2004b) 'Harnessing Informal Volunteering: Some lessons from the United Kingdom' *Journal of Policy Analysis and Management* 23(3) pp. 613–616.

Wilson, A. and G. Pimm (1996) 'The Tyranny of the Volunteer: The care and feeding of voluntary workforces' *Management Decision* 34(4) pp. 24–40.

Wilson, J. and M. Musick (1997) 'Who Cares? Toward an Integrated Theory of Volunteer Work' *American Sociological Review* 62(5) pp. 694–713.

Wilson, J. and M. Musick (1999) 'Attachment to volunteering' *Sociological Forum* 14(20) pp. 243–272.

Wilson, R. (2003) *The A-Z of Volunteering and Asylum: A practical handbook for people managing volunteers who are, or who work with, refugees or asylum seekers,* Volunteering England: London.

Wilson, R. and H. Lewis (2006) *A Part of Society: Refugees and asylum seekers volunteering in the UK,* Tandem: Leeds.

Wolfenden, J. (1978) *The Future of Voluntary Organisations,* Croom Helm: London.

Yates, H. and V. Jochum (2003) *It's Who You Know That Counts: The role of the voluntary sector in the development of social capital in rural areas,* NCVO: London.

Young, C. and D. Young (2008) *Sustainable Paths to Community Development: Helping deprived communities to help themselves,* School for Social Entrepreneurs: London.

Zaltauskas, M (undated) 'Lithuania' in Spes – Centro di Servizio il Volontario del Lazio (Ed) *Volunteering Across Europe, Belgium, Lithuania, Slovakia. Organisations, Promotion, Participation,* Spes – Centro di Servizio il Volontario del Lazio: Rome.

Zimmeck, M. (2001) *The Right Stuff: New ways of thinking about managing volunteers,* Institute for Volunteering Research: London.

Zimmeck, M. (2007) *The Crop is Worth the Seed,* unpublished paper prepared for the Commission on the Future of Volunteering, London.

Index